THE
PRINC

THE
PRINCE & I

Life with the motor racing Prince of Siam

Princess Ceril Birabongse

VELOCE PUBLISHING PLC
PUBLISHERS OF FINE AUTOMOTIVE BOOKS

DEDICATION

To Evelyn

ACKNOWLEDGEMENTS

I began to write this account of my life for my family but, thinking that it might be of interest to others too, I sent the early draft to the successors of Bira's and Chula's publisher, G.T.Foulis & Company, for consideration. As it turned out Rod Grainger, one-time editorial director of that company, subsequently formed his own publishing concern - Veloce - happily now my publisher; thus maintaining a link with the past.

I wish to express my thanks to Mr Grainger for his interest in my work and to my editor and agent, Robin Read, without whose help and encouragement this book would never have been finished.

The photographs used are from my private collection, taken over the years. Frequently, photographs accumulate in such a way as to make it difficult, or even impossible, to accurately trace their origin. If there are any unacknowledged illustrations within these pages I extend my apologies, and thanks, to the photographer concerned.

Ceril Birabongse
Riva Del Garda, Italy

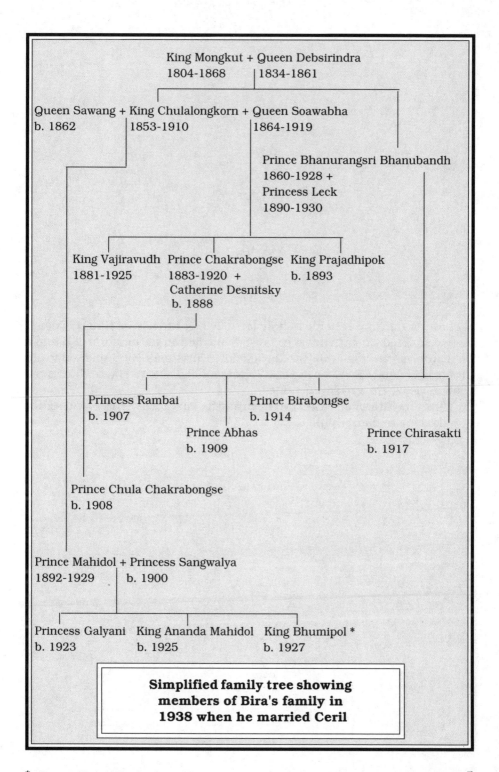

King Mongkut + Queen Debsirindra
1804-1868 | 1834-1861

Queen Sawang + King Chulalongkorn + Queen Soawabha
b. 1862 | 1853-1910 | 1864-1919

Prince Bhanurangsri Bhanubandh
1860-1928 +
Princess Leck
1890-1930

King Vajiravudh   Prince Chakrabongse   King Prajadhipok
1881-1925   1883-1920 +   b. 1893
    Catherine Desnitsky
    b. 1888

Princess Rambai   Prince Birabongse
b. 1907   b. 1914

Prince Abhas   Prince Chirasakti
b. 1909   b. 1917

Prince Chula Chakrabongse
b. 1908

Prince Mahidol + Princess Sangwalya
1892-1929 | b. 1900

Princess Galyani   King Ananda Mahidol   King Bhumipol *
b. 1923   b. 1925   b. 1927

**Simplified family tree showing
members of Bira's family in
1938 when he married Ceril**

---

* *Present King of Thailand*

My brother rang me at home in Italy late one night to tell me Bira was dead. He had suffered a heart attack, collapsed and died on the platform of Baron's Court underground station two days before Christmas 1985 -just opposite the block of flats where, for the last 20 years, I had always stayed during my London visits. He was seventy one.

I first met Bira when I was seventeen and he was twenty. Three weeks later he asked me to marry him ...

CHAPTER ONE

On the day I was born in October 1916 my father, then a captain in the Royal Marines working at the War Office, was sent to inspect the wreckage of a Zeppelin that had been shot down. Later, he suggested to my mother that 'Zeppelin' might be a good name for the new baby. Fortunately for me, my mother disagreed and I was named Ceril after her youngest sister, to compensate her for not being able to be my godmother (she was a Roman Catholic). Ceril - one of the names for Sarah - had been chosen for her by her Jewish father. My mother had recently become a Christian Scientist but, as my father belonged to the Church of England, I was christened near to where we lived at St Mary Abbots in Kensington. Later, I married a Buddhist but never followed any religion myself.

My parents came from very different backgrounds: my mother's family were city merchants, my father's military people. My father's mother had one daughter followed by eleven sons, of whom he, Percy Raworth, was the tenth. My grandfather was a Justice of the Peace, active in local politics, a hunting and shooting country squire who had joined the Gordon Highlanders in the days when commissions were bought and officers retired without a pension. Captain Charles Hensman Heycock and his wife lived at Pytchley House in Northamptonshire. Their daughter went to Cheltenham Ladies College and the sons to public schools. There was never any question of any of them going into trade and they would have been cut off by their father if they had. Seven sons went into the services and at one period four were serving in India at the same time. My grandmother's family was also military based and her brother, Colonel John Chard, won the Victoria Cross at Rorke's Drift in the Zulu war. My father and his brothers were all extremely fond of one another and kept in close touch; meeting as often as possible.

My mother's father was Samuel Henry Phillips, eldest son of Sir Benjamin Phillips. With his friend, Henry Faudel, he started a wholesale business called 'Faudels' in Newgate Street near St. Pauls in the City of London, and later married Rachel Faudel. Sir Benjamin Phillips had many other financial interests, was chairman of the Union Steamship Company, elected Alderman in 1847 and Lord Mayor of London in 1865.

Sir Benjamin's second son, my mother's Uncle George, was Lord Mayor of London in Queen Victoria's Diamond Jubilee Year of 1897 as Sir George Faudel-Phillips, the family by then having added Faudel to its name. During the time he was Lord Mayor the King of Siam, King Chulalongkorn, came to London on a state visit and was entertained at a banquet in his honour at the Mansion House. Some forty years later when my engagement to Bira was announced, a Bangkok paper commented on the fact that Bira's uncle had been entertained in London by my great uncle.

My grandfather, Samuel Henry Phillips, married Sarah Georgina White, eldest daughter of George Frederick White, Deputy Lieutenant of the City of London and senior partner of a company started by his father, John Bazley White. The company premises were next to the Tate Gallery and were amalgamated with the Associated Portland Cement Manufacturers Limited in 1900. My great-grandfather - Sir Benjamin Phillips - amassed a considerable fortune and was well known as an art collector.

After their marriage, my grandparents went to live at 17 Grosvenor Street and there Rachel, Henrietta Norah (my mother), Ceril and Henry, known in the family as Ray, Norah, C and Harry, were born. As children they saw very little of their parents, only being taken to the drawing room each day for a short time after tea, but, their mother never failed to go up to say goodnight to them, the train of her evening dress spread out behind her with the nursery cat sitting on it. The cat always waited for her at the top of the stairs to jump on and glide along into the bedrooms and back down the corridors, jumping off at the last moment when Sarah returned downstairs.

The three girls never went to school and were educated at home by French, German and English governesses. Harry was sent to Eton. Their father went to the City every day where he and his brother George worked and lunched together, and went on frequent business trips abroad. Their mother, who was very beautiful and a superb needlewoman, able to work exquisite flower embroideries with the narrowest ribbons and gold thread, was most severe with her daughters but spoilt her son. When his regiment (the 16/5th Royal Irish Lancers) was stationed in Ireland Harry met a woman many years older than himself, fell madly in love and, at the age of twenty, announced he was going to marry her. His father refused permission and warned him that he would cut off his allowance and disinherit him if he disobeyed. So Harry went to his mother, made her believe he would fall ill and die if he couldn't get his way, and she forced her husband to give in. His wife, Aunt Nell, was to become my godmother.

However, when my mother fell in love and the young man proposed, her parents refused permission. I never knew why, but the fact that she was not allowed to marry the man she loved so upset her she vowed she would never stand in the way of any daughter of hers. She kept this vow, although was naturally not at all happy when I wanted to marry an oriental, which then was a very different thing to marrying one in these modern times. Nevertheless, to the surprise of many, she gave me her support, albeit very reluctantly.

My mother, Norah, met my father when she was about thirty five. Her family were not pleased by the idea of her marrying a younger son with no prospect of inheritance, while his family were not pleased at one of their son's marrying into 'trade'. However ,the difficulties were overcome, the Heycock family came up to London, Captain Heycock gave his son a most generous cheque and, on Saturday 26th November 1910, my parents were married at St. George's, Hanover Square, with a reception at Claridges.

My father had seen a great deal of service abroad and seemed likely to return there, but my mother did not like army life so eventually, to please her, he retired.

My brother, Raworth Henry Faudel Heycock, was born in 1914 two years before me, and was known to us all as 'Way'. We lived in Evelyn Gardens, just off the Fulham Road, and had a French governess, Marie Antoinette Welsch, whom we loved and called Maddy. Way went to school in Sloane Street, and when I was five I was sent to Challoner School in Queen's Gate, where I made two friends in my class, Daphne Lewis and Lisba Hunter, who later married Bira's cousin Chula. We were very different to look at, Daphne with dark, curly hair and brown eyes, Lisba with short, straight blonde hair and deep blue eyes and me with green eyes and long, reddish gold hair parted in the middle, hanging down the sides of my face and making me look, according to my friends, just like a spaniel. Daphne was my best friend as she was very kind and gentle, Lisba being too inclined to boss me about; but what drew Lisba and me together was our love of painting and we persuaded our parents to let us have extra painting lessons at school.

Both my maternal grandparents died before we were born.The house in Grosvenor Street was sold and the contents divided among the family; Uncle Harry taking a lot to his villa on the Riviera near Grasse, while some came to our house and some to the new home of my mother's sisters, Aunt Ray and Aunt C, at 54 Cadogan Place. There was a sale of the remaining things which fetched very good prices: the Rembrandt, a small panel *Head of the Artist's Sister* which my grandfather had bought in 1876 for ten guineas, sold for £1890, a portrait of Mrs Jordan by Sir Thomas Lawrence £504 and an Angelica Kauffman £130 ... I wish we still had them today!

Most of the staff moved with the Aunts from Grosvenor Street but Frampton, the butler, lived out: it was not considered correct in those days for a man to sleep in the house of unmarried ladies.

The Aunts were not at all alike. Aunt C was tall and stern, hated any form of show and would have much preferred to live a simple life in the country but felt it her duty to stay with her sister. Aunt Ray was small, auburn haired, an excellent painter who brought back sketch books of charming watercolours from her frequent visits to Italy and Switzerland. She insisted on being treated very much as the elder sister and never let an opportunity go by to sniff at her sisters' religions, Aunt C being a Catholic and my mother a Christian Scientist. Aunt Ray was a great sniffer of disapproval yet ,when in London, the three of them met or telephoned each other constantly, and when on holiday wrote to each other every single day!

We saw Uncle Harry and Aunt Nell when we visited them in the South of France and when they came to stay at the Hyde Park Hotel. This was always a big event for Harry's sisters who loved him, and for me too. I was terrified of him but loved his wonderful presents. When I was five he bought me a pony at Tattersalls and it was kept at Roehampton Club, where my father went nearly every day to play golf. I rode her in Richmond Park for many years until I outgrew her. Since Uncle Harry and Aunt Nell had no children, Way and I were the only ones in my mother's family. We were in some ways spoilt, and very much loved; but we were also much criticised; every little transgression was at once pounced on by our mother, the Aunts, or Maddy.

Our elders were all extremely strict, had the highest standards and biting tongues which, in a way made me very shy and uncertain of myself all my life, leaving me with a slight inferiority complex. Only with my father could I seem to do no wrong: he was kind and easy-going, although in one case he did put his foot down. He would not allow me to have a dog, saying he did not approve of them in London. One day, however, my mother brought home a tiny black and white kitten that the caretaker at the Seventh Church of Christ Scientist in Marloes Road (where I went to Sunday School) had found drowning in the gutter. I called him Whiskey and for nineteen years he was my love and came with me when I married. He was a clever cat as, although my father made a rule that he must live in the basement with the servants and never come upstairs, he gradually crept upwards a little at a time. He was sent down when seen, but eventually wore out my father and was grudgingly accepted. Thereafter he slept on my bed when he could. He walked to school with me, never at my side but behind me, weaving his way across the roads; luckily the traffic was very light in the 1920s. On the way home I would never know when I would meet him as he would suddenly spring out from some corner where he had been waiting and follow me back. My walks to and from school and to the park with Maddy gave me great pleasure as she always told me stories in French. I had Victor Hugo and Dumas day after day in instalments, and the worst punishment she could give me if I misbehaved was a silent walk.

Daphne, Lisba, and I were together at Challoner until I was eleven and they were twelve and thirteen respectively when they went to boarding schools and I moved across the road in Queen's Gate to Miss Spalding's who offered a higher standard of teaching but not so much fun. Consequently, for several years the three of us lost touch.

By that time Way, now thirteen, was at Eton. He was in Mr. M A McNeile's house and after about two years Bira arrived at the same house. He was a late arrival because, although exactly the same age as Way, Bira had only come to England from Debsirindra School in Bangkok (which was founded by his grandmother Queen Debsirindra) when he was thirteen, and firstly had to learn English and attend preparatory school for two years to prepare for the Eton entrance exam.

We heard from Way that a Siamese prince had come to his house but nothing much beyond that, because although they saw each other every day in term time, and always got on very well at school and, later as brothers in-law, they had very little in common. Bira simply loved his time at Eton and always told me how happy he had been there, whereas Way disliked it. Bira was friendly, very popular and good at all games; Way was shy, clever and hated games, though he was a 'wet bob' and enjoyed rowing. Bira was not studious at all and only just kept his head above water in that respect, but was in one of the best junior cricket teams, got his house colours at football and won the school long jump.

Bira's father was HRH Prince Bhanurangsri Bhanubandh, son of King Mongkut and Queen Debsirindra and full brother of King Chulalongkorn. He was the uncle of King Vijiravudh, HRH Prince Chakrabongse (Chula's father) and of King Prajadhipok, and great uncle to the present King of Thailand. He married young and had children then, late in life, married again and had another family; a daughter - Princess Rambai - and four sons: Prince Abhas, followed by a mentally handicapped boy, then Bira and the youngest son Prince Chirasakti. When he sent Bira to Eton, Prince Bhanurangsri already had a grandson there, son of a daughter of his first marriage. When, years later, Bira and I went to Siam, another son of one of Bira's half-sisters was Regent for the boy king and used to tease me that I was now his Aunt.

Bira's father had taken him to Singapore to see him off when he came to England; to his great sorrow Bira never saw his father again. Prince Bhanurangsri died while Bira was at Eton, leaving him an orphan as his mother had died when he was four. His younger brother, Prince Chirasakti, had been living in the Grand Palace with King Prajadhipok and Queen Rambai when their father died and, as they had no children, they adopted him. Bira, on the other hand, was taken into the care of his cousin, Chula, who had been at Harrow with Bira's elder brother Abhas and was now with him at Cambridge. The two of them used to go to Eton to take Bira out and away with them in the holidays. It was then that the friendship began between Chula and Bira, and Chula quite soon began to love the boy so intensely that Bira became the centre of his life. HRH Prince Chula Chakrabongse was six years older than Bira and had just inherited an immense fortune.

When I was twelve my mother suffered a nervous breakdown and I was sent to live with my aunts for two years. At Cadogan Place the owners of the houses had keys to the gardens in the square, and these became my playground. In the shrubbery at one end there was a clearing with swings and a seesaw, and here the children of the residents gathered. I had a particular friend who spent most of the year with her grandmother, who lived a few houses away from my aunts. She was going on holiday to Biarritz to stay with her much-married American mother, and as I was going to St Jean de Luz with Aunt C we were very excited at the thought of meeting there. I went abroad with Aunt C every holiday; mostly to St Jean de Luz as she had French and Spanish friends there. She agreed to send me over to Biarritz with Louisa, the maid who travelled with us and Vincent the chauffeur. I spent the afternoon with my friend at the Polo Club where her mother's latest husband was playing and we had a wonderful time, but it was never repeated. That evening Aunt C questioned me closely, and after hearing my excited account decided my friend's mother lived the same kind of rich, polo-playing life that Uncle Harry enjoyed on the Riviera, to which she had no intention of exposing me!

My mother recovered, I went home when I was fourteen and was sent to Claremont school at Esher in the beautiful house and grounds that had once been the home of Queen Victoria's uncle, Prince Leopold of Saxe-Coburg.

By now Way was seventeen, had passed the Cambridge Entrance Examination and gone abroad for a year to study languages. Bira, on the other hand, having gone late to Eton, stayed on for another two years until he was nearly nineteen. Like Way he was down for Trinity College, but had not passed the Cambridge Entrance Exam when he left school to go and live with Chula in London. Chula found a tutor to coach him but Bira unexpectedly changed his mind and decided he wanted to learn sculpture instead of going to university. Of course, he had to get Chula to agree as, by now, Chula had adopted him and was his legal guardian, but this was not difficult as Bira was always able to get round Chula. In any case, Chula was only too glad Bira would be staying in London with him instead of going to Cambridge. So Chula looked for a sculptor who would take Bira on as a pupil: because he always wanted only the very best for the boy, he asked Charles Wheeler ARA (later Sir Charles Wheeler PRA) to have him at his studio.

At Christmas the family joined Way in Munich and went skiing, then stopped in Paris to look for a family where he could go in the spring. Through friends my parents met Madame Armand Delille, who was English and lived at Ville d'Avray with her artist husband. It was decided that Way would go to stay with Pastor Paul Perrelet - Madame Delille's brother-in-law - and his family until he went up to Cambridge in the autumn and that, in the summer I would also go there and study painting with Monsieur Armand Delille.

The following Christmas I returned home for two weeks and went skating at Hammersmith ice rink with David Foster, a friend who often stayed with us in the holidays. There, by chance, I met Lisba Hunter again, with her younger sister Clare and their nanny Jessie, who I remembered well as she used to wait for us outside the school with Maddy. I hadn't seen Lisba for some years and hardly recognized her: her blonde hair was now permanently waved and she was very smart and very pretty, far more grown-up looking than I even though she was only one year older. We were pleased to see each other and catch up on our news - she was at a finishing school in Florence and was shortly to return there. As I was going back to Paris, we arranged to meet in the autumn when she was planning to go to art school in London and asked me if I would join her. So, in September 1933, Lisba and I enrolled at the Byam Shaw Art School on Campden Hill near her home, and my father taught me to drive and gave me a second-hand car.

CHAPTER TWO

Lisba invited me to her eighteenth birthday dance at her home in Upper Phillimore Gardens. I went with Way and David Foster and it was the first really smart grown-up dance I had been to, with a marquee in the garden and a band. Lisba looked ravishing in a pink dress from Harrods while I, of course, wore a dress made by Mrs Sherlock who lived in a country cottage - one of the last old cottages left in London - down the Fulham Road. She had made my dresses since I was a child. Daphne's family lived only a few doors away from Lisba and, as her elder sister Irene was married to Ferdinand Quittner that day, Daphne came to the dance in her bridesmaid's dress.

During the winter I was invited to a lot of dances, which was a problem for my mother as most hostesses wanted girls to bring a partner, there always being a shortage of men. Way and my own friends were at university, so my mother had to fall back on the sons of her cousins, who were all much older than I and mostly working in the City. Family feeling was strong and they couldn't refuse to come, but I was tongue-tied with them and they were bored stiff.

In the spring my mother presented Daphne and me to King George V and Queen Mary at Court, as Daphne's father had died recently and her mother was still in mourning. Lisba and her mother went to the same Court, too. It was the custom to give a small party before going so that friends could, one hoped, admire your finery. It would have been impossible not to admire my mother, who looked quite beautiful in a dress of black lace over silver and wearing the emerald and diamond necklace that had been her mother's which, many years later, I was to sell to buy my villa in Italy.

Despite all the dances and May Week at Cambridge, I went regularly to the art school. I was asked out quite a lot by the son of friends of my parents who was in a Scottish regiment. I went with him to the Royal Tournament at Olympia where we had a box from which he took the salute as his men marched in to participate in the show. I was very impressed by this, but when he came to ask my father if he could propose to me (as did a friend of Way's at about the same time) I told my father I did not like either of them enough to marry them. My parents were most understanding and consoled themselves with the thought that there was plenty of time ahead for me to find a husband. They never even contemplated my having a career of any sort: their only idea, like that of the parents of most of my friends, was that I should make a suitable marriage.

A few days after the autumn term started at the art school in the first days of September, Lisba and I were sitting side by side drawing in the life class when, to everyone's surprise, the Principal, Ernest Jackson, came in with a young oriental boy and settled him down at an easel. In those days it was fairly unusual to meet people from the east and we had certainly not had one at the school before.

It was still warm in London and during the morning break Lisba and I used to take the buns we had bought at the school canteen and walk up and down the road munching them. That morning we saw a most exciting-looking sports car parked there, an MG Magna - very different from the second-hand MGs Way and most of his friends owned. This one was painted a deep hyacinth blue, the chrome-work gleamed and the front was decorated with club badges. We went over at once to examine it, and saw that on the dashboard there was a small silver plaque inscribed with the words 'Prince Birabongse'. I told Lisba I now knew who the new pupil was.

I told Way about Bira and his car when I went home to lunch (Way was still there as he was not due back at Cambridge until the end of the month). He said I must go up to Birabongse in the afternoon and say I was Heycock's sister, as he would probably be feeling rather lost on his first day at the school. I was too shy to approach him alone so Lisba came with me. He seemed delighted to have someone to talk to and later asked if he could drive me home in that beautiful car. This was a problem as my mother had a strict rule that I must never go out with any boy whose parents she had not met, so until she had met Bira's parents, or in his case his guardian Chula, I was told not to accept any invitations from him. I explained all this to Bira at school and he was most understanding about it, although very disappointed as he had just bought a model yacht and was taking it down to the Harrow School outdoor swimming pool with Chula and a few friends to launch it. He wanted to invite Lisba and me and, as Lisba's parents were less strict than mine, she was able to accept while I had, very unhappily, to refuse. This did not please Bira at all and he asked Chula to invite my mother and me to tea as soon as possible. So we went to their modern and, to me, very luxurious flat in Cornwall Gardens where their manservant Ives served tea and my mother and Chula talked together.

My mother was favourably impressed by Chula's seriousness (he seemed

15

much older than twenty six) and his European good looks inherited from his Russian mother. Also it helped that he had known several of her cousin's sons (of whom I been so shy) at Cambridge. After that tea my mother allowed me to go out with Bira, but with certain reservations that she and Chula agreed on together. She was relieved to find Chula as worried as she was, if not more so, that Bira and I would become too friendly, and was glad that he too made rules about our meetings. In the end we were allowed to go alone to the cinema in the afternoon, but if we went out to the cinema or theatre in the evening we could only go in Chula's Rolls, with Calligan the chauffeur driving and taking me home afterwards. If we wanted to go on to supper and dance after a show then we could only go to the Savoy or Berkeley and nowhere else, and never, never, to a nightclub. That was absolutely forbidden by both Chula and my parents. To their relief, Bira and I neither drank nor smoked. If we wanted to drive out into the country at weekends together we could only go alone if we were going to friends of Chula's or my parents and told them beforehand where we were going.

So we started going out together, very carefully obeying the rules, and after a short time Bira said he loved me and wanted to marry me. He told Chula, who met my parents to discuss this, and new rules were laid down. There was to be no thought of marriage for three years until I was twenty one, as my parents told me that to marry a man of a different race would be such a serious step I must be of age. The decision would be mine alone and, if I still loved Bira then, they would not stand in my way. They hoped, as did Chula with all his heart, that we would grow out of this infatuation. Chula had known that Bira might one day become seriously interested in a girl but had hoped it would not be too soon; in fact, not for many years so that they would go on living together for a long time.

Chula had been in and out of love from an early age: a little princess in the Grand Palace in Bangkok, in London with Rosemary, daughter of Lord Falkland who later married Aubrey Essen-Scott the racing driver, and in Paris with Marina Chaliapin, daughter of the Russian opera singer. All three had remained his friends and in both London and Paris he took out other girls; but this part of his life had taken a back seat when he met his young cousin Bira and became totally infatuated with the boy. Bira, on the other hand, having been extremely spoilt by Chula who pandered to his every whim and loaded him with the most unbelievably expensive presents, had had very little time to think of girls. Now that Bira's interest had suddenly awakened, Chula's attitude was one of if he couldn't stop it he could at least console himself that it had happened with a harmless and obedient young girl with nice parents.

On my eighteenth birthday in October 1934 Bira took me to have supper and to dance at the Savoy after the theatre. Although I had been there before to parties I had never been taken alone by a man and it was a great event. We were by then terribly in love and fast becoming real friends. Bira was twenty, only a few inches taller than I, beautifully proportioned with slim waist and

16

hips, broad shoulders and very strong arms and legs: I found him incredibly good looking. His black hair shone with Brylcreem, he had smooth pale gold skin - so lucky as many of his Siamese friends and relations were marked by smallpox - and he was a wonderful dancer.

Bira didn't stay long at the Byam Shaw art school. He every day went to Mr Wheeler's studio in Tregunter Road, Chelsea, and Charles Wheeler said he showed considerable talent, although he felt Bira needed to learn to draw, which was why he sent him to the art school. Bira always came back to the school, though,to drive me home. At that time, besides his MG Magna he had an open 3 1/2-litre Derby Bentley and a two-seater Riley Imp. Bira drove very well and gained valuable experience driving Chula (who didn't drive) about Europe on holiday. He was now trying to persuade Chula to let him race.

In winter my mother took a small party ,including my brother and several of my friends, to Zürs and Bira asked to join us. David Foster was a good skier and we had all done a little before, so felt superior to Bira who had never been on skis. But not for long. All his life as a natural athlete Bira took any sport he attempted most seriously: he engaged a private ski instructor and by the end of the holiday could ski better than any of us!

When we returned to London Chula was waiting to welcome him back. It would never have occurred to Chula to go skiing - he was bad at all games and generally disliked them. The only sport of any kind he had enjoyed was coxing at Cambridge. Now Bira began again to persuade Chula to agree to allow him to go motor racing and, as always, Chula gave in. The first step they took was to consult Thompson & Taylor at Brooklands to ask if it would be possible to strip the Riley Imp and tune the engine, which Mr Taylor thought could be done. So the car was prepared and its colour changed from white to Bira's favourite hyacinth blue - later to become famous in the racing world as 'Bira Blue'- and entered for two handicap races at Brooklands on 16th March 1935. That day, Bira drove Chula, Lisba and me there and we picnicked by the Bentley. Not that any of us ate much, for we were all rather frightened. Bira left us to go to the Riley while we three climbed to the top of the Member's Hill to watch.

Bira chose to race under the name of 'B. Bira'. His full name - Birabongse Bhanudej Bhanubandh - was too long and, in any case, everyone always called him Bira. He finished far back in both races and *The Light Car* wrote "B. Bira, a Siamese Prince driving a standard-looking 1098 Riley obviously enjoyed the whole thing hugely, despite his modest pace". Bira's motor racing career had begun.

Not content to continue at that level, Chula and Bira bought an MG Magnette. When they had first gone to see Mr Taylor about preparing the Riley Imp he had warned them that racing was a very expensive sport: luckily, Chula was rich. He had not always had money to spend as when his father died Chula was only twelve years old and Prince Chakrabongse's great fortune was taken under the control of the Monarchy, first by Chula's uncle, King Vajiravudh and, after his death by Chula's other uncle, King Prajadhipok.

Chula's education was paid for by the Kings and he received a modest allowance. It was only just after he left Cambridge that his fortune was released and he became rich overnight.

Bira's father had also been an immensely rich prince like his nephew, Chula's father, but whereas Chula had been an only child and so inherited the entire fortune, Bira's father had eight children, including a son and two daughters who were grown up by the time he had five children by Bira's mother. Nevertheless, Bira had a large enough fortune of his own, although everyone thought he was much richer than he was. This was because the amount of money he had available to spend was almost limitless as Chula continually told him that now he was his brother and his beloved companion, everything he owned was equally his. He begged Bira never to touch his own money at all, just to let it accumulate so that if the time ever came when Chula could not go on supporting him Bira would still be a very rich man. Sadly, things in life often fail to turn out as planned. On the rare occasions when Chula felt he had to say no to something that Bira wanted, Bira disobeyed and used his own money. This sowed the seeds of Bira's financial disasters later in life; when he found himself on his own at last he had stupidly frittered away his money.

One cannot entirely blame Bira for this because he had simply not been brought up to appreciate the value of money at all. When his brother Abhas left their father's palace to go to school in England, Bira was seven and the adored companion of his rich and ageing father. Then, before Bira in turn went to England, he was sent to spend a year in the Grand Palace as honorary page to the childless King Prajadhipok in order to learn court manners. The King also loved and spoilt him - and then came Chula. Bira had just never thought about money at all - it was something that had always been there in vast quantities to be spent at will. However, this, surprisingly, did not spoil his character at all; he was always modest and charming, even at the height of his motor racing fame, and was very gentle and kind. Chula said no Siamese boy had ever been so popular at an English school as Bira had, and certainly all my friends loved him at once. It was only that no-one had thought to teach him the value of money and when he did finally learn it was too late.

While the Magnette was being prepared by Thompson & Taylor, Chula and Bira went off on a long tour of Spain and Portugal and, when they returned Bira created his 'train room'. The flat above theirs had become vacant so they took it, partly to give Bira space to lay out his large collection of model trains, but also as a home for a friend who had come over from Paris to live with them and act as Chula's secretary. We now had to get my parents to relax their rules a little to allow me to spend evenings with Bira in the 'train room' where he built a table to occupy almost the entire room, leaving a central space in which to stand and work the controls. He loved music, so bought a radiogram, and we would spend the evening listening to classical music while we worked; he laying the tracks and working out new timetables, while I painted the scenery and made farms and villages with trees constructed from sponges dyed green and mounted on twigs.

The friend who came to live in the upper flat was Alexander Rahm, always known as 'Shura'. He was one of the sweetest-natured men I have ever met. His grandfather was a Swiss from Geneva who had gone to Russia, married a Russian and started a business, making a large fortune. His son, Melchior, Shura's father, also married a Russian, and Shura and his sister Valerie were at school in Russia when the 1917 revolution broke out. The family escaped across Siberia and thence via Japan and China to Paris. Although they had left all their money and property in Russia, the Rahms were more fortunate than most of the Russian refugees as they still had some money in Switzerland. Chula's Russian mother also lived in Paris and knew the Rahms well so Chula and Shura, who were the same age, became friends. Shura, a very talented pianist, was studying at the Paris Conservatoire and at the same time studying Science and Astronomy at the Sorbonne. In his spare time he designed and built an astronomical clock of Meccano supplied free by the factory after the director, Mr Frank Hornby, had seen the plans Shura had sent him. It took Shura one thousand hours to build it and, when it was finished, he was asked to lecture on it to the French Astronomical Society. The clock is now in a Paris museum.

Unfortunately, the Rahms continued their Russian lifestyle in Paris without taking into account the fact that they no longer had their Russian income, so soon had to go and live more modestly in Switzerland. It was just the wrong moment for Shura to have to leave the Sorbonne and give up his musical studies. His sister Valerie had by then married Prince Alexander Obolensky, but they were unable to help Shura as the prince had also lost everything and had enough difficulty providing for his own family. So Chula asked Shura to come and work for him and he became the much-loved friend of us all.

Chula's mother lived in Paris with her second husband, Harry Stone, known to us all as 'Hin' which is Siamese for a stone. He was a tall, good-looking American from Portland, Oregon. Chula's mother was born Ecaterina Ivanovna Desnitskaya, daughter of an important judge from Kiev, with one brother, Ivan Ivanovitch. Her brother had died but his widow lived in Paris with their two sons, the younger of which was to become well known as Ivan Desny the film actor. When Chula's mother was a girl she had been sent to St Petersburg to join her brother who was studying there. She met Chula's father at the house of mutual friends when she was seventeen and he twenty two: like Bira and I, they had fallen in love.

Chula's father was the second, and favourite, son of King Chulalongkorn and was sent abroad to be educated like all Siamese princes. He left Siam when he was thirteen, travelling with his uncle, Prince Bhanurangsri (Bira's father), to England. Bira's father spoke good English, having first had lessons in the Grand Palace as a child when his father, King Mongkut, engaged the English governess, Anna Leonowens, to teach his children. This episode was made famous by book, play and film as *Anna and the King of Siam* and *The*

King and I.

Chula's father stayed with a family in England for two years and then went to Russia. The Tsarevitch Nicholas (later the last Tsar) visited Siam in 1891 and became friendly with King Chulalongkorn who subsequently visited S. Petersburg. While he was there the Tsar told him he would be very pleased to take charge of the education of one of his sons, so Chula's father was sent to Russia. The young prince joined the Corps des Pages and lived at the Winter Palace until he passed out first in his class to serve as an officer in His Majesty's Hussar Guards, based then at Tsarskoe Selo.

Chula's parents married without telling anyone or getting permission from the King . Prince Chakrabongse left his wife Ecaterina at Singapore and returned home alone, but the news leaked out so he sent for her to join him in his palace. King Chulalongkorn was very angry indeed but the Prince took no notice and simply carried out all his royal duties, while his young wife lived quietly at home learning almost perfect Siamese and studying the very complicated court etiquette. Chula was born when Ecaterina was twenty. Queen Soawabha wanted to see the baby - her first grandchild - so invited Chula's mother to visit her, liked her at once and adored the child. Then the King, too, began to soften but only saw his grandchild once as he died soon after, without having had time to give the baby a title. The King's eldest son came to the throne as King Vajiravudh and, as he had always supported his brother's marriage, at once gave his little half-Russian nephew the title of Prince.

The new King was unmarried and seemed to prefer the company of his courtiers. When eventually he did marry he only had one daughter who could not inherit the throne, so Chula's father became Crown Prince and Chula was now in direct line to the throne. When Crown Prince Chakrabongse died and Chula was twelve, Chula's uncle, Prince Prajadhipok, became Crown Prince; as he had no children it seemed possible that Chula would succeed him as King. Chula very much wanted to be King; however, while he was at Harrow his mother came to see him to tell him that she had remarried. Chula often used to say that he found it very difficult to forgive her for this because, although the Siamese had absolutely accepted her as the wife of the Crown Prince and would probably have accepted Chula as King, despite his being the son of a mixed marriage, he knew they would now never accept him with an American stepfather.

Whether Chula was right or wrong he felt strongly about it. He always had a complex about his mixed blood and told us that as a child he had never known where to stand at royal ceremonies. His grandmother used to treat him as the most important of the young princes, and would see to it that in royal processions he was placed up in the front. Then his father would come and pull him back to walk with the princes of lower rank saying that this was his place as his mother was a foreigner. It was all very muddling and humiliating for a small boy and the memories and bitterness stayed with him all his life, making him seem aggressive and self-assertive. He always insisted on his rights above all and felt very royal. This often made him unpopular, especially in motor racing circles, while Bira, with his good humour and placid nature, who never felt royal at all, was always liked by everyone. It was really very unfair.

When Chula and Bira came back from their Easter tour of Spain and Portugal King Prajadhipok abdicated. There had been a peaceful revolution in Siam in 1932 and the absolute monarchy had been abolished. The King stayed on as a constitutional monarch but now in 1935 as a result of further unrest in the country, and years of failing eyesight due to cataracts in both eyes, the King signed an Act of Abdication and came to live in England. The throne then passed to the elder son of his half-brother, Prince Mahidol, who had died at the age of thirty seven, leaving a widow and three young children: Princess Galyani, who was then twelve, the new King Ananda Mahidol, ten and Prince Bhumipol, the present King of Thailand, aged eight.

King Prajadhipok bought a house at Virginia Water and moved there with his wife Queen Rambai, known as the most beautiful woman in Siam and Chula's old love from the days when they were children together in the Grand Palace. Bira's youngest brother, Prince Chirasakti, their adopted son, came with them and I met him then for the first time. He and Bira's eldest brother Abhas were fascinated by Bira's racing.

Bira had two more races with the Riley then he ran-in the new Magnette at Brooklands and took it there to the Whitsun meeting, and then to the British Empire Trophy, a memorable occasion for me as it was the first time I watched a race from the pits and where I began to learn about time-keeping. Chula had decided to be Bira's pit manager himself, so had to keep a chart to be able to see the position of all the cars in the race and their lap times. He gave me a scrap of paper on which to note the number of each car as it came past and the time on the watch. I would pass it to him to enter on the chart and was also ready to take over the chart for a moment if his attention was needed by the mechanics when important decisions had to be taken, such as which lap Bira should come in to refuel or whether it was necessary to signal him to go faster or slower in order to nurse the engine.

My job as assistant required the greatest concentration as often two or three cars would come roaring past, the nearest hiding the numbers of the others or, in wet weather, sending up spray which covered the cars, so I had to learn to recognize them by shape and colour almost out of the corner of my eye in a split second. I used to take care to wander around the paddock before the race to memorize the numbers on each car.

Now my years of chart keeping began, first as an assistant and later on my own. It would have been impossible for me to do if it hadn't been for Chula's strict and excellent training and being forced to be careful and accurate at all times, even in the midst of the shouting and excitement. To have made a mistake would have meant facing one of Chula's earth-shattering, carpet-biting rages and I was quite frightened enough of him in those days without that!

21

People always ask racing drivers' wives or girlfriends whether they are frightened of an accident happening to their man. I found that the enforced concentration on the stopwatch took my mind off the danger during the race and, in any case, at such a young age (I was only eighteen) the excitement of the whole racing atmosphere overwhelmed any anxiety I might have felt. When I was thirty it was different; then I began to mind rather a lot.

After the 1935 British Empire Trophy at Brooklands, where Bira didn't finish due to plug trouble, they took the Magnette to Donington Park where he finished fifth. People were becoming intrigued by him and the idea of a rich oriental Prince arriving in his Rolls-Royce or Bentley, dressed in Siamese silk overalls dyed specially to match the colour of his cars, and receiving pit signals in Siamese. *Motor Sport* wrote "Bira handled his Magnette well to gain fifth place, his pit signals with their Siamese characters causing great delight".

CHAPTER THREE

Chula and Bira began to realise they had made a mistake in buying the Magnette, as a new and exciting car had appeared and Bira wanted one badly. It was the ERA, financed by Humphrey Cook and built at Raymond Mays' home at Bourne. Their idea was to run an ERA works team with Mays as its chief driver and to sell cars to other drivers to help with their expenses. The first successful private owner was the South African, Pat Fairfield, closely followed by Dick Seaman. At the 1935 Eifelrennen in Germany, ERAs finished 1st (Mays), 3rd (Rose-Richards), 4th (Seaman) and 5th (Cook).

Now that Bira had gained some experience in England he wanted to start racing abroad where the courses were better and more exciting, so they entered the Magnette for the Dieppe race to be held on 20th July 1935. Bira knew he would have no chance against the ERAs so, without telling Chula, he went to Bourne to ask Mays if they could have a car ready for him before Dieppe -Mays thought it would just be possible. Luckily for Bira, his twenty-first birthday fell on 15th July, just five days before the race, and Chula, generous and loving as always, said he would give him the ERA as a birthday present.

Charles Wheeler told Bira he could hold his birthday party in his studio; the Berkeley were to look after the food and send waiters and a band was ordered. There were friends of Chula's from Cambridge days, Bira's from Eton, some Siamese and some of the principal dancers (friends of Chula and Bira) from the Russian Ballet. Massine came to the party with Madame Massine, Tatiana Riabouschinska with Lichine, Danilova and the two 'baby' ballerinas Tamara Toumanova and Irina Baronova, who both wanted to go and see Bira race (Toumanova actually did go to Brooklands with her mother that year). Chula and Bira both adored the ballet and when the De Basil

Company were in London I often went with Bira to watch at least one ballet from the wings during the evening.

At midnight the ERA was wheeled in and guests queued up to sit in it. Bira, Raymond Mays and Peter Berthon were photographed with the car and, later, Massine gave an impromptu cabaret, dancing to the *Blue Danube* with Danilova and performing a Spanish dance with Toumanova. It was a wonderful evening.

The following morning the lorry came to fetch the ERA and take it straight to Dieppe, while Bira drove Chula there in the Riley Imp and Shura went by train with the luggage. There were 20 cars in the race: five ERAs, some Bugattis, a Delage, Frazer Nash and MGs. Fairfield won and Bira came second. The *Light Car* wrote "I remember few novices who have acquired real proficiency in the handling of fast machinery so quickly". The *Motor* said "Bira was driving amazingly well".

Attaining second place at Dieppe had shown that Bira really could drive well so Chula and he became more ambitious. They decided to go to the Tourist Trophy Race at Belfast in September, only none of their supercharged cars would be suitable as the race was for unsupercharged sports cars. Another car had to be bought and sprayed Bira Blue, this time a 1500cc Aston Martin.

Before now going to Berne where they had entered the ERA, they visited the new little King of Siam and his family at their villa near Lausanne, and then went on to Geneva to see Shura Rahm's family. From there they did a tour of mountain passes - the Grand St Bernard, Furka, Oberalp, Julia, Stelvio and the Brenner Pass - for Bira to acquire some hillclimbing experience. Bira sent me a card from the St Bernard Hospice saying they were going to see the St Bernard dogs and that perhaps he would smuggle home a pup or two! He and Chula simply loved dogs and owned an adored wire haired terrier called Joan. Then from the Bellevue Hotel at Berne Bira wrote "In this hotel it is so terrific, full of famous drivers".

In those days two races were held at most of the big continental meetings, one of which was for *voiturettes* (light cars) which was usually held in the morning before the Grand Prix. As Bira was driving a 1500cc car he drove in the *voiturette* race, the *Prix de Berne*, where the majority of entries were private owners. The Grand Prix races were dominated by works teams whose factories were subsidized by their totalitarian régimes - the Auto Unions and Mercedes by Hitler's *Nazis* and the Ferrari Alfa-Romeos by Mussolini's *Fascisti*. The Swiss papers were kind to Bira. *Sport Illustrierte* of Basle published a big photo saying he was the sensation of the day and *Automobile Revue* of Berne said Bira was the best of the younger generation of drivers.

A telegram after the race said "SECOND **STOP** BEST LOVE" and in the evening Bira wrote from Interlaken -

So you don't think I ought to be jealous about your friends dar-ling? I am very greedy and selfish and want you all to myself and

24

*everyone else can do without you, even your dearest cat Whiskey! I
sent you a wire about my success on Sunday and hope you got it
in good time as when I got off the ERA, Chula and I practically ran
to the telegram office on the course ... I was so pleased to have
come in second behind another ERA (Dick Seaman) instead of
some other make of car. It was a marvellous run as I was having a
long tussle with a works Maserati for over three-quarters of the
race. I was terribly pleased when I found that I was still second at
the end of the race! I beat Mays who stopped and Lord Howe who
came third ... It was the greatest fun going through the last 2 or 3
laps when people were waving their hats and scarves all along the
circuit when they saw my blue car scuttling along up through the
woods and down by the bends. Everyone was excited to see me
coming in second. The Siamese who came were very proud. The
King's mother and her daughter enjoyed themselves immensely,
especially when I came over to the tribunes to say hallo to them in
my overall which was half-soaked with oil!! ... Before I stop I want
to give you this message: I love you with all my heart.*

My mother and I were going to France and, as Chula and Bira were also
passing through on their way back from Berne, Bira planned for us all to meet
and stay in the same hotel at Abbeville for one night. We were very much in
love and looking forward so intensely to this meeting that Chula and my
mother agreed. They still hoped we would fall out of love but didn't have the
heart to interfere, being thankful that the heavy programme of racing would
keep us apart most of the summer.

Bira wrote once more from Interlaken -

*I have just woken up this morning feeling miserable and abso-
lutely in agony missing you. I am counting the hours to Abbeville
and so look forward to it, and will not be happy until I see your
face with my eyes. The weather is none too good and that makes a
love-sick person much worse.*

My mother and I crossed from Dover to Calais on 30th August and Chula
and Bira came from Paris, where they had stayed the night with Chula's
mother and stepfather Hin. Bira and I flung ourselves into each other's arms
and Chula and my mother put up with a very boring evening!

At Berne, as at other Grand Prix meetings, all racing cars had to be
painted the national colour, green for Britain, white for Germany, blue for
France and so on. Of course, Siam had no national motor racing colour yet
because they had never before had a Siamese racing driver. Chula, therefore,
got the organizers at Berne to agree to let their ERA remain its Bira Blue, but
with a large Siamese flag painted on each side of the tail. It was seeing these,

and their national flag flying above the grandstand with the flags of the other competitors, that made such an impression on the Siamese who were at the race.

After they returned from Berne Chula began to take Lisba out quite often. I had changed art schools and now went to the Chelsea Polytechnic which was nearer home, while Lisba had given up painting. She had been unofficially engaged for some time but it was broken off and she had now fallen in love with a Swiss she had met skiing.As he lived far away, however, she was pleased to go out with Chula. She was a good companion for him; intelligent, well read and a music lover. More importantly to Chula, she was also very pretty indeed! The only thing to stop him falling in love with her, apart from the fact that he was far too taken up with Bira to be seriously interested in anyone else, was the fact that Lisba was a sporting type and had always admired tall, athletic men, which could hardly have been more the opposite of Chula, and he felt he would never have any chance with her. Still, she loved being taken to all the smart places Chula frequented and also loved motor racing; she began to come with us to the pits and Chula got her to film the races. Bira and I were pleased as we got on well with her, though Bira found, as I had at school, that she could be very bossy and full of herself, which he didn't like.

They now took the new Aston Martin to Belfast from where Bira wrote -

I am at this moment thinking of you hard and loving you terribly. I find you so very attractive and wonderful in every way I shall love no one else more or even in the same way as I love you, ever. It is my real feeling and time alone can prove it to you, my darling Ceril. I want you to know I am serious and in earnest about it.

He wrote again before the race -

Thank God I am left alone now for an hour or so and what do you think I'll spend the time on? There is tons of news which I will have to squeeze in ... every place in Belfast is packed with motor enthusiasts. Everywhere I go I feel like being the Prince of Wales or someone as people whisper, stare, stop and turn round, and sometimes point!!! It's being done so frequently now that I am beginning to get used to them because I realise they do it out of interest and good-naturedly. The prospect of the race is very low as the Rileys have something extra under their bonnets and went 30 or 40 seconds faster than us Aston Martins in practice, so all I can hope for is to finish as well as possible, but to win outright I have very little chance. Nevertheless a race is not won until the flag drops. I am quite calm today but expect I shall be as nervous as anything in the morning as usual! I wish with all my heart you were here to comfort me as I can never be really happy and com-

forted with anyone else, and that's saying a lot as you know how fond I am of Chula. He might be coming now for he has just gone to call and give cards to all the important people we know in Ulster.

A telegram followed the letter. "ENGINE BROKE DOWN AFTER THREE QUARTER LAP MOST DISAPPOINTING RETURNING LONDON SUNDAY NIGHT LOVE BIRA".

While Bira had been writing to me Chula had been leaving cards, because although they were there for the race they were still members of a royal family and etiquette in those matters was strict. Chula was a great one for etiquette and left cards with the Governor-General, the Duke of Abercorn, Lord and Lady Londonderry (with whom Chula and Bira lunched before leaving Ulster) and the Prime Minister and Lady Craigavon, with whom they had tea. They then drove back to London with their dog Joan and took the ERA down to Brooklands to tackle the class F Mountain record held by Mays. The following day they left England for a tour of European capitals they had not yet visited. Bira and I hated to be parted again so soon but I was consoled by his letters which arrived almost every day.

Calais, 11th September 1935. *About Donington, I want to ask you to do me a favour. Could you ask Mummy nicely to allow you to come and spend a night with the Pinney family, as Lisba is preparing to do, if we don't all return to London? You see sweetheart, you can say that it is tiring driving back to London after the race, that it would be nice to have a rest at Chula's best friend's house, and that you have already been introduced and all that to George Pinney, who will be glad to invite us all to stay. Then Sunday we can spend the day together again! It would be so wonderful if you can manage that. Darling, yesterday I saved our sorrow after the downfall at Belfast by beating Mays' record for the Mountain Course of 1500cc class. Now I am the holder of 1500cc Brooklands Mountain Circuit!! My name will remain in gold on the board of honour outside the club house as long as no one beats it up!!! Actually I am the 3rd fastest man that ever lapped the course, beating Sir Malcolm Campbell with his big Sunbeam car! This will allow me to race in the Brooklands last meeting in the record holder's race!!*

Heidelberg, 13th September. *No sign of life from you. I have become more and more in love with you, darling. I don't know where it will end, perhaps never unless I should burst and that would be so very unpleasant wouldn't it? We are being very energetic on this trip and taking full advantage in educating ourselves. Yesterday, we saw the actual spot where le Maréchal Foch signed the Armistice for the Great War. We saw most of the Western Front* trenches and the battlefields. This morning we visited the famous university. The road from Frankfort to Darmstadt is a newly built road called the 'Autobahn'. It has a partition in the middle of it to prevent accidents and Chula went to sleep when we were travelling at 90 mph! The Bentley ran from Frankfort to Darmstadt in 9 minutes and the distance was about 13 miles so the average was about 80 mph.

Munich, 15th September. *We reached Stuttgart about one o'clock and after wandering through this vast city we found a place for lunch ... and after having fed in a Germanic way, we scrambled out into the open and just managed to pack ourselves into the large blue car! We then left the city and drove towards Hochstadt, where the famous battle of Blenheim took place. Marlborough was the hero of the story, and he completely routed and shattered the French army under Louis XIV within 6 hours fighting and set them running in the other direction towards the river. I believe the French were driven to take refuge in drowning themselves. Bad luck for them, but I think it was wiser than getting swords in the back.*

Vienna, 15th September. *Vienna! What a romantic name and lovely city. I adore Vienna. Oh darlingest Ceril, you can't imagine the glory of this place. First I want to thank you for your letters and wire more than I can express in writing.*

Budapest, 18th September. *Thank you so much for writing such a lot. Oh sweetheart you are so wonderful to me to be so much in love with me still after 11 months!!! We came pretty fast from Vienna today, but we left so late that we didn't reach here until 4.30. Chula is dog-tired and is sleeping. I will wake him up at 7.00 pm. The reason why Chula is so fed up is that Lisba and other people have not written to him a single line, so he feels rather depressed. Poor him. Chula's greatest fear now is that Swiss friend of Lisba's, but as far as he knows he will fight it out this winter!! Thank goodness it is not my case else I would have passed out completely, as I cannot stand any competition as I have a tremendous inferiority complex and always think I am beaten at once, even when I stand an equal chance. Chula on the other hand I think enjoys competition.*

Prague, 21st September. *You simply must visit Prague with me whatever happens for I think it is a marvellous city. It is so beautiful. There are masses of sculptures for me to see and already it has inspired me, and I promise myself when I go back for the autumn I shall work like a Trojan. I am so keen on art and sculpture, you can't imagine it. It is no more idling around. I will take work more seriously for I don't see any better way of passing the time when I am not with you, my dearest Ceril. I wish you would* *come to lectures with me for I think I shall attend quite a lot of them. It will be so good for both of us because we could discuss about it, as well as about ourselves!!! Oh sweetheart, isn't there such a lot of things we can share together? I think it would be a pity if we don't live together for there are so many things in common, besides our terrific mutual admiration.*

Berlin, 27th September. *Today we got up late. After lunch we visited museums and art galleries. Now we are back and Chula is having a bath. Apparently he is in the same boat as me but much worse; he can't see Lisba until Monday night, she is away in the country for the weekend. I gather they are getting on most rapidly. I am very glad for Chula's sake to have found amusement in some other person when I am not free.*

Lisba and I went to Donington together by train on Saturday 5th October, two days after my nineteenth birthday. The Nuffield Trophy race was to be the first time a Grand Prix was held in Britain and the public were looking forward to seeing some of the big names in continental racing although, in the end, only Gino Rovere and Nino Farina came from Italy with Maseratis and Raymond Sommer from France with his Alfa Romeo. The rest of the field was made up of British drivers who owned Grand Prix cars. Chula and Bira did not own one but Chula thought that as the circuit was short and twisty Bira might have a chance with his much smaller 1500cc ERA of at least putting up a good show, but they wondered if the engine would last the 300 miles.

We joined Chula and Bira in the paddock to share their picnic; Bira, as usual, ate nothing. He was always frightened on the day of a race and would only swallow a raw egg in the morning. He was terrified of making a fool of himself; stalling the engine at the start or something like that. He was never afraid of danger, whether sailing, gliding, piloting his plane or racing, but like all Siamese boys he was really frightened of ghosts!

Farina and Sommer led the race and Bira lay seventh. A few laps later Chula signalled that he was doing well, which was a pity as it distracted him for a split second and he swerved, braked hard and the engine stalled. In the pits the mechanics said that was the end as even they experienced the greatest difficulty cranking an ERA and always push-started it if possible. However, Bira managed, first with his chewing gum, then with a small pebble, to keep the throttle open. With his extremely strong arms he swung the starting handle, the car started, nearly ran over him and he was in and off again. He drove well and came fifth. *Sporting Life* said "The Siamese, with a 1488cc ERA which was the smallest car in the race, put up a fine performance in finishing fifth".

Bira and Chula gave an end-of-season cocktail party in their flat for racing drivers which was, of course, a great success - everyone talked cars!

On 20th December,the *Autocar* printed an interview with Bira headed Sculpture his work, motor racing his hobby. Prince Bira of Siam has risen to motor racing fame in a single season".

On 27th December the *Light Car* wrote "Back in the spring a quiet little Siamese appeared at the track in a standard-looking Riley Imp. If omniscient Fleet Street hadn't seen through his alias, 'B Bira's' presence might have passed practically unnoticed. A month or two later everybody was noticing his driving; he had become a very noticeable young man. His ERA début at Dieppe created something of a stir. It was difficult to believe he'd never driven in a race before.and that this was his first year in motor sport of any kind ... good as he was then he is far better now. The coming of Bira is one of the events by which we shall remember Anno Domini, 1935".

Bira drove my mother, Way and me to ski at Lech in Austria and, whilst there, I received my first letter from Chula -

29th December, 1935. *My dear Ceril, I hope you have made a pleasant journey and that your holiday will be most agreeable.I send you my very best wishes for 1936 during which I hope you will enjoy great health and happiness. In fact for 1936 as in all years to come I send you our old Buddhist wish (in Pali!): Long Life. Beauty. Happiness. Strength. Yours very sincerely, Chula.*

CHAPTER FOUR

For 1936 Chula and Bira planned an ambitious racing programme. To start with they sold the Aston Martin and bought a second ERA exactly the same as their first one: Bira called them *Romulus* and *Remus*. Their programme would have been impossible to carry out with only one car and, by having two cars the same, the spare parts and even the engines were interchangeable. They engaged Wuyts, the works ERA mechanic who had looked after Bira's car at Dieppe, and also a second mechanic. They rented a garage in London at Hammersmith, bought a van and decided Shura would work full-time looking after the secretarial side. He threw himself into it all with his Russian enthusiasm and Swiss thoroughness, ending up not only doing the secretarial side but, when needed, driving the van and even helping in the pits as a mechanic.

Over the garage door was a big sign saying *White Mouse Garage*.which was the name of their team. When Bira had first started racing he had painted a little white mouse on each of the cars, because he, and all Chula's close Siamese friends, called Chula *Nou*, Siamese for little mouse and a nickname given often to Siamese children. Bira wanted to show that the cars also belonged to Chula. The British press, however, always referred to "Bira's Mickey Mouse Mascot".

They planned participation in seven races in Britain, four in Ireland, one in the Isle of Man, Monte Carlo, Nürburgring, Péronne, Albi, Berne and Pescara on the Continent, which would mean that I would see very little of Bira during the season. In April I was going to St Jean de Luz with Aunt C and Bira was trying to persuade Chula to go there too between races, holding out the bait that his mother and Hin would be at Biarritz then and the Chaliapins at their villa in St Jean.

In the summer my parents were taking Way and me on a tour of the Austrian Tyrol, Bavaria, Venice and Lake Como. It was to be my first visit to Italy which would eventually become my home for over forty years. The one place we never went to was the French Riviera; my family didn't like it and had only gone there when Uncle Harry had his villa near Cannes. Subsequently, he had sold it and come back to live in England, so now that Bira was going to race at Monte Carlo I was unable to persuade anyone to take me to watch the race. Lisba was much more fortunate as she was going on holiday near there with her mother and very beautiful eldest sister Eileen, and Chula's mother was also going to watch as they wanted to show her what all this motor racing was about. Monte Carlo was holding two races, one for 'light cars' and one for the Grand Prix cars as at Berne, but here the light car race was being held on the Saturday and the Grand Prix on the Sunday.

In the end Bira very nearly didn't go to Monaco at all. The weekend before a stone had hit and splintered his goggles while he was going along the straight at Donington and pieces of glass had entered one eye. He had seen a specialist in London who had been very against him driving again so soon, but Bira had insisted on at least trying. Instead of being with Bira I had to content myself with his letters -

Monte Carlo 9th April 1936. *Your letter, received when I arrived here, was heavenly and I can't describe what joy I had in reading it. My eye is better now.* Friday night *You're an absolute darling to have written so much. I received one letter every day ... I also got two parcels for Easter! I chose some flowers to send you from the Riviera. Now it is just 10.30 and I am told to go to bed as it is my big day tomorrow!*

Telegram 11th April. "WON BRILLIANTLY SO SORRY YOU NOT HERE CHULA"

12th April. *I couldn't wait any longer to write to you. It is only 8 o'clock and I have slept 5 hours. I am so excited to tell you all about it. Darling, after I wrote to you I felt like death waiting to go to the course. We left the hotel at 2 o'clock. Lisba was so smart in her pink dress which she wore to the big race at Brooklands some time ago. Mother was equally smart in her white raincoat, and Chula dressed like he always has been doing on race days. I must have looked like a frightened rat, but soon got out a smile when I saw Romulus standing outside the garage ... Wuyts and Shura were in overalls and looked very distinguished. The equally smart blue lorry then set out after me to the circuit ... After the preparations at the pits the cars were moved to the starting line. The tense excitement of the start was even greater than anything I have known.*

continued on page 41

Bira's uncle, King Chulalongkorn, with Ceril's great-uncle, Sir George Faudel-Phillips (when Sir George was Lord Mayor of London in 1897, Queen Victoria's Diamond Jubilee Year) at a banquet at the Mansion House held in the King's honour.

Ceril's parents pictured before going to Court in 1910, the year of their marriage.

Bira's mother in Siamese dress with Chirasakti on her knee and Rambai behind her. Bira, dressed as a cub scout, is on a stool with Abhas beside him. 1917.

Ceril and Way in 1917 in Cadogan Place gardens with their nurse.

Ceril, aged five, in Rotten Row with Uncle Harry and a friend the day he gave her Tatty, the pony.

Girls of Challoner School in 1924 in the play
Quality Street. Ceril is sitting in front, with
Lisba kneeling beside her on the right of the
photo.

Ceril in 1933, aged seventeen.

Bira at Zürs, winter 1934.

Chula and Bira at Brooklands with their cars in September 1935. Left to right: Aston Martin, ERA, MG Magnette, Riley Imp, Rolls-Royce, Bentley, Voisin, MG Magna, MG Midget, Ford.

Chula and Bira at Brooklands with their three MGs in September 1935.

Bira with King Ananda Mahidol of Siam and his mother at Lausanne in 1935.

Bira after winning the Grand Prix de Monaco at Monte Carlo in 1936 ...

... and after narrowly beating Raymond Mays to win the JCC International Trophy at Brooklands the same year.

Uncle Harry (Major Faudel-Phillips) at the Islington Horse Show with Princess Elizabeth and Princess Margaret in 1936.

Shura (Alexander de Rahm).

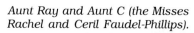

Aunt Ray and Aunt C (the Misses Rachel and Ceril Faudel-Phillips).

HRH Prince Umberto, Crown Prince of Italy, visiting the pits before the race at Turin in 1937.

Bira and Ceril and the Rolls that Bira bought with the money Chula gave them as a wedding present (which was intended for furniture!).

Bangkok 1937: Bira in the uniform of a Second Lieutenant in the King's Bodyguard.

Bira working on a head of the Hon. Sir Steven Runciman, a close friend of Chula.

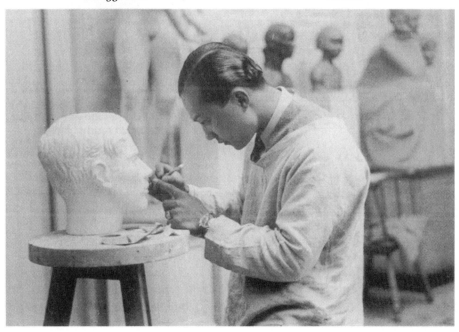

Bira and Ceril leaving the Siamese Legation after their marriage on 12th January 1938

Bira and Ceril with Whiskey - who lived until the age of 19 - in the kitchen after a party.

Bira outside his father's palace in Bangkok.

40

I was third row although I made equal 3rd fastest time with Ray (Mays), Bianco, and Zehender. The flag was up, the smoke was fuming out of people in front and behind. The last 10 seconds would never go. Chiron was by my side signalling me to get off the mark. He was sweet, behaving like my father. The flag flashed down, noise and fumes increased as cars surged forward and left the line. The race was on and a big thrill! I got off the mark but my Italian rival Villoresi pushed me nearly into the gutter. I had to give him the corner.

As cars roared up the hill of the Casino the order was Tenni, Howe, Ray, Zehender, Bianco, Villoresi, Pat (Fairfield) and me. It continued like that until the third lap as I roared up behind Pat and a red Maserati in front of him, and when we reached Tribune U the red car skidded wildly in front, then Pat in endeavouring to avoid him skidded broadside, and as he accelerated a bit he was crossing over towards the inner curb to where there was 3 yards of room, and I shut my eyes and stamped on the pedal and just cleared his nose like a miracle. I left them struggling to get away, and another chap came plum into them and there was a fine mess, but not serious. Soon Villoresi was driving like a devil as he passed me into third place and promptly burst his car in doing so. Ray and Howe and Zehender apparently conked out so it left me in 2nd place after about 19 or 20 laps. Romulus was running like an angel with wings. No splutter, no popping, just fine. My pit people seemed to be pleased and jumped about. After 25 laps I still remained second and thought it was about time I opened up again. All this time I had been playing the waiting game. The road became more and more disgustingly slippery and now skill and carefulness were needed. I was closing down on the leading car, Tenni, by about 2 or 3 seconds per lap. He was then given the 'faster' signal which he promptly took and turned a complete circle on the 30th lap, and this loss of time gave me my way into 1st position. I passed him struggling to get his engine moving. I then had to hurry and made quite a fair speed. Poor old Tenni in trying to catch me up hit a sandbag and the opposition from him was no longer felt.

Then there were some 8 laps to go and it seemed like 10 years. On the 45th I came to that sharp corner before the hill rather fast and slid right across the road gently, but I corrected it miraculously. When I looked up I saw there had been a collision of two cars before I came, who apparently had flooded the whole road with oil and water, worse than anything I had been on. An awful mess it was, and as I roared up the hill I vowed to myself that the next time round, whether being chased or not, I *would crawl along that part. Then 3 laps before the finish that erratic Villoresi came up behind me again, and he tried to go fast there. When I looked in my mirror I saw him mounting the sandbags and his two front wheels lifted up like a circus horse. He was lucky not to have turned over. I came flashing by for the last time with everything ready to receive me ... and the crowd! The chequered flag came down and I won!.*

I had a nice chat with the niece of the Prince of Monaco and it was she who presented me with the beautiful Challenge Cup. I also got a 4 foot bouquet which I gave to Mother who had brought me luck. I pinched, or rather Mother picked out for me, a dark red rose to take back to someone. I am afraid it won't last but I will press it. Dearest, in spite of all this dream you can rely on me that I am just your dearest Bira and nothing else. It has not changed his attitude towards life in any way. You must believe that darling.

The Motor wrote "One of the most brilliant young drivers in this country". *The Autocar:* "He certainly deserved it, for he not only drove finely, but his car is beautifully kept, and his équipe extremely smart". *Light Car:* "Hats off to Bira! Was there ever such a rapid rise to the top rung? Last year Bira was a pure novice, driving sports cars with a slightly timorous air as though to say: 'I hope I am doing this properly and not getting in anyone's way'. Now he ups and wins the world's most important small car race".

The next race was the class handicap International Trophy Race at Brooklands held on 2nd May, the day after the Private View at the Academy where Chula, Bira and I went to see the fountain in the form of a seal with a fish in its mouth that Bira was exhibiting. In the afternoon they went to Brooklands for the practice session.

Chula had a big staff in his estate office in Bangkok and always one or two of them in London to deal with his Siamese correspondence and type the manuscripts of his books, as Chula was a historical writer by profession. At that time his life of Frederick the Great had been published in Bangkok and he was working on the life of Catherine the Great of Russia, books which were later used by the university. One of Chula's Siamese secretaries, Banyen, had just arrived in England, excited at the prospect of seeing his first race. That day at Brooklands, Chula told Banyen to stand with me and help me take down the numbers of the cars as they passed as there were to be 44 starters and they would come round in bunches. He also wanted Banyen to start learning about racing charts so that he could take my place when they raced abroad. The race was won by Bira and turned out to be one of the most exciting I remember and I felt quite ill afterwards from the emotion, due not only to the spectacular finish when Bira beat Raymond Mays on the finishing line, but also because Chula had lost his head after a display of temper and nearly cost Bira the race. Fortunately, Bira had remained calm and obeyed

Chula's signals blindly, even though he could not understand them and thought he was a lap behind Mays right up to nearly the last moment.

When Bira stopped for fuel a pit official rushed up to Chula and told him there was one more mechanic helping than was allowed by the regulations. Chula screamed at one of the mechanics to get back into the pit, then lost his calm altogether and began shouting at everyone and, of course, lost his place on the lap chart. Despite my very timid attempts to put him right he wrote Raymond Mays down as having already come past, so gave him an extra lap on paper. He now thought that Mays was over a lap ahead of Bira when really he was only just in front of him. Then Bira had a stroke of luck because the official ERA pit had also made a mistake: when Mays came in for his pit stop, in their hurry to get him off and keep his lead over Bira they had not put in enough fuel, forcing him to stop again for a couple of seconds to tip more in and allowing Bira into the lead.

However, Chula's chart showed Bira second and he gave him that signal, instead of a signal to go faster as Mays was catching him up. Dr Benjafield, a special friend who had dropped out of the race, rushed up to Chula to tell him to get Bira speeded up or he would be caught, but Chula was by then in such a state of nerves he wouldn't believe him. Then Mays' pit made the most extraordinarily sporting gesture of putting Chula right, so Bira got his 'fast' signal at last, obeyed it and just won.The Light Carwrote "Of course, whenever the issue is as close as that, one hears 'ifs' by the score ... if Bira hadn't driven a simply superb race from start to finish, he would never have been in a position to win the International Trophy at his first attempt". Tommy Wisdom wrote in Sporting Life ""Bira beat Mays in a great finish. It was the finest finish ever seen at Brooklands in a long-distance event". After the race they had to rush up to London without time for Bira to wash or change as he was due to broadcast at the BBC where he spoke very well.

On the day after the race Chula blamed himself terribly for that mistake - he was always humble and miserable when he had lost his temper, which I fear he did frequently. He then told me about Madame Hoffmann, who had been Chiron's girlfriend and was much admired in racing circles for her accurate charts. After one Grand Prix she had been able to go up to the official time-keeper's box and prove that they had missed Chiron's car going past on one lap, and so had put him down as having done one lap less and not given him the chequered flag when he had, in fact ,won the race. The officials had to admit she was right because it was clear after looking at the times she had recorded for each car on every lap that they were in the wrong, and the race results were corrected. Now the beautiful 'Baby' Hoffmann was married to Caracciola and when I went to watch the race at Berne that summer with my father I could hardly take my eyes off her. She had become my heroine and the centre of my daydreams.

Having had two successful races with Romulus the team now left the car in the garage to be overhauled and went to Donington with Remus ,where Bira was second in one of the short handicap races and then on to Cork from where

I received this letter -

> **15th May.** Remus *is so troublesome. This morning we got him going but after 4 laps he refused to shift and so I did not practice much. The fuel pipe was blocked and there was a leak in the radiator. However, thank goodness we cleared the main trouble which occurred at Donington last time i.e. the carburation. This afternoon I think we will go to try and kiss the Blarney Stone near here to wish for something I want to have badly! It is supposed to work quite well so you better look out Ceril darling. You better make up your mind to marry me!!*

The car broke down when he was leading and Bira was sad that *Remus* was proving less reliable than *Romulus*. He realized now that if his car was running well he could hold his own with any of the other ERA drivers, even Mays. As it turned out, Bira was the only ERA driver to win not just one but three races on the Continent that year.

There appeared a new rival to the ERAs in the form of Dick Seaman with his completely rebuilt and modernized 1927 Delage. The ex-racing driver and mechanic, Giulio Ramponi, had come over from Italy to supervise the work and the car was ready, perfectly tuned and going beautifully. By the end of the season it was to be a close contest between Seaman and Bira as to who would win the British Racing Drivers' Club Gold Star for 1936 which, in the end Bira won by one point. In order to qualify for the Gold Star one had to be a member of the British Racing Drivers' Club, and Bira, resident in Britain, was elected an honorary member in 1935. Points were awarded after each race rather as for the present Drivers' World Championship.

In the end Bira was to win the Gold Star three years running - a record. After he won it for the second consecutive year, Chula gave each of his intimate friends a silver cigarette case designed and made by Cartier. As I didn't smoke I was given the lid of the case set in onyx as a paperweight.

Bira went on accumulating points, but more with *Romulus* than *Remus*, with whom the mechanics experienced constant trouble. They took *Romulus* to the Isle of Man for the race on 28th May which Seaman simply ran away with whilst Bira was second, but Dick said Bira's was the only car he couldn't shake off. It was true that the Delage was faster than the ERAs but it must be remembered that Dick Seaman was one of the greatest British drivers of all time. He and Bira were friends and had spent the evening before the race playing table tennis together, both being fine players.

After the Isle of Man came the Eifelrennen at the Nürburgring and the day before leaving London Chula's first book about Bira's racing was published. It was an account of the races in 1935 and Chula had written it for his friends. It was published privately by Lisba's father's firm, the Sun Engraving Company. Chula never thought the general public would be interested but was obviously mistaken as the whole edition sold out and was later republished by G.T Foulis. The book *Wheels at Speed* was very well and clearly written, as were all Chula's excellent motor racing books.

Bira wrote from Germany -

Adenau. *We arrived here from Brussels yesterday and found the little village of Adenau quite charming. Today after lunch we went to the circuit to practice. All the big cheeses were there and for once since Monaco I felt I was a nobody, and so did Ray and Dick!! Those big heroes were terrific with their big cars. I did 5 laps only during the 3 hours as the car was not properly prepared. Once it got going I was cutting down my time and I think mine was one of the best times the ERA produced, if not the best. However, Seaman and one Maserati beat us up hollow. He can't help winning on Sunday unless something goes wrong with the machine. He's got the speed, the driving, and the knowledge of the circuit. I shall be quite happy if I beat up the works ... I miss you like <u>anything</u>. I am so jealous of people like Chiron and Martin and Howe who have their girlfriends with them.*
Adenau.*This morning I received a lovely long letter. I do love your drawing illustrations, they make me laugh a lot and keep me amused. If I was the kind of swelling headed fellow you would not recognize me by now as everywhere I go people make a hell of a fuss of me.*

Telegram - "THIRD AFTER TWO ITALIANS **STOP** GOOD RACE".

Adenau. *We are just setting off for Paris and everyone is in a fine mood as the result of yesterday's racing. I was beaten by two Maseratis. They were both a brand new design¹ and tuned and driven by an ex-Alfa Romeo captain (Count Carlo Felice Trossi, who was for some years the President of the Scuderia Ferrari) and Tenni the champion motor cyclist! I was terribly bucked as I had beaten up all the others. The course was exceptionally difficult and all the big car stars were amazed by my performance because of the first time out and all that. Nuvolari said I ought to join up with the firm and drive big cars!!! Secretly, I may be given an Alfa to drive at Ulster!!! Don't spread it around yet, but what fun!!! Darling I must go now, but I worship you. I must fly. In haste.*

Firstly they were going to stay with Mother and Hin at *Le Mesle* near Rambouillet, the lovely house and beautiful garden that Chula had given his mother some years before. Then on to the Picardie race, which they feared might be cancelled because of the wide-spread strikes in France. The 1936

¹Trossi's car was a new design (the 6CM) but Tenni, in fact, drove the earlier Tipo 4CM.

Le Mans 24-hour race had already been cancelled, but the situation later improved.

Bira wrote -

Le Mesle, D'Adainville. *Life here is very restful and so we are quite quiet and peaceful. Mother asked me this morning to bring you here when Lisba's coming in July.*

Then they went to Péronne and, in order to get more speed from *Romulus* to try and keep up with Dick's Delage, sent to England for *Remus's* larger supercharger.

Telegram - "WON SPECTACULARLY **STOP** PHONE ME WHEN YOU COME IN MONDAY".

They came back for the Nuffield Trophy at Donington, and as *Remus* was still being overhauled and *Romulus* needed a rest, Lord Austin lent Bira one of his 750cc 'Twin Cam' racing cars for the handicap race. Bira simply loved this little car which was like a toy to him after his own bigger ones, and if there was one thing Bira adored it was toys. Unfortunately ,it ran into trouble, but Bira still managed to finish fifth. Next was Albi on 9th July. All the usual cars were there with the exception of Seaman who had gone off the road at Péronne putting the Delage out of action.

Albi. *Chula and I have talked a great deal more about you than before. I think he felt I was miserable a little. He said all very nice things about you especially that you were such an honest 'A1' girl! That if you say something you're sure to mean it. I am awfully glad you both like each other as I love you both so much. It would be a tragedy otherwise ... Yesterday's practice hasn't been successful as I couldn't get much 'revs' owing to the new back axle, but the mechanics changed it last night. I hope I can do better next time.*

Telegram - "WON HAPPILY WISH YOU WERE HERE".

The Light Car wrote "So Bira has done it again! What Caracciola was to formula racing in 1935, Bira is to voituretting this year. Bravo! And again, Bravo! What a man this is!"

Bira, luckily, remained totally unspoiled by all this adulation!

CHAPTER FIVE

Chula and Bira now had two free weeks before the race at Limerick and before my family were going abroad. Chula intended taking Lisba to *Le Mesle* to introduce her to his mother and asked Bira to bring me too; he thought it would be fun for the four of us to spend ten days together in France. Bira, quite unthinkingly, put paid to any hopes of that. One evening when he was having dinner with us at Evelyn Gardens we were talking about Paris, and Bira told us what had happened to him there some years ago. He and Chula had been staying at Neuilly with Chula's mother and Hin in their lovely flat, and Mother had given an Easter party for her Russian friends, serving Russian food she had prepared herself (she was a superb cook) and a lot of vodka and good wine. As the evening wore on the party became somewhat noisy, and Bira, who hated parties unless there were games or dancing, got very bored with the whole thing and slipped away to bed. In the night he was woken by Chula's mother shouting at him and trying to pull him out of bed. How dared he leave her party without her permission? He was ill-mannered, spoilt, and so it went on until she became quite hysterical. She flounced out of the room saying he was to get up at once and return to the party. He did get up but quietly left the flat instead and walked round the corner into the Avenue de la Grande Armée where there was a small and very modest hotel. He asked the night porter for a room where he slept until morning. When he returned to the flat for breakfast he found pandemonium. After the party had finally broken up, Chula had gone to his room to find Bira gone. The shock sobered him up at once, he got out of his mother what had happened and was very angry with her indeed, also frightened. Bira was just a boy; where had he gone - what would he do alone in Paris at night? He was about to ring up the police when Bira calmly walked in, surprised at all the fuss.

Bira thought it was a very funny story but my mother most certainly did not. Paris, Russians, drink, wild parties - she was certainly not going to allow her daughter to go and stay with people where that kind of thing went on. During the telling I had signalled to Bira frantically to stop; he hadn't seen and now the damage was done.

So Chula and Lisba went to *Le Mesle* alone. Lisba got on very well with Chula's mother during the visit - sadly, that changed when Mrs Stone became her mother-in-law. While there, Chula proposed. He said afterwards that he felt he had to do so because he realised the time would soon come when Bira would leave him and he would be alone. He definitely did not approve of mixed marriages after his experience as the child of one, but although he did not want to get married just yet he knew that if he didn't make the effort then to try and get Lisba away from her Swiss friend he might lose her for ever. However, Lisba said no, she was not yet sure enough of her feelings and wanted more time to think about it.

Consequently, Chula didn't return from his mother's in a very good mood and certainly not in the right mood to face the run of bad luck they would have in August. At Limerick Bira ran into a wall taking a corner on the course that ran through the town with, fortunately ,no harm to him and only repairable damage to *Remus*, but there was terrible tragedy as the Duke of Grafton was killed in that race: it had been his first racing season.

After returning to their flat for a few days, Chula and Bira set off again to race in Italy. While there they learned that Bira's fountain had been sold at the Academy; later it turned out that it had been bought by Gracie Fields for her home in Capri. The other event of note was that they bought a Maserati, an ex-Whitney Straight 8CM 3-litre complete with many spare parts. Bira wrote to tell me about it, sending the letter to Munich.

> *Dearest heart what do you think I have done? I have sold my work for a hundred guineas!!! Oh darling I am so thrilled!! The Seal cost £36 to cast and I get 70 pounds!! Its my first earning too. Isn't it wonderful? Chula is so excited about it as it is such an encouragement ... We have just bought the Maserati and tomorrow we are going down to Brooklands to try it out. I hope I can drive it after all that effort and expense.*

They were due at Pescara in the south of Italy on August 12th, where *Romulus* ran into trouble halfway through the race and caught fire in the pits. The Duke of Bergamo was presiding over the race and came down from the tribune to sympathise with Bira for having to drop out when he was second to Seaman.

From Pescara they went to stay with Crown Prince Umberto in the Royal Palace at Naples, and he took them to Capri in his motor boat. A pity the Seal hadn't arrived or Bira could have gone to see it. A letter from Pescara read -

Pescara. *I am looking forward to your visit to Berne every minute that goes by ...The Bentley has been admired by every single person who has seen it, even by the most blasé of all blasés (Raymond Mays and that crowd) ...We leave here after the race tomorrow and go to Naples to stay with Prince Umberto until Monday morning, and sleep somewhere that night on our way to Berne. Wednesday I shall motor up to where you are and stay with you 2 nights. I suggest bringing you, and perhaps Poppa, to stay in Berne for the race until Monday morning. It is the only way of seeing each other as much as we can. Chula and I will be back in England after Biarritz. I must work for the Siamese section of the 1937 Paris Exhibition.*

As *Romulus'* engine had been damaged by the fire at Pescara, *Remus'* engine had to be rushed out to Berne to replace it, but Bira broke down again when lying second to Seaman. We said goodbye at Berne as they had to rush back for the Junior Car Club handicap race the weekend after at Donington. Bira failed to finish for the fourth consecutive race and gloom descended on the team.

Meanwhile, my family were having a marvellous holiday; we four enjoyed being together. My mother and Way paired off to go sightseeing everywhere, while my father and I tended more to go swimming and rowing on the lakes and for walks in the mountains looking for flowers. I also loved the shops, especially in Vienna and Venice, though having to manage on the small allowance my father gave me meant I could only window-shop. My father loved and spoilt me, but not with money, and if I ran out before the end of the month it was no use asking for more: the answer would always be no. Soon after I met Bira he came to fetch me in the Bentley; it was Armistice Day and a poppy seller happened to be standing on the pavement just outside our house as he arrived. Bira at once chose the largest poppy on the tray and fastened it to the silver tiger mascot on the car; a mascot he had sculpted himself as he was born in the year of the tiger. Then he discovered he had come out without money so asked me to lend him five pounds. I did, but how I regretted it; I'd given him half my month's allowance and he promptly forgot all about it. Of course I never said anything, and couldn't ask my father for more, so spent a very lean second half of the month.

Meanwhile, Chula and Bira had gone straight from Donington to Belfast for the Tourist Trophy Race for sports cars in which Bira drive one of the BMW team cars.as they had sold the Aston Martin. From there he wrote to me on holiday -

Belfast. *We are returning to London Saturday 19th so please hurry home. In yesterday's race it was terrible bad luck, but I did complete the race in 7th place and our team of BMWs won. I should have been second at least. I had a very bad start, the*

*starter motor refused to work so I didn't know what to do. With
great desperation I got the car going but not until the last car of
my group was out of sight. I was terribly put-off by that, and also
the rain was pelting down cats and dogs. It was quite a disgusting
day. When I got going about the 4th lap I broke Nuvolari's record
of the 2-litre class 3 times, then my brakes wore down. However I
look at it philosophically and thanked the stars I could finish a
race after those last 4 disasters. Tomorrow we are going to
Donington to try out the Maserati. I must get some more points at
Phoenix Park and Donington. We must beat up Seaman whatever
happens. It would be heart-breaking after having led him for 30
points before. Chula wants to eat now as we have been out all day
on a social lunch on a millionaire's yacht, and Lady Londonderry!!'*
London. *Let me know when you will be arriving at Dover so that I
can fetch you to bring you up to London, and you will be floating
on the wings of a dove! With me beside you! The Maserati is being
painted Bira Blue and I saw half of the job done when I went down
to inspect the Bentley. She looks incredibly nice, and so will the
Bentley on Monday when I shall go and fetch her. I am so excited
at the prospect of seeing you again so soon before I go away to
Phoenix.*
*Next Saturday Henry and Chula and I will go up to Manchester to
stay the weekend!! It's quite mad ... on Sunday we are going to
drive over to Blackpool and enjoy ourselves at the fun fair ...This
morning I started a mask of Freddie Dixon as I intend to do as
many masks as possible of famous racing drivers. I worked at it all
day, but with no result. It looked like ER Hall instead! I have just
left it with disappointment and I will remodel it when I wake up
tomorrow.*

The excuse for going to Blackpool was that Chula had been asked to write
a book in Siamese on England and English customs and said he wanted to
include Blackpool. The real reason, however, was that Bira simply adored
funfairs and very much wanted to visit this giant one and visit it with Henry
Maxwell (son of the well-known writer W B Maxwell), quite one of the wittiest,
most amusing and kindest men it is possible to meet, who had been at Harrow
and Cambridge with Chula. He was their much loved friend and Bira's
favourite playmate; model ships, trains, aeroplanes, in fact, models and toys
of all sorts were a passion for them both. From there they went to Ireland for
the first event with the new Maserati, a handicap race at Phoenix Park.

Telegram - "SECOND TO SMALL MG **STOP** BROKE LAP RECORD **STOP**
ENJOYED DRIVE **STOP** BEST LOVE."

The Autocar wrote "...driving from scratch he handled the 3-litre Maserati
in masterly style". *The Light Car* "He was unquestionably the most polished

car driver on the course, and on corners there was no one to touch him for skill and speed".

They rushed back from Ireland in order to be at the practice at Donington for the Grand Prix, their last long distance race that season, but the Maserati failed at the start and Bira only achieved fifth place. As the race was on my 20th birthday we all stayed with the Pinneys and I went back to London the following day with Bira. There was one more Brooklands meeting and then they entered for the Brighton Veteran Car Run with a 1902 Peugeot, taking Henry as a passenger. Thus, the 1936 season ended and Bira won the British Racing Drivers' Club Star.

After that life calmed down, and we both worked at sculpture and painting. Bira did an excellent portrait bust of Chula and started his designs for the Paris exhibition.

Bira would sometimes go with me to see my Aunts and they thought him a most amusing boy with beautiful manners. He and Aunt C would talk about their mutual love of France and the friends they both had in Paris and S. Jean de Luz. With Aunt Ray he talked about Italy and art, and also a lot about Siam.

Aunt Ray had collected stamps since she was a child and by now had a large and important collection. She was a girl when King Chulalongkorn had come to England on his state visit and her Uncle George had entertained the King at the Mansion House. Knowing she collected stamps he had given her all those from the correspondence with Bangkok before and after the visit. That had started Aunt Ray on a specialized collection of Siamese stamps in a separate album, because of which she had become very interested in the country itself. She and Bira would study the album together while he explained his relationship with the various Kings on the stamps and told her how his father, Prince Bhanurangsri, who had been in charge of the army as well as several ministries including Post and Communications, had also been a keen stamp collector. Eventually Aunt Ray gave Bira her album of Siamese stamps, which was a pity as Bira never took care of his possessions and some very valuable examples indeed passed through his hands only in the end to disappear altogether.

Bira also discovered the Aunts' toy cupboard and it was an Aladdin's cave for him. They had brought all their childhood games with them when they moved from Grosvenor Street and Way and I had been allowed to play carefully with one or two on Sunday afternoons. Now Aunt Ray and Bira had them all out. Aunt Ray loved playing with toys and Bira said they were exactly the same kind of games his father had brought back from visits to Europe for him.

We didn't go skiing that winter because the racing season was due to start again in February and Bira didn't feel he should interrupt his work until then. We met as often as possible in the evenings and our favourite place was the small room just off the restaurant at the Berkeley Buttery, where we always had the same table and the wine waiter would come up at once with our big jug of fresh orange juice decorated with little pieces of fruit. Sometimes Bira had to leave me alone while he went to the cloakroom to give himself an injection. I always hoped people didn't think the very worst if they saw him doing it, but about a year before he had suffered violent food poisoning from a bad oyster, and now suddenly without warning his face would begin to swell until his eyes disappeared, and his hands and face would become covered in rash. Dr. Pettivel had discovered the antidote which, when injected, would bring down the swelling at once, and had told Bira to come to him whenever it occurred. However, as Bira pointed out, if it happened when he was away racing, or was out in the evening at a theatre, he couldn't get to the doctor. He had therefore persuaded Dr Pettivel to teach him to inject himself and always carried a full syringe with him. It was several years before Bira got rid of this complaint altogether which, in the meantime, often caused him considerable distress.

CHAPTER SIX

During the winter of 1936 Chula and Bira made their plans for the next season: we were to be married at the end of it when I would be twenty one and then the three of us planned to go to Siam for six months.

The first thing they did was buy Dick Seaman's Delage, which had been so successful in 1936 and which he offered for sale as he had been asked to join the Mercedes-Benz Grand Prix team. He was also selling all the spare parts and an extra engine. Chula managed to buy a second Delage from Captain J. C. Davis and their idea was to modify and rebuild both the cars with the co-operation of Lory, the original designer, so that for the 1937 season they would have two Delages and one spare engine. They sold their ERA *Remus* but kept *Romulus* and also the 8CM Maserati to use as spare cars just in case the Delages didn't work. Which they didn't! They were an enormously expensive mistake: the cars were not ready until June and then were too heavy and never finished a race that year. It was indeed lucky they had kept their ERA *Romulus* and the Maserati and had bought a sports Delahaye, or the season would have been a very sad one. As it was, *Romulus* won three races and was second in three, the Maserati won one race and was third in three and the Delahaye won one race which meant, at least that Bira won the Gold Star again, despite the Delage failure.

Their programme was for twelve races in England and Ireland with eight abroad and Chula and Bira left for Pau on 17th February, very reluctantly, as Chula had a streaming cold. Their reason for going was to decide whether to buy a sports Delahaye and to try one out in the race there first.

Bira wrote -

Darling, I was kept so busy before the race, and after Chula felt so rotten, we left as soon as we came off the course. I was the first to get off the line behind Wimille's Bug. I was behind him the whole time until I blew up. However it dispelled my usual doubts before each season that I could not really drive a racing car!!! I think personally we were "had" by the works people at Delahaye because other "independents" went out with the same trouble. Anyhow we must do some good in our own show next month, and darling, thank heaven I am going to be with you again soon.

However, they did later buy the Delahaye. At the Easter meeting at Brooklands Bira managed a second and third place in handicap races with *Romulus*, after which they went to Donington with the Maserati for the British Empire Trophy but retired with a broken gearbox. Two days later they were on their way to Turin in the Bentley, taking Henry with them.

Turin, 15th April 1937. *We all got up at 7.30 this morning to practice and you ought to have seen Henry's face at that hour!! It was too good to be true. I made the fastest time of the day and the car, so far, sounded very nicely. I don't want to tell you too much darling about the race as I am very shaky about how long the car will last!! Nuvolari crashed this morning, so won't be driving on Sunday which is a pity as he alone would have given a spectacle in the big race. Our small race will be more interesting as far as racing is concerned.*

Turin, 18th April. *I take this opportunity to write a few lines before going out to race. I always feel the greatest need of your company when I am excited before a race, but this time I have to content myself by thinking about you. Last night after I wrote to you we went to Biella where Count Trossi lives in his beautiful castle ..and it was simply wonderful. Very old and has a draw-bridge!! Inside the courtyard the moon was shining on a fountain. Oh darling, what a bliss of a place. When we go near there I will take you to stay with them. Oh how I would love to have a place like that as it was just like in a book or a film. A starlit night, with moon shining on an old castle, and a very charming young couple of Italian Count and Countess!!!! I think she is terribly in love with her husband but seemed rather depressed because she is not very well with the same complaint as mine. Rash on her hands and feet. Also she terribly wants a child and her first child died. Aw-fully sad thing as I never met anyone who wanted so much to bear her husband a child and heir. He has a garage in the stables where he is building a special racing car. I will now go and dress up and prepare for a fight with the Italians!! They are pretty fast this year, but good old Romulus must try and beat them. It will be my joy to see him do his tricks again!! I wonder what sort of*

54

weather you are having in St Jean. Write to me often and love me as I love you, although I know it is nearly impossible. Prince Umberto arrived last night to attend the race this morning, but we have not seen him yet. I think it will be a good race with equal chances for everyone.

Bira started the race at Turin in the front row and led for 30 out of 40 laps before retiring with gearbox trouble. He told me he had asked Countess Trossi at dinner the evening before if she went to watch her husband race. She said that not only had she never seen him race, but that she was too frightened even to listen to the race on the wireless. When he was racing she always stayed in the family chapel praying.

From Turin they went on to race at Naples.

It was stormy when we reached the beautiful city of Naples. Vesuvius was hidden by clouds of rainstorm and so robbed us of one of the wonders of the world. The hotel is packed with people, but beautiful rooms were reserved for us by il Principe, so everything is nice and comfortable. I shan't write any more as I guess you will be leaving St Jean on Monday. I shall send you a wire letting you know how I got on in the race on Sunday. Umberto is so busy we have not had a glimpse of him yet. We are however supposed to be lunching with him tomorrow at the palace.'

Telegram: - "SECOND TO TROSSI VERY GOOD SHOW **STOP** MISS YOU SO MUCH **STOP** YOUR BUST ACCEPTED ACADEMY **STOP** PLEASE TRY BE BACK THURSDAY".

I went with Chula and Bira to the Private View at the Academy to see the portrait bust he had done of me cast in green bronze on the morning before the Campbell Trophy Race at Brooklands, and in the afternoon we watched Bira practice. After he had finished, Chula and I sat together in the car while Bira was making his report to the mechanics and had one of our first serious talks. Chula said that he needed my help and wanted to explain exactly why. He said he had taken Lisba to Paris after Christmas to stay with his mother and step-father, and that while there she had told him she was now willing to marry him even though he had not asked her again. It was he, this time, who hesitated. He had decided that after Bira and I married in October and the three of us went out to Siam for the winter, he would take a look at Siamese princesses with a view to perhaps marrying one of them instead of Lisba. He knew that he was probably the most intelligent of the younger princes and had begun to feel it might be both a duty and a pleasure to fill the gap in his life, left after Bira married me, by working for his country. In that case, a Siamese wife of his own rank would be more support to him than a European wife, especially as he was only half Siamese. Before making up his mind, however, he wanted to know what, if he did marry Lisba, her position would be in Siam.

The only way he could discover this was to use my marriage to Bira as a test case. He thought it would be much better if we could delay our marriage for two months and for Bira to go back alone to ask the Council of Regency's permission to marry in person, not just send the request by letter from England. Chula did not think they would then withhold their permission, but he badly wanted to know what rank they would give me because whatever position or title they gave me would then be given to Lisba if he married her. He very much wanted to know this before making up his mind.

Chula knew that all this made no difference to Bira and me as all we wanted was to be together. We neither of us liked a social life and planned to live as artists with Bira's racing as an amusement for as long as it lasted. Bira was really only interested in art and sport. We hoped to have a house and studio in London where we could both work during the spring and summer between races, and in the winter find another studio in Bangkok where I could paint and Bira carry out the many orders for portraits he knew he would get, as he was already getting them in England. I was now painting portraits and, like Bira, exhibiting in a small way. It was the kind of life we liked; neither of us wanted any sort of smart or grand life but for Chula it was different. He very much wanted to live as a royal person and wanted the same for his wife. He deeply hoped I would be accepted as a Siamese princess which, as it turned out, I was, because then it would mean that Lisba would also be accepted as such if he decided to marry her. It was most important to him and for this he needed my help. He knew that if he asked Bira to postpone our marriage he would refuse at once, because we were both counting the days to it, whereas if I sided with Chula and helped to convince Bira, maybe he would agree.

Chula said he and I must work together over this and went on to give me two more reasons. The first was entirely in his favour, the second in mine. He very much wanted to share with Bira alone the wonderful welcome that would be waiting for them. The Siamese people were so proud and enthusiastic about their racing successes, especially all the young people, that they were only waiting for Bira's return to give him a hero's welcome. As Bira's successes had been due to Chula who had made it all possible, it seemed to me quite natural that he should want them to go back without me and, as by now I liked Chula very much, for this reason alone I would have helped him. The other reason I also thought sensible, but didn't really like at all. Chula pointed out that Bira had not been home since he was thirteen, ten years ago, and had met very few Siamese girls in Europe. Now when he went home the loveliest of them (and Siamese girls are very lovely) would be falling at his feet. What would happen if he were to discover he preferred them to an English girl after all? Would it not be better to find out before marriage than after? I didn't relish the idea of all that competition, but couldn't deny that Chula was right.

I felt very sympathetic to Chula's concern about what Lisba's position would be if they married, as I knew it would mean a lot to both of them, so agreed to do all I could for him. By now I was beginning to like Chula more and more, and above all to admire and completely trust him. Whether he chose Lisba or a Siamese princess to be his wife was, of course, his own business, but I felt it would be sad if he lost Lisba: she would obviously be a wife to be very proud of, she was so beautiful and I thought she would make - as indeed she did - a wonderful hostess.

I had been quietly observing Chula over the last two and a half years and privately thought he had a Jekyll and Hyde character; he seemed to me a complicated and mixed-up man. He could, if he wished, be the kindest, most generous, loyal and unselfish person imaginable, and there was nothing he wouldn't do to help a friend. He was a brilliantly clever man, a charming and interesting companion but had an awful 'Hyde' side to him. He could be cruel, almost sadistic, often to people who could not defend themselves or were dependent on him. His tempers and rages would flare up and were appalling, as were his bad moods (often fuelled by unwise drinking) and this I decided must be his Russian side showing through as his mother could be the same - all the Siamese I had met up to then were the gentlest of people. Shura was often one of Chula's 'victims' but because of his sweet nature, and because he loved and was grateful to Chula, he never answered back, but then Shura was a saint. Lisba, unfortunately, answered back later, but Bira took no notice at all of Chula's moods, which was the best way to treat them.

Anyhow, I did what Chula asked and put it to Bira, giving Chula's reasons, that we might perhaps wait to get married until after his return from Siam. At first Bira agreed, then changed his mind and said he couldn't wait, so it wasn't until the summer that we finally told Chula we would do as he wanted.

They had taken both the Delage and the Maserati to the practice at Brooklands that day, but it was obvious to everyone that the Delage was not yet ready. The steering was unsatisfactory and the brakes not working properly. In the race the following day Bira drove the Maserati and had a spectacular duel with Lord Howe; he and Bira taking it in turns to lead for a quarter of the race. Then Lord Howe, who was in front at that moment, took his eyes off the road for a quick glance back to see where Bira was and crashed. This upset Bira for a long time afterwards as he had seen the whole thing happen so close in front of him. Bira went on to win the race and, in time, Lord Howe completely recovered.

The next event was the Coronation Mountain race at Brooklands and Chula, Bira, Henry and I went there together. The week before had been a busy one for Chula as he was representing his young King at the Coronation of King George VI and Queen Elizabeth, going to Westminster Abbey with his Siamese equerry and to the banquets at Buckingham Palace and the Foreign Office. He had arranged for Bira, Lisba and I to watch the procession together from a building on the route. Bira raced *Romulus* in the Coronation Mountain Race, a handicap, just failing to catch one of the small cars and finishing second. They went on to Cork for another handicap race and from where, as usual, Bira wrote -

Cork. *After lunch I drove round and round the circuit and just stopped to let Joan have a run. Later I flew my model aeroplane.*

During the night Bira woke up in pain and was very sick; something he had eaten at dinner must have disagreed with him. Nevertheless, he decided to race and made a good start from the front row with the other scratch car, C E C ('Charlie') Martin's Alfa. Then after fifteen minutes his arms went quite numb, he had no strength to get the car round the next corner and crashed into a wall. By some miracle he was practically unhurt but the Maserati was wrecked. It was Bira's first real crash; the first of many, and the *Daily Herald* next morning carried the headline "... taken ill at 90 mph".

Despite this they went to the Isle of Man a week later for the RAC International Light Car Race on 3rd June, an important race as it was the chief 1500cc race held in Great Britain during 1937. They took both the Delage and the ERA *Romulus* with them, hoping they would be able to use the Delage at last. It was there that Bira first met Baron 'Toulo' de Graffenried - with whom we were later to become friends - as he and Villoresi, with Maseratis, were the only foreign drivers. The ERA was much faster than the Delage so Bira drove *Romulus*. He led straight away from Raymond Mays and Pat Fairfield, who were both driving official ERA team cars, and the race was held in pouring rain. *The Times* wrote "Bira drove a superb race throughout. He thoroughly deserved his victory, having driven a grand race under such very difficult conditions".

A few days later they were on their way to Italy for what, it transpired, were three very disappointing races beginning with the Florence GP. To add to that it was on this trip that they heard the dreadful news that Pat Fairfield had crashed at Le Mans and died of his injuries. It was an appalling blow for everyone in racing to lose this magnificent South African driver, so liked by everyone. Bira was very touched when he was given the order to design and execute the Fairfield Memorial, which was unveiled the following year at Donington by Lord Howe.

Bologna. *Darling, when we left Paris we slept at Sens. The next morning we left for Aix-les-Bains, but I suddenly had a wish to buy a baby Rolliflex so we decided to go to Geneva for it, but arrived there about 6 o'clock so could not buy the camera.*
We thought we might as well go and call on the small King at Lausanne. We arrived there about 7.45, by which time the children were preparing for bed. Both Ananda and Leck (little brother) were so excited to see 'B.Bira' they ran round and round the room. They were simply sweet. They showed me their press cuttings and all sorts of things about me and the racing cars. They were too excited to go to bed then, so were allowed to stay up for a little*

*King Ananda Mahidol Rama VIII acceded in 1935, aged 10.

longer. In the end they persuaded their mother to put us up for the night so that they could sleep next door to 'B.Bira'!! At nine o'clock we heard awful noises going on upstairs and their nurse came down and told us they refused to go to sleep, so at once I went upstairs and told them they had better get to bed as they had to go to school in the morning. They at once obeyed and then I tucked them up in bed!! The sister was allowed to stay up a bit longer as she is older.
When Chula and I came upstairs we found our names written on the wall in chalk with arrows showing our rooms. Wasn't it sweet? The next morning they came and woke me at 7.00!! and begged me to take them to school in the Bentley which I did. I managed to buy the camera there before we left for Italy.

Florence 13th June 1937 , telegram - "LED THREE LAPS SECOND FOR ELEVEN LAPS THEN BRAKES BUSTED VERY TIRING RACE BEST LOVE".

Ceril my darlingest I am most terribly sorry I could not send you a more cheerful wire, but after a breakdown like that it was rather disheartening as we did not know whether it was possible to be mended by Milan race. I jumped into the lead, then led Trossi by miles. After 3 laps he came up and passed me as I expected, then after 11 laps I saw Bianco coming up in the mirror so speeded up, but found it impossible as I had less power for braking. I dropped to 4th, even then I struggled on but it was apparent after 30 laps I had no brakes at all.we will run the Delage at Péronne and send Romulus back to England straight after Milan. Darlingest if you can't come to Péronne for the race don't bother as I have no chance anyhow to do any good as the Delage is so slow.
Villa D'Este, Lake Como. *I have just come back from Milan and now practically have to jump into the bath as we have Count Lurani coming to dine with us. Today Romulus was not ready so Johnny Lurani lent me his car and I did 4 secs faster than him each lap!! He's rather distressed about that!!*

Romulus again failed to finish a race and the Delage failed at Péronne in the Picardie GP. Wuyts, the mechanic, resigned, he and Bira having had a disagreement because Bira, seeing the car was going so badly and the clutch slipping, came in and retired whilst Wuyts thought he should have continued.

Now Raymond (Lofty) England came to them as chief mechanic with Stanley Holgate as assistant mechanic, while Shura continued to help everyone. Chula and Bira realised what a big mistake the Delage had been and that it was the indirect cause of *Romulus'*two failures in Italy. There had been nothing seriously wrong with the ERA, it had just not been prepared as well as usual as too much time had been spent on the Delage. They gave orders to put it completely on one side and give all attention to the ERA, rebuilding the Maserati after Cork and the Delahaye: the season started to improve.

On 15th July 1937 Bira celebrated his 23rd birthday and on 17th won the London Grand Prix with *Romulus* at the Crystal Palace which cheered them up again. The following week Chula introduced Bira to the King and Queen at the Royal Garden Party at Buckingham Palace. King George VI was most interested in motor racing but told Bira to be careful and not get himself killed. On 24th July Bira won the 12-hour sports car race at Donington in the Delahaye with H G Dobbs as his co-driver.

In August Chula went to stay with his mother and Hin and did not come back for the Crystal Palace Cup race because Lisba was passing through Paris with her mother on their way to Salzburg. For the first time he trusted me to keep the chart alone. Bira came second, after which he joined Chula for the journey to Berne.

Bellevue Palace, Berne, 20th August. *In the evening we came down to dinner late and just sat around gossiping to people. In the bar here there are four very good caricatures of drivers: Rosemayer, Nuvolari, Caracciola and 'B'. Mine is rather fun as they only had a 'B' and a crown on the top! I can't tell you about our chances yet or if we have any until after this afternoon's practice. I think we have none anyway. Tomorrow Ananda's party are coming to lunch. The two boys want so badly to watch a racing car at close quarters. They are simply sweet, especially Leck.***
This must be just a line dearest as we are in a terrible jam. The ERA has blown up twice, in both practices, and we are rather in a dump. I wish you were here to cheer me up. The King and his family turned up today; yesterday we had Prince Chichibu, the brother of the Emperor of Japan. Poor mechanics, they have to put Romulus *right by tomorrow but I don't think there is any hope to win as the car won't last more than 3 laps at the most.*

Telegram - "THIRD AFTER DOBSON MAYS **STOP** WHILE RAIN FIRST **STOP** GOOD RACE **STOP** LOOKING FORWARD TUESDAY BEST LOVE".

**The present King Bhumipol Adulyadej of Thailand

CHAPTER SEVEN

The summer of 1937 our family stayed in England and my parents rented a little house at the mouth of the Beaulieu River looking across the Solent to Cowes. My father hired a rowing boat with an outboard motor for us to use together.

Between races Bira came to stay and for the first time discovered how much he enjoyed being on the water. He took over the boat completely when he was there, and then decided he must have one of his own. He bought all the yachting magazines and while driving Chula to Berne apparently talked of nothing else. He saw an advertisement for exactly the kind of boat he was dreaming about, a very expensive cabin cruiser, and asked Chula if he would give it to him as a wedding present. Chula quite firmly said no, he had already decided his present for us would be furniture for whatever house we found in London. Bira said, in that case, he would buy the boat himself. In the end they compromised and agreed to share the boat and pay half each: Bira would use it the following summer in England and then the boat would be sent out to Siam for us all to use there.

After their return from Berne Bira ordered the 37-foot motor cruiser. He now made new plans for our honeymoon: no longer a trip to Italy, we would cross the Channel and go along the canals through France. He bought nautical maps to study, completely disregarding the fact that neither of us had had any boating experience at all, except for outings on the river in that small rowing boat. It certainly worried me - I was a very bad sailor.

My brother seldom came to Beaulieu, spending most of his time with Uncle Harry. After my uncle had come back to live in England he began writing books for children on riding, gave talks on *Childrens Hour* at the BBC, became one of the founders of Pony Clubs and did a lot of judging at horse shows. He bought a house in Hertfordshire and opened the 'Major Faudel-Phillips Ltd. Riding Academy.' Aunt Nell had died and he lived there alone with his staff of teachers. My brother was then working on the Stock Exchange and, thinking he was getting too little exercise, my parents sent him to stay with my uncle from where he travelled to London each day. Way had never been interested in sport or exercise of any sort and I don't think he particularly liked riding, but he did like one of my uncle's very pretty young instructresses very much indeed!

After Chula and Bira returned from Berne they had seven races in seven weeks; Chula said it was like living in a circus. There were two races at Donington, two at Dublin, one at Brooklands, then Czechoslovakia and back for Donington again and the last race of the season at the Crystal Palace. Before they left for Czechoslovakia, Bira burnt his face and arm rather badly during the BRDC 500 mile race on the Outer Circuit at Brooklands when acid from the Delahaye's battery sprayed over him so, together with Henry, they went to Brno by train instead of driving there.

Bira wrote -

Brno, Czechoslovakia. 24th September 1937. *We had quite a long and tiring journey from London and changed trains no fewer than 5 times. We were met by a very smart Czech who came to receive us at Prague and accompanied us to Brno. He came to receive us in proxy for the Prime Minister so altogether we felt quite grand!! The whole journey by train I did little else except reading all about the coast of the English Channel!!! and I learned quite a lot more about the sea. My face is nearly peeled off now but it is pretty patchy! So I hope you won't be ashamed of me. Do you know I am at the present moment nearly 3000 miles away from you and yet I simply worship you ... It will be something like hell when I go away next month to Siam, but I shall console myself by saying to myself that I shall be doing the right thing. Please give my love to Mummy and Daddy and Whiskey.*

Telegram - "FIRST AFTER TWO THIRDS BLEW UP CAME FOURTH ALL LOVE".

The day after the Donington Grand Prix, where Bira was sixth with the 8CM Maserati, was my twenty first birthday which meant I was free to marry him, although we had decided to wait until after their return from Siam as it meant so much to Chula. Bira won the last race of the season, the Imperial Trophy at Crystal Palace, with *Romulus*. What a wonderful car! Three firsts that year, three seconds and two thirds. For 1938 they were planning to get another ERA and call it *Hanuman* after the monkey-god hero of the Ramayana, the ancient Sanskrit epic poem. Now they arranged to take *Romulus* to Siam to put on show and for Bira to give a demonstration run in.

They sailed from Marseille on 16th October, George Pinney and Banyen went with them. For Bira it was his first return home since he was thirteen.

Over the next few months I received many letters from Bira, telling me all about his visit -

In-flight to Paris on Imperial Airways airliner. *You were a complete darling when you wept. It nearly stopped me coming altogether ... I have a front cabin seat, and so am left to myself to ponder over these ten dream years I have spent in this wonderful land, and before I know where I am, I am en route back home.*

P&O Rajputana 19th October 1937. *Before we reached Malta, the sea got rather restless and we were just saved by the ship coming into port quickly. About 60 passengers got off then and just before the ship arrived at Malta the daughter of Lord Howe summoned up her courage and walked up to me and introduced herself. She said all her friends had chaffed her for not coming to speak to me before because I knew her father on the track and all that. Besides she said that had she gone without having spoken to me her husband, who is a great enthusiast of motor sports, would never have forgiven her. She was sweet about everything and we had a nice long chat. She was coming out to be with her husband who is at Malta on one of the torpedo boats .... As soon as the boat was outside the harbour again she began to heave and roll like a small pea in a soup pot! Chula at once rushed downstairs.*

23rd October 1937. *By the time you get a mail from me from Bombay you will have to read it in series as it will be so long!! After I wrote you last there have been quite uneventful days. The sea was merciful and calm, but it became terribly warm. We got to know three or four young men, and an old Admiral and his staff, two lieutenants called Chubb and Proffet. We made a poker party with the friends I mentioned and George and Chula, and we had a very amusing evening as I bluffed like anything. In the end I won about four shillings. I nearly finished the book by Cecil Roberts and will begin on* Wheels at Speed *as I have not read it yet. Chula has thought of writing another one and it will be called* Bira Blue. *Tomorrow we arrive at Aden.*

26th October 1937. *After I wrote to you we prepared to give a small film show for a few enthusiasts who wished to see the motor racing films, the Captain, the Admiral, and 10 other male guests. We showed the first and second years of racing and it was a great success. After the show it was about 10.30 so we had a small gathering for drinks and then went to bed ... Yesterday it was announced that there would be a fancy dress dance, and Proffet came and asked whether he could be B.Bira, so I lent him my blue overalls plus the wind cap and dark goggles. I of course wore my*

Tyrolean costume.

I had a good game of deck tennis with the Admiral, Fox, and Proffet. I like that crowd, you know, as they are not at all spoilt and quite sweet in their way. We then went to a small cocktail party given by the Purser; there were males only. He mixed Chula a very potent one and he was laid out before the fancy dress parade! I am very glad I am an absolute teetotaller as it saves a lot of bother! Proffet of course looked very trim in my kit, with George and Chubb as the mechanics, although they looked more like stokers! Poor Chula by this time was prostrated in his cabin and could hardly say a word when I went down to see him from time to time. The whole thing went on until midnight, altogether the brightest evening we have had so far on this trip.

28th October 1937. *I played deck tennis with the Admiral and Chubb and Fox, also the General and Proffet joined in. I have never yet met anyone who cheated more than those two, the Admiral and the General!!! They cheat at games like troopers!! I played just three games and came down to see Chula. He was not feeling terribly well as he had a shade too much to drink the night before and this was the effect. He swore he would not touch another drop until we get back, but I know him so well. I just told him he shouldn't make such a bold resolution. All the same I must watch him.*

3rd November 1937. *We arrived in Ceylon port about 8.30. There we found five or six members of the Ceylon Motor Sport Club waiting to greet us. The drive to Kandy was a heavenly one. We went to visit the temple but weren't allowed to visit the sacred shrine where Buddha's tooth is now placed, so we went to see the library instead. The librarian was a very intelligent priest and showed us everything. He remembered my uncle King Chulalongkorn very well as he was already in the monastery when the King came to visit Buddha's tooth. We had an appointment in Ceylon to go to visit Prince's College, the monastery school which was founded by a Ceylonese priest, and carried on by a Siamese prince who became the abbot. That was why we were invited to visit the school and the monastery. We entered the small temple and at once Chula and I knelt down on the floor and did homage to the Buddha. I was very thrilled as I have not done it for ten years! George was sweet and he just kept very quiet and respectful in the background. Then we had eleven priests saying their prayers and it was enchanting.*

5th November 1937. *Tomorrow is the last day already and I am too excited for words!! I am longing to go ashore as I am sure there's something waiting for me from you. Yesterday at 7.30 Chula and George and I were invited to the Admiral's cocktail* *party which was given to those who are leaving the ship at Penang. He's a very nice man and his son was at Eton with me and I knew him well.*

CHAPTER EIGHT

Bangkok 9th November 1937. *I was simply overwhelmed with the reception over here. We were received grandly by the Siamese people all the way from the frontier in the Malay States to the capital. It has been most thrilling and touching, so much so I was moved to tears several times. The Siamese people do love to have their princes back. We reached Bangkok at 12.00 noon after 3 hours' nap on the train on account of having to get out of the train to receive people at the stations even as late as 5.00 in the morning. It was Saturday, and this allowed people to come to receive us in millions. In fact it was so terrific people never saw anything like it since King Chulalongkorn's return about 60 years ago. We were taken to Udorn Palace, where we are staying, to wash and clean up, then at 1.00 we went to have lunch with the Council of Regents, and were terribly grand. At 3.00 we went to the Old Palace to pay respects to the ashes of our ancestors which was a very impressive ceremony. We drove to see some Wats (temples) and Bangkok town, and also my palace and the old school. Everything was like a dream to me. Before dinner I saw my old nurse Sihn who wept at my feet. At 9.30 we went out in the car to see places at night and also went to Chula's house near the river. Chula and I loved it as it is just like an Italian villa. Chula said if he was given another place to live in he would give us his house!*
Darling I am sure you would love it here and would soon make friends with people. Siamese women especially, they are all terribly chic over here. Everyone is so charming to us, I believe they are terribly impressed by us two, not because of cash alone. So dar-

ling, when you are my wife you must make up your mind to become a charming SIAMESE wife of a charming Siamese hero! I think and believe that you can do it sweet.

On Sunday I woke up early, and at 10.00 we received all the important officials. In the afternoon we were free. I went out with Bisdar alone to order some 100 coloured fighting fish to take back to Europe for our new house. Monday morning we received the Prime Minister and such people, then went to pay our respects to High Princes. We lunched at home, then in the afternoon I called on my half sister and was very warmly received. But I didn't know how things leaked out, she seems to know I have an English girl!! She teased me about it all. She said all the hearts of Siamese girls are here fluttering for me. After that I went to the docks to try and borrow a small speed boat to use while we are here.

In the evening we went to the Siamese ballet and there were several very attractive Siamese girls, all well dressed and smart and high birth, but this did not seem to make the old heart flutter. We did not get back until late as ballets in Siam go on nearly all night. This morning we did our routine, receiving people until lunch, then in the afternoon I went to visit my palace, and 200 of my father's old servants. It was great fun, only to be completely put off for me when I saw my crippled brother and I nearly wept. I only controlled myself because there were hundreds of people around. I did not leave them until 5.00 and then picked Chula up and together we went to call at the old Queen's palace. We stayed with her until late, then Chula came away to prepare to make a speech on the wireless, while I went to my half sister's palace to listen in.

Bangkok 15th November: Chula and I are being received in a most grand manner. We are absolutely thrilled beyond words. We are simply overwhelmed by the generosity of the people out here, practically every meal we are asked out, and several nights we couldn't even get back until well into the night. That's why tonight I have taken free so I could write to you. I now know that if you want to be a success as my wife you've got to become completely Siamese, like Chula's mother was when she lived here, and this I will help you to be. Actually George is now nearly arranging to become naturalized Siamese because he loves Siam and the people so much, so if George could have such feelings for us here I am sure you would do so much more as your future husband is a Siamese. I am sure if you really set your heart to make our life together a success it will be a huge success. I have seen my full sister and even she has already heard the rumour I was marrying an English girl. She said my wife must feel she's a Siamese otherwise it will be a failure.

Since I have been here I have bought for myself a teddy bear!! A baby living bear! With a little white 'waistcoat'. This is the mark of the sort of bear he is. He's called Teddy Thai and he's only 4 months old! He's already big enough to be naughty. I am keeping him here in the palace! I miss Joan so much I had to buy a pet. Yesterday was Sunday so we went away to the country to rest at Ayudhya where the whole town is founded on river just like a miniature Venice. It was lovely, but I will bring you to all these places. This evening I have just broadcast so I'm excited to hear what the papers will say tomorrow. Chula did his brilliantly last week.

23rd November. *Chula has already started asking the Prime Minister about our marriage. Tomorrow I shall go to the head of the family, then to the Council of Regents.*

27th November. Ceril my very own, your wire is too wonderful for words!! 'Accept with all my heart'. How very sweet and how like you. I am so happy I can hardly speak. Thank you a billion times dearest for making me so wonderfully happy. I will never forget this day.

Darling will you then marry me on Wednesday 12th January 1938 please? I have chosen this date as a fortune teller said it would be a good day. I will have to send you the list of my guests we will ask to our wedding reception. I quite agree with you to have it done properly and in grand style! I am determined that our love should never be broken ever. I want to have a diamond wedding, that's my ambition now. You remember the first lunch we had together? My heart was beating so fast I hardly knew it was over when I took you back to school?

30th November. *Bira's engaged! Bira's already found a girl! Prince Bira's proposal. All these rumours and news are spreading fast all over Siam! I don't think Reuter has sent the news of our engagement from Europe yet, but somehow news has leaked out, and one paper has plastered my name all over the front page!*

I am so very busy you can't imagine, Darling, with these state functions and going to Thanksgivings of our ancestors and so on, and I shan't be really free now until we get on board the Rajputana again, what with the Constitutional Fair coming on and the speed trials to show off Romulus and so on, and the farewell parties next week. They have taken our engagement pretty well. I am saving up all sorts of stories and I noted down things which would interest you.

7th December 1937. *The photo you sent me from England everyone admired so much when they saw it. They are all thrilled and are longing to see you in person! The general opinion here is that it was a pity I couldn't wait a little longer as they thought I was* *rather young and therefore I ought just to remain a dashing young hero for a little while more. They don't particularly mind a foreigner because they are pretty broadminded. Everything is passing off most smoothly. I am rather pleased that some of my nice relatives are even taking the trouble to send you presents! They all want to see you and make friends with you.*

9th December. *The opening of the Constitutional Fair took place last night. I can't begin to describe to you the magnificence of the whole show. We can come next year together and we shall stay in there until dawn every night shall we?*

13th December. *This is the last letter you will get from me from Bangkok. Its such a lovely country and quite the best in the Far East. Tomorrow I will be setting back to you again. I adore you and goodbye from Bangkok.*

The papers reported their departure in an article in *The Bangkok Times* on Tuesday 14th December, 1937. "It was a very busy day for both Prince Chula Chakrabongse and Prince Birabongse Bhanudej yesterday saying goodbye to relatives and friends. Last evening, we understand, they were guests of His Serene Highness Prince Varnvaidyakara Voravarn at a farewell dinner. Others present included members of the Diplomatic Corps. There was a large attendance to see the Princes off from the Chitra-lada station this morning. Boy Scouts, Sea Scouts, and schoolboys and girls lined up on the road, and in addition to the Council of Regency, we noticed HRH Prince Narisra, most of the members of the Council of Ministers and the President of the Assembly of the People's Representatives. Seats were reserved in the saloon of the Hua Hin train. At Nakon Pathom both Princes bowed to the assembled officials and the guard of honour, and the train stopped long enough to enable both of them to light candles of worship to be conveyed by an official to the big pagoda".

15th December. *Ceril my darlingest fiancée! It is more than I can stand! I thought Bangkok was my idea of heaven but Hua Hin seems to put it in the shade. I love it. By the way you will be called 'Mom Ceril Bhanubandh' by the Siamese over here, and in Europe 'Princess Birabongse! I don't know for certain what day I shall be arriving in London. It's either 8th January evening by plane at Croydon or 9th. I am so sorry I can't send you a photo of Teddy Thai because he won't let us photograph him. Anyhow you will see him when he comes to London with us ... it's a lovely rest here by the seaside but alas we have only nine hours more, and then we take the train to the south.*

Sonkra.16th December 1937. *This is the last town in Siam before we leave. I have just come back from a dinner given by the people of Sonkra. I hope you will send me lots of letters as I am* now starting on my last lap for home, and I shall be so glad when I see the chequered flag and I win a huge prize!! It's a perfect heaven in Siam especially when the whole of Europe is in the middle of winter. I should be jolly surprised if you don't like it here. I have taken tons of films, but it's colour so I hope the exposure in Siam was correct. Anyhow the main thing is that I am well away from Bangkok and as you see there was not one person who could keep me there.

SS Rajputana 21st December 1937. The boat is practically empty compared with coming out. Every day I visit Teddy Thai!! He is sweet but has grown enormously. Soon he will be a big, big bear!! Still he is just like a baby yet, and the cook brings him out for a walk to go and look at the sea. The fighting fish seem to be very happy in the aquarium in my cabin and lots of stewards have asked to see them, and they admire them very much as they are so colourful.

23rd December 1937. I arrive at Victoria on the 8th at 5.00 by the Golden Arrow. Chula arrives on Monday 10th. On Tuesday I shall just see you for the afternoon and tea, then I shall dine with Chula and you spend your time with Mummy as it is our last day with them.

Then comes the glorious day, the day of our lives, the 12th. I intend to sleep late, then pack everything, and perhaps a little phone to my darlingest future wife! Then have lunch (or at least nibble a little bit of bread) then I will meet you at the Siamese Legation at 2.30 accompanied by Chula and Abhas. You will bring Daddy and Way. There will be a group of Siamese officials and the Siamese Minister. He will shake hands with us both and then when everything is quite ready we will sign our names in turn and I give you my ring, and kiss you.

Then I would like Chula to perform a little Siamese ceremony as I do really believe in our Holy Water. It is alright for you to take it too as it does not have anything to do with vowing to become a Buddhist or anything like that. It is only a blessing with water on the happy occasion. He will pour the water on our heads from the Sacred Shell which is very old. We brought it from Bangkok with us for this purpose. Then Chula will put three dots of powder mixed in this water on our foreheads, three each. It symbolises all the happiness we are to receive. I think it is a very beautiful thought, and ever since I was a child I saw it happening at weddings. I always think that anything to do with blessing in any religion is a good thing, and as I am such a naughty boy I need all the blessings on me!!

Then we two will thank the Minister and get in the Rolls which Chula is lending us. He says he will follow in the Minister's car to

the reception. There we will stand and receive all the guests and
when it is all finished we will cut the cake with my military sword
as I am a second lieutenant in the King's Bodyguard.

After Bira had sent a telegram to say that our engagement was official my father put the announcement in *The Times* saying that the marriage would take place with the permission of the Council of Regency as Chula had asked him to do.

When Bira left for Siam in October I went to look at various houses for us but had so far found nothing suitable. I had also kept in touch with the boat builders and, to my great relief, found out that the boat would not be ready in time for our honeymoon. My mother and I started to get my trousseau ready, but it seemed to tire her, though she never once complained, and gradually she took to staying in bed more and more. It was obvious she was not well at all. My father was very worried and insisted on having his doctor to examine her who told us there was nothing to be done. Our old nanny came back to help look after her and, though I was missing Bira dreadfully, I was in some ways glad he was away so that I could spend all my time with my mother.

The family now took over the shopping for our wedding, Aunt C going to the Army and Navy Stores for our linen, Aunt Ray to Peter Jones for china and glass and Uncle Harry gave us our silver. My father left all the details for the wedding reception to an old school friend of his who was a director of Searcy's in Sloane Street - they used a house in Belgrave Square for receptions. My father, determined to give his only daughter a good wedding, sent out 500 invitations.

CHAPTER NINE

Bira came home at last. Calligan the chauffeur had been looking after Bira's dog Joan in his absence and he took her and me to meet Bira at the station. I don't know who was happiest to see him - his dog or me! We went straight to my home, where my father was waiting in the hall to welcome us, and Bira rushed upstairs to greet my mother, shocked to find such a change in her. She was weak, lying in bed in the room next to the drawing room where we had moved her as it was easier for the nursing. She was happy to see Bira, even though hating the idea of us marrying and maybe having children of mixed blood. She had hated the idea from the beginning but had become as fond of Bira as he had of her.

My poor mother had always pictured me married to an Englishman, one of Way's Eton friends if possible - ideally a Christian Scientist - and leading a traditional English life. The idea of me going to live in the East with a Siamese husband was something terrible for her to accept. My father, on the other hand, was not against our marriage in any way. He was an unusually tolerant man with no religious or race prejudices whatever who liked Bira immensely. As he and all his brothers had always been madly keen on sport he admired Bira for being the same, and was proud and delighted at his motor racing successes. The only thing he was not certain about was whether Bira was mature or responsible enough to marry yet.

My brother's feelings were that it was entirely my affair who I married; he just hoped I would be happy. He himself was deeply in love with the girl from my uncle's riding school and was also hoping to get married, having already brought the very attractive Ygerne Harris to meet our parents.

Chula came back from seeing his mother in Paris two days before our wedding, very disappointed that Lisba was away skiing. The following

72

continued on page 81

Bira and Ceril arrive at Bangkok railway station at the start of their visit to Siam.

Bira takes Ceril, in Siamese costume, to see his relations during their visit in 1938.

Bira takes the royal children out in his motor boat: Bira, Prince Bhumipol (the present King of Thailand), King Ananda and Princess Galyani.

Above left: At the palace of Prince Naris; all in Court mourning for his niece. Standing is Prince Naris with Chula and seated are Ceril, Abhas, Bira and Lisba.

Above right: Bira and Chula in Siamese costume on their way to a tea party.

Some of the cooks at Ta Tien.

Left: At Colombo, Sri Lanka.

*Above: Ceril and Bira
with some of their
friends.*

*Bira, on the garden
wall at Hua Hin in
1939, wearing the
Chinese pyjamas he
always wore when at
home in Siam.*

*Ceril, Bira, Chula
and Lisba at the
opening by the King,
in early 1939, of the
new military centre
at Lopburi.*

Ceril launches Macharnu with champage whilst Bira's left holding the handbag!

Chula reading the war news to Lisba and Ceril at Hindhead in September 1939.

Chula pours holy water on the cabin cruiser Macharnu.

Bira's bust of Aunt Ray which he sculpted in 1949 whilst at Lynham House, Rock.

Ceril in the jungle at Angkor during their visit to Indo-China.

Way, Ygerne, Poppa, Ceril and Bira, plus dogs!

77

Lisba and Ceril.

Prince Svasti and Bira working the trains in the Train Room Bar.

Bira and Titch in the glider.

Chula at home at Lynham House with
Romeo, Bira's dog.

Bira starting a stone carving of Thai
dancers.

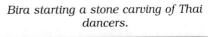

Chula's mother, Mrs Harry Stone
(formerly HRH Princess
Chakrabongse) dances with Corp
(Evan Davies), a family friend.

Lisba's birthday. At the table are Ceril, Bira with Titch, Shura with a friend, Lisba's father, Lisba and Joan and Chula. Ceril's portrait of Chula hangs on the wall behind.

Ceril with Chula, Lisba and Bira celebrating Christmas at Tredethy.

morning he gave Bira a cheque that was to be his present to us to furnish our home when we found one, and furnish it very luxuriously. That evening Bira rang up and, knowing him so well, I could tell from his voice that he was bubbling over with excitement. I could tell that something had occurred, something even more exciting than the thought of our big moment the next day, and at last he confessed, very shyly, what he had done. He had spent part of our wedding present from Chula on a new car. It was, and even then I felt it, a foretaste of things to come, a realisation that Bira, whenever he had money, could never resist spending it at once. That afternoon he had bought a Rolls Royce he had been admiring in Jack Barclay's showroom window in Berkeley Square ever since his return: as he explained to me, it was quite the loveliest Rolls Coupé he had ever seen. Just the shade of blue he loved, like the racing cars but a little more of a smokey blue, and the most modern, low, sporting Rolls yet designed. As the cheque had come into his hands temptation had won and he had gone straight off to buy it.

He told me he had invited Jack Barclay and his partner to our reception, and that they would arrange for the car to be parked outside. Shura would put our luggage in it and it would be ready for us to drive away in. This information nearly ruined my wedding: not the thought that we would now have a less luxuriously furnished home, or that Chula would be angry and upset; not even the thought that this sort of thing would very likely be repeated often in the future. It was the horrible realisation of who would be driving the new car away from the reception in front of our friends and relations, as Bira had been banned for six months for dangerous driving. I would have to get into a car I had never seen before, in a state by then of great emotion and excitement and, gears crashing, drive us away in jerks and jolts. Of course, once we got to France Bira would drive using his Siamese licence. As always Bira's charm was so great and I loved him so much that, despite these horrifying thoughts, I couldn't be angry with him but suffered instead in silence.

The morning of our marriage Bira rang up as usual, now in a cloud of happiness at getting both me and the new Rolls on the same day. He had told me it would be he who would be giving me my wedding bouquet as he wanted it to be entirely of orchids, a Siamese flower, which he would choose himself as he wanted them to be exactly like the ones he had seen on his trip. A beautiful bouquet was delivered by Wills and Seager, together with the biggest basket of flowers I had ever seen. It was for my mother, with a little note saying goodbye to her and sending his deep respect and affection, hoping she would look at these flowers while we were getting married and think of us as we would be thinking of her. He really loved her and she was terribly touched.

I went with my father and brother to the Siamese Legation in Ashburn Place near our house - in those days, Siam only had a legation in London - not yet an embassy. The legal marriage and the mixed Buddhist and Brahmin ceremony, with the pouring of holy water from the sacred conch shell, took place as Bira had described to me in his letter from Bombay - and when it was over the Minister handed me a Siamese diplomatic passport made out in my new name, Princess Ceril Birabongse. I had now given up my British nationality and was a Siamese subject.

The reception was beautifully done, and when it was over all my family, Chula, Abhas, the Siamese people and our guests crowded out of the house to throw confetti and see us drive away. So came the moment I had been dreading, but Bira leaned over and started the car, helped me put it into gear - and off we went.

After a night in Dover our first stop was Paris at the Hotel Crillon, for me to at last meet Chula's Russian mother and American stepfather Harry Stone - or Mother and Hin, as they at once said I must always call them. They looked on Bira as a son and when Mother had lived in Siam she and Prince Chakrabongse had been very fond of Bira's father, who was then the senior prince there. They were sweet to me, as they were always to be, and gave us a beautiful china breakfast set for a wedding present. I found Chula's mother quite fascinating. A tiny person, much smaller than I (she didn't come up to Hin's shoulder), but with an enormous personality. Hin was exactly as I'd imagined tall blond American cowboys might look like, and was completely ruled by his wife. She was domineering, moody, unpredictable - very like Chula - and always smoked black Russian cigarettes in a long holder. She sat at the head of the table at dinner that night, talking several languages at once - Siamese to Bira, English to Hin and me, Russian to relations who had come to meet us, French to her neighbours Monsieur and Madame Dubois (who had looked in for coffee), and Italian to her maids. A large portrait of her first husband hung on the wall behind her and the cabinets were filled with priceless Siamese porcelains.

We drove on to the Hotel de Paris at Monte Carlo. Being together was perhaps even better than we had anticipated; Bira was in seventh heaven driving his new toy all along the coast and up into the mountains every day, and in the evening we would dance in the hotel. The casino and other sorts of nightlife held no charms for us at all - we just liked dancing together. Bira thought I ought to have a little wrap to wear over my evening dresses and his eye was caught by a small mink cape in one of the display windows in the hall - put there to tempt the guests. I found it on my pillow one night - but again it was a temptation Bira would have done better to resist, as after he had paid our hotel bill he found he had hardly any money left. Consequently, when we stopped for a night in Paris on our way home it was not at the Crillon but the very modest little hotel where Bira had gone when he was a boy to escape from Mother's rather noisy Easter party. The Rolls looked most out of place parked in the street outside.

Bira had agreed to cut short our honeymoon as I wanted to get back to be near my mother as soon as possible. She died two weeks after our return.

One of the first things we did on our return was get married again. Our solicitor, John Stanton, felt it wise to be married by British as well as Siamese law. We went to the Kensington Registry Office in Marloes Road and Henry Maxwell and Charles Wheeler came with us as witnesses.

We were staying at a hotel while we went house hunting and soon found by chance exactly what we wanted - several artists' studios which had been beautifully converted into one apartment. These studios, in St Albans Grove just off Kensington High Street, were built round an Italian-style courtyard, with a wide staircase at the end of the garden leading up to them. The first thing we did was to get Wills and Seager to fill the flower beds with spring bulbs, and Bira moved one of his larger Rodin-inspired stone carvings there. A wooden balcony stretched from the top of the staircase along outside the four studios, and there we hung baskets also filled with spring flowers. Bira took over the biggest studio for his trains, and the others were to be our bedroom, the living and dining room and our working studio. There were two more studios on the ground floor and these had been converted into kitchen and living quarters for the staff - by the time we had spent the remains of Chula's cheque to furnish our new home, we had acquired a 'staff'. Aunt C, through the nuns, had found a young Irish valet to look after Bira's clothes and wait at table - and through an agency, Mrs Amy Healey arrived. Mrs Healey was an inspired cook, did all the housekeeping, brought a niece to help her daily and she and our valet took life very easily, as we were out or away so often. On the other hand, we could bring friends home - even at the last moment - and a superb meal was always served.

For me, Mrs Healey was ideal - she was a cat lover. Bira bought a small tabby kitten one day as he passed through Harrods' pet department to give Whiskey a friend - and whenever I went downstairs to see Mrs Healey she would be sitting in a low armchair, her short fat legs spread apart, a glass of whiskey beside her, reading the horse racing results with a cigarette hanging from her lips and the two cats on her wide lap covered with ash - the picture of contentment.

We also had a dog - a funny little fellow we had chosen at the Battersea Dogs' Home - called Popski. Bira took him to the Dogs' Bath Club at the top of Beauchamp Place (where Joan had been going for years), to have him shampooed and trimmed. Popski got on very well with the cats. Not so Joan, who was a cat hater - so we had to be very careful when she came to the studio. Bira had left Joan with Chula to keep him company - only this meant buying her a car, as it had been Bira who had driven her to the park in the morning to have a run. Now Chula told Calligan he must take her, but Calligan said it would be impossible as the Rolls was always being washed in the mews at that hour in the morning - so Chula bought Joan a Ford.

Chula never got up much before lunch if he could help it. This was a habit he acquired when he lived with his grandmother, the old Queen dowager, in the Grand Palace in Bangkok. She turned day into night there - most inconvenient for her family and the Court. She slept all day and during the night expected visitors, entertainments and meals. She was almost bedridden, so all this had to take place in her bedroom - and as by then she doted on her grandson she wanted him always with her. Realizing, however, that the boy had to go to school during the day and must sleep at night, she arranged for him to have a bed just behind hers, separated by a curtain. Chula would have his supper with her while she had her breakfast, often waking in the night to listen to fascinating conversations. This had greatly appealed to him and now one of his favourite amusements was to sit up most of the night; talking and drinking with friends and, if he was alone, it was at night that he wrote his books.

The fighting fish came to the studio with Bombay Duck, a canary Bira got from a sailor in India. Teddy Thai went to live at the *White Mouse Garage* with the racing cars and was looked after by the mechanics, as Bira had to admit that he really couldn't come to live with us and be looked after by Mrs Healey with the cats. He was a sweet bear, but growing at an alarming rate - when I saw him first, he was almost as tall as I was! Stanley Holgate re-christened 'him' Freda, as Bira had been mistaken about the bear's sex, and Holgate and the others used to take her out of the cage to play - luckily, they were tough men and stronger than she was. They liked her, looked after her well and she seemed content, but obviously couldn't spend the rest of her life in the garage. When we went to Siam the following autumn she came with us and Chula had a big enclosure built for her in the grounds of his seaside house at Hua Hin, where she could enjoy fresh supplies of her favourite sugar cane.

The 1938 racing season had now been planned. Chula and Bira sold the Delahaye as they did not intend to enter any sports car races, nor race much abroad. They felt that to be successful it would be better to concentrate on fewer races - most of them in Britain - and so cut costs and improve reliability. Their cars were to be the ex-Whitney Straight Maserati 8CM and the two ERAs - old *Romulus* and the new C-type *Hanuman*.. Now that Dick Seaman had gone over to Grand Prix racing and Pat Fairfield had been killed, the star drivers in England at that moment were Raymond Mays, Arthur Dobson and Bira. There were to be eighteen races for Bira in England, three in Ireland - and only two abroad at Péronne and Berne.

At the beginning of the season I drove Chula and Bira to Brooklands, Crystal Palace and Donington, as Bira did not get his licence back until the first of June. He was always sweet to me when I drove him; never criticized or gave advice - but then fortunately, he saw me through very rose-coloured spectacles. The only thing that irritated him was if a Lagonda passed us when I was driving him in the Bentley, then he would plead with me to put my foot down and try and overtake at once. Not easy, as I was a very average driver with no fast driving or racing inclination or experience at all. I looked with the deepest admiration at glamorous Kay Petre and slim Doreen Evans when we ran into each other in the 'ladies' at Brooklands before a race - but had no wish to emulate them. I would anyhow have only been like Madame Itier, the *moving chicane*, as the drivers called her, crawling round the circuits and getting in their way.

The car of Bira's I liked driving most was his Fiat *Topolino*. On his last birthday he had been very disappointed to wake up and not find any toys from Chula on the bed - only an enormous round box of *Charbonel et Walker* chocolates - as big as the wheel of a car, Bira told me later on the telephone. But he wanted toys - not chocolates - like the wonderful scale model of the cross-Channel boat, the *Canterbury*, he had been given the year before. Then Chula said casually that he had actually bought him a little car but had hidden it on the window sill and was afraid it had fallen down on to the road. Bira jumped out of bed so fast he scattered the chocolates all over the room in his dash to the window. There in the street below was a new baby Fiat 500, painted Bira Blue and wrapped in cellophane, with an enormous satin bow on top. Bira pulled on his trousers and shirt in record time and tore downstairs, left the wrappings in the street for the porter to pick up and drove round the block. Back he came to thank Chula, have his breakfast and telephone me. He said Chula was on his knees, trying to get the chocolates back into the box.

Now Chula was alone in the flat and thought he would be very lonely without Bira, after living there with him for five years. He threw himself into his writing - his book on Catherine the Great of Russia (published while they were in Bangkok) had sold out already - and now he had started on the life of Camillo Cavour. He had plenty of friends like Lisba and Henry to go out with, but still felt miserable until we came back from our honeymoon - when to his surprise and happiness, he found he was seeing Bira almost as much as before. After my mother died I was so sad to feel my father was alone that Bira and I had come to an arrangement where I spent several evenings a week with him, while Bira went to Chula. It was then that I realized, somewhat with surprise, that Chula now seemed to like me. I had feared he might be resentful and even a little jealous of Bira's love for me, but happily it didn't turn out like that at all. Chula quite soon lost his fear of losing Bira, became my friend and began to spoil us both.

Bira's boat was now ready and we brought it down the Thames from Walton to moor at Chelsea. When there were no races we would spend the weekend cruising up and down the river - Bira learning to handle the boat and I, as crew, leaping about at locks and cooking the sausages and eggs which Bira loved. Bira's great rival, Arthur Dobson and his white ERA, also owned a boat, so when he came on a trip with us I was under strict instructions not to let our side down. Our favourite companions on the boat were my friend Delia Hunt, who was just about to marry Lindsay Sowerby (later editor of *Amateur Photographer*), and Bira's friend Michael Lambart (later Earl of Cavan). We four enjoyed many outings together.

During the week Bira worked in our new studio on the Pat Fairfield memorial, which was due to be unveiled in July by Lord Howe at Donington. He was modelling Pat's head in bas relief, to be cast in bronze and mounted on a stone drinking fountain he had designed, with Pat's wins written on either side and a line drawing of South Africa's symbol, the springbok, engraved beneath the basin. Bira was also working on a self-portrait in racing overalls with goggles round his neck. It was to be exhibited at the Royal Academy that summer - described in the catalogue as "B Bira; Siamese racing driver" - by Prince Birabongse of Siam.

Towards the end of March Bira felt he had gained enough experience on the boat to venture out to sea. During the week we moved the boat to a mooring nearer the mouth of the Thames and the plan was to drive there early that Saturday morning and sail a little way round the coast. If this was successful, on another occasion we would cross the Channel.

It was a cold, windy day with showers when we passed Tilbury and headed towards the open sea. There it began to blow in earnest and became really rough, so after a while Bira thought we ought to turn back. To say I was thankful for this decision would be an understatement. He said he was worried the little rowing boat we were towing might break loose, so asked me to take the wheel while he went up on deck to secure it. I had never had anything to do with sailing the boat before, but he told me just to steer straight ahead and left me to it. A second or two later a large object fell past the cabin door into the sea. "Oh God; dear God", I cried, "it's Bira".

Everything that followed must have happened quickly but seemed to take hours. I tore up on deck and, between the mountainous waves, just caught sight of his upstretched arm for one second; then it disappeared as I sailed away from him. I dashed back to the cabin - by now sobbing and petrified - not knowing what to do, but instinctively turning the wheel back in his direction, and rushed up again to try and pull a lifebelt away from its bracket. By the time I had it free, i had passed him again and had the greatest difficulty finding him - it was only possible to glimpse his head now and then between the waves. Down again, turn the wheel once more towards him, up on deck to fling the lifebelt - which by some miracle reached him -down to turn the wheel and back to throw a rope and this time he got to it. At last we were reunited - and now I didn't care how much we were being tossed about,or where the boat was heading.

I stopped sobbing and praying and pulled him to the side - but then came the hardest part. Bira was tired, had swallowed a lot of seawater, was weighed down by his heavy winter clothing and I could only just reach his hands by lying flat on my stomach, with arms stretched down. How could I pull his weight up the smooth side of the boat? There was no time to go and look for the steps - it was obvious Bira's strength was exhausted. I never knew how we managed but we were both desperate and somehow he got on board and collapsed on the deck. I dragged him down to the cabin - where he quickly recovered, put on dry things and was his old self in no time; taking charge of everything. Back we went to our mooring, with Bira saying cheerfully that we'd have better luck the next day after a good night's rest on board. That was one of the extremely rare times I ever said no to him - I said I hated the boat, hated the sea and I wanted to go home. He said he understood - and home we went. As we drove round the corner of St Alban's Grove we came face to face with our valet on his way out for the evening - wearing one of Bira's favourite suits - his tie, shirt, shoes, everything. We lost our valet but were soon back on the boat again.

Now the racing season started and Bira went in for two races at Brooklands - one with the new ERA and one with the big Maserati. He was second in both and it was at this meeting that I had my first experience of being stared at as Bira's wife. I was proud to be seen with him, but a little embarrassed until I got used to it. He then won the Coronation Trophy at the Crystal Palace and the *Motor* said "Bira was driving with all his mastery, steady as a rock, more polished it seemed than ever". This pleased Bira, as he told me when we got back from the race that several people had warned him he might not drive so well - now he was married. I couldn't think why this should make a difference as he was no more fond of me than he had been during the last three racing years - and certainly didn't now act like a responsible husband - he never did ...

The week after I drove Chula and Bira to Donington where we stayed as usual with the Pinneys. Bira crashed the new ERA *Hanuman* in practice, so Shura and Holgate drove up to London to fetch *Romulus*. Bira was second to Charlie Dodson and blamed himself all the way back to London for having gone off the road with the faster *Hanuman*. Then at the Easter meeting at Brooklands, Bira won from Arthur Dobson with *Hanuman*, and they both outpaced the Maseratis of Villoresi and de Graffenried.

Chula and Bira went to Cork on their own where on 23rd April 1938 there were two races on the same day as was frequently done on the continent - a *voiturette* 1500cc race in the morning, where Bira was driving *Hanuman* - and a Grand Prix race in the afternoon in which he was to drive the Maserati. Dobson had now taken Pat Fairfield's place in the ERA official team with Mays - and Villoresi, de Graffenried, Soffietti and Hug had come from abroad with Maseratis. Bira won the race and was the only driver to take part as well in the Grand Prix in the afternoon. Two Delahayes had come from France with Dreyfus and Comotti, and Jean-Pierre Wimille with a Bugatti. Bira was second to Dreyfus - the *Motor* wrote "Unruffled as ever". The *Daily Telegraph*: "Brilliant cornering by the Siamese Prince". The *Cork Examiner* said "The Siamese Prince won the light car race and finished second in the Grand Prix - a truly wonderful performance".

In May we went to the Private View at the Royal Academy for the third year running, where Bira was showing his self-portrait. It was there that Chula told us we would be going to Ascot the following month and had been invited to tea in the Royal Box, explaining that I would be presented to the King and Queen as the wife of a foreign prince. Of course, I began to worry about what to wear and how to pay for an expensive outfit without bothering Bira. Aunt C, as always, came to my rescue.

It had been arranged with my parents before I married that they would continue to give me an allowance - but larger than before. This meant I would be able to be quite independent of Bira for all my personal expenses - which I knew would be an advantage as although he had a great deal of money, at the rate he spent it he needed it all for himself. In the end I never had an allowance because instead I came into money from my mother's estate - but probate was slow and my bank account was getting low, so I wondered if I ought to get the new dress and hat that I wanted. It was then that Aunt C - who always, without saying anything, seemed to know whenever I had a problem - took me out shopping. I am glad to say the results met with Chula's and Bira's approval and the day at Ascot was wonderful. At tea, the King talked to Bira about his racing while the Queen, with her enormous charm, put me at ease at once and asked (as did everyone else) what it felt like to have a husband who continually risked his life?

Bira's way with money was impossible to follow, as there was no constant factor; no rhyme or reason to it. He was immensely generous, spent more than freely, then suddenly would decide we must economize. One morning soon after we were married we had the painters downstairs freshening up the servants' rooms, so I suggested it might be a good idea to take advantage of this to re-paint our tiny guests' lavatory. The men quoted £5 for the job. Bira said he absolutely wouldn't hear of it - it would be extravagant, unnecessary - and we couldn't afford it. He then left to go out shopping and lunch with Chula. In the evening he returned in the highest spirits to tell me all about his day and how he had popped into Hamley's and bought a model steamer for £25, which after lunch he and Henry had taken to the Round Pond to launch. After several crossings, to Bira's amusement the boat had sunk and was now at the bottom of the lake! I remember this incident especially as it was then I realised I would never understand Bira's reasoning over money.

Sometimes Chula would tell him he had put £1000 into his account, which always set Bira off doing his sums. He would sit down and write a list of several things he would like - each costing about £1000 - only instead of finishing by deciding which one he would go out and spend the money on, he would end by buying **everything** on the list. At first I thought we would go broke, but somehow or other after a meal with Chula and a very mild ticking off, the accounts were always in order again. Early on in our marriage I made the decision - and kept to it all the time we were together - that Bira's money arrangements were his and Chula's problem, and I would never refer to them or interfere in any way, thanking goodness I was now quite independent of it all.

After Cork it was apparent that Bira was leading on points for the BRDC Gold Star again - and the papers said that to win it for the third year running would be a record.

The JCC International Race at Brooklands came next, for which they entered the now-ageing Maserati. The cylinder head cracked in practice, with Bira crawling into the pits in a cloud of smoke. There was great dismay as although they had ordered a spare head from the factory at Bologna, it was not yet ready - so no race for Bira. Arthur Dobson came to their rescue by offering them the cylinder head from his brother's car, which was up for sale. There was a rush to fetch it, with all-night work by Holgate and the others to fit it - helped by Lofty England, who had left the *White Mouse Garage* to join Alvis, but came back to help that night just for the fun.

The race was a handicap with 22 entries, and a big crowd gathered to watch them go off as it was a rolling start. Bira and Mays were the scratch men, but worked their way through the field to come round at the end of the first lap in the lead; the fourth man being the French driver, Joseph Paul. To everyone's horror, his car was in flames, with the driver standing up trying to steer clear of the spectators. The car following him was unable to avoid hitting the blazing Delage and the Frenchman went off the road into the crowd by the starting line. It was one of the most terrible accidents in motor racing as people were ploughed down, killed, burned, pinned against the railings and the driver very seriously injured.

Chula had been standing in that group at the start a few seconds before; talking to Murray Jamieson, one of the designers of the ERA, but had just moved off with Shura to return to the pits. Murray Jamieson was among those killed. The race continued, with Bira leading, but seven laps from the end the back axle went. The *Autocar* wrote "The gallant old car had to retire". It was hard on the mechanics who had worked all night, but that was racing and anyhow, the horror and tragedy of that dreadful accident was all one could think about.

The Crystal Palace meeting for the Sydenham Trophy was on 21st May, and everyone looked forward to a duel between Bira and Arthur Dobson, but Arthur had to scratch as he was unwell. Bira just failed to catch a small MG in the handicap race so all the headlines read "Bira beaten". The *Motor* said "We are rapidly nearing the time when a win from Bira, driving one of Chula's racing cars, is ceasing to be news - but when he loses, that is news indeed".

Chula and Bira went to Péronne together and, even though *Hanuman* blew up, they seemed to enjoy themselves immensely, staying at St Etienne together with Raymond Mays and their friend Johnny Wakefield. Back to the Crystal Palace to do battle with Arthur again for the London Grand Prix. Bira won but Johnny Lurani had a bad crash, and Bira and I visited him several times in hospital. The Gold Star points were mounting up - Bira now had 48 against the second man, Dobson, with 18.

When we three went to Donington on 9th July where *Hanuman* was entered for the Nuffield Trophy, Lord Howe unveiled the Pat Fairfield Memorial, which the British Racing Drivers' Club had commissioned from Bira. Everyone said it was an excellent likeness and the *Motor* wrote that it was "brilliantly executed". Bira won the race - mainly because *Hanuman* was able to go through without refuelling, and the *Autocar* said "Unbeatable Bira. It is rumoured freely and with candour, that man and car are practically unbeatable - so that races will have to be organized with one class for Bira and another for the remaining drivers. The point is that he deserves his wins".

There was a sports car race at Brooklands where Bira was lent an HRG. It was held on the day after Bira's 24th birthday - and on the morning of the race, I received a letter from Chula.

July 15th 1938. *My dear Ceril, This being Bira's first birthday since he has become married to you, I feel I should like to say a few words to you about yourself .I do honestly think Bira is very lucky indeed to have met you and won your love. I think you have in every way been a most wonderful wife and companion to him, and from what I have seen of him, you have made him gloriously contented and happy. What is still more unusual and remarkable, is that far from interfering adversely with the deep-seated and extraordinarily affectionate friendship between Bira and myself, you have on the contrary <u>increased</u> it, and I do not think I have ever loved Bira as deeply as I do now. I have in the past accepted you, as you must know, because Bira loved you. Now I have had the opportunities to know and appreciate you for yourself, I should like to be allowed to tell you that I have the deepest affection and the greatest admiration for you, and I think you are worth your weight in gold. If there is anything I can do to assure your full happiness, which you far more than deserve, I should only be too honoured and too pleased to do so. Yours very affectionately, Chula. PS. Will you and Bira please call for me for the race at 12.00?*

This was the first step towards the great love Chula and I were to feel for each other.

CHAPTER TEN

There was a gap of over a month before the race at Berne and Bira wanted to take me on our real honeymoon then, as the one after our wedding had been cut short due to my mother's illness. Having decided he wanted to go faster on the water, Bira bought a ChrisCraft speedboat and Lisba's father, Edward Hunter, told Bira they had passed a beautiful lake surrounded by mountains on a recent tour of northern Italy with his brother Noël which he thought would be ideal for the new boat. It was Lake Garda, just north of Verona. Bira got out his map, ordered a trailer for the boat and had a tow bar fitted to the Rolls. Before leaving, Chula blessed the ChrisCraft with holy water and named it *Romula*.

No wonder Mr Hunter had been impressed by the beauty of the place! We found our first view of Lake Garda quite breathtakingly lovely and Bira said at once that here was the only place he had seen in Europe to compare with Siam. We stayed in the Hotel Lido at Riva, which had a large park and private beach. Bira enquired where he could put the boat in the water and was sent to see the captain of the local yacht club, Bruno Tomasoni. I went to unpack and when Bira got back, his face shone with happiness. He said it was paradise.

The next morning Bira introduced me to Bruno, a nice-looking, smiling young man a few years older than we were, who bubbled over with enthusiasm and efficiency. *Romula* was in the water in front of the yacht club with a group of admirers waiting to see us go out. The members of the club were fascinated by Bira - here, suddenly had arrived a racing driver who they had all read about with a speed boat faster and more modern than any on the lake, who was full of fun and friendship.

Bira found out that Bruno owned a dinghy, asked if he would take him out and so discovered one of the great passions of his life. Bruno's family owned a large villa next to the hotel and Bira started getting up at five in the morning and running over to the hedge of their garden to throw stones at Bruno's window so they could go out sailing in the early morning north wind. He soon got the hang of it and hired a dinghy from the club. Upon discovering that Bruno was the local champion, Bira spent his time trying to beat him at sailing and table tennis (neither of which he succeeded in doing). Bruno, like Bira, was a natural athlete, but now had a stiff leg after an accident to his knee at football which had put an end to skiing and tennis for him, so he had taken up sailing instead. He was very self-conscious about being lame.

When Bira went out again in the afternoon I would often bathe from the hotel beach and then find a quiet place in the shade to paint or read. Bruno would always come to look for me and sit and talk. He was intrigued that I was shy and retiring with people and I explained that if I was not with Bira or my family or close friends, I was happier on my own. Bruno said he hoped one day he would become one of my friends.

The month slipped by far too quickly and Bira used the speedboat less than he had planned because of his new love of sailing, but he saw what fun *Romula* would be in Siam that winter so instead of towing it to Berne with us he asked Bruno to send the boat to Bangkok. Before we left, Bruno said he would very much like to write to me and from then on we corresponded regularly except for during the war years.

Chula and Lisba came by train to join us for the last two days in order to drive with us to Berne. They had at last decided to get married in September so that we could all go out to Siam together, but we found them very nervy and on edge and not getting on at all well. It seemed that they were now both having second thoughts about it all and quarrelled and bickered all the way to Berne. It ended in a real row when we discovered there had been an error over the booking of our rooms at the Bellevue. The hotel had been asked to reserve a double and two single rooms and must have concluded they were for a Siamese prince and his wife and their maid and valet. In consequence, Bira and I were shown into a magnificent suite overlooking the Bernese Alps, while Chula and Lisba were given two tiny rooms across the corridor. Lisba was furious and normally Chula, so efficient in all these things, would have gone to the hotel reception and even though the Bellevue was full for the race somehow or other would have secured alternative accommodation. Instead, having worked himself up into one of his worst moods with Lisba, he just laughed and did nothing. Bira and I were extremely upset and embarrassed and assured them most sincerely that we didn't at all mind taking the small rooms, but Chula refused, Lisba sulked and the atmosphere was strained; this was not helped by Bira failing to complete even one lap of the race. The stay in Berne was such a contrast to our happy month in Italy.

We had to hurry back to England as the Junior Car Club's 200-mile race took place the following weekend. It was on that long drive that Chula began for the first time to tell me about his and Bira's family. Lisba, still upset, said she was not interested; nor was Bira who was too busy thinking about his own exciting life to bother about the lives of his forebears, but I was curious Like everyone I had heard stories of the Kings of Siam and their numerous wives and children. Up to fairly recent times, polygamy was practiced in the country and a man could have as many wives as he could afford. I told Bira I was very relieved it was now against the law.

King Vajiravudh and King Prajadhipok had each only one wife, but King Mongkut and King Chulalongkorn both had a great many, though only a wife who was herself of Siamese royal birth could become Queen. King Mongkut, the monarch portrayed in the play and film *The King and I* which Chula assured me were both incredibly inaccurate, had only one Queen who had three sons. One died young and the others were King Chulalongkorn and Bira's father. Queen Debsirindra was the King's niece, because for a King to have a royal wife meant she had to be a close relative. This was a system used in other Eastern countries; in ancient Persia, and by the Pharaohs in Egypt in order to keep the royal blood pure.

King Chulalongkorn had four Queens who were his half-sisters. One died tragically with her children in a river accident when her barge sank, because none of her servants could rescue them as it was forbidden to touch a royal person. The other three Queens lived in the inner part of the Grand Palace where only women lived and their sons left when they were twelve years old. The inner part was like a small town, about a mile square which even had its own women police. It was there that Chula had stayed for long periods as a child with his grandmother, Queen Soawabha, who was the chief Queen, the only one of the King's wives who shared his private apartments in the Chakri Building in the Grand Palace. All the other wives had their own houses in the inner part with large households of female servants, relations and attendants.

It was considered a great honour to become one of the King's wives and brought many advantages to their families. For this reason, girls from important families all over the country were given to the King. Ripley once wrote in his newspaper strip *Believe it or Not* that King Chulalongkorn had 3000 wives and 370 children, but Chula told me that in the official records he had 36 wives by whom he had issue and they gave him 77 sons and daughters. Queen Saowabha had nine children and Queen Sawang, the grandmother of the present King of Thailand, had eight. Wives who had not had children could leave if they wished to and in that case were given money. It was thought there had been some fifty royal wives who had not had children. I was quite fascinated by this and over the years, Chula was to spend hours telling me about his boyhood in Siam and his family, as he knew I loved to hear about it all.

After we got back to England Chula wrote to Lisba at Aix-les-Bains, where she had gone to join her mother, and broke off the engagement. He then became desperately depressed and Bira persuaded him to telephone her and the engagement was 'on' again. The trouble was not that Chula did not love

Lisba, for I am certain that he did, just that he didn't really want to get married at all. He would have much preferred to be able to go on living with Bira.

Now that he and Lisba were back on good terms again, Chula said she must have some jewellery as all his cousins' wives wore a lot on important occasions and he did not want his wife to be outshone. Many years before when Chula's mother Ecaterina had lived in Siam, she had been given beautiful jewels by her mother-in-law, Queen Saowabha. Then it happened that when Ecaterina returned from a long visit to her brother Ivan (who was in the Russian Diplomatic Service and had been appointed First Secretary at the Russian Legation in Peking in order to be able to visit his sister from time to time in Bangkok), she found Chula's father had fallen in love with one of his own young nieces. It was a great shock as until then he had been completely faithful to her. He refused to give the girl up so Chula's mother left Siam and went to live in Shanghai. Before leaving, she took all her jewellery to the Queen's apartments and threw them down on the floor in front of her in a truly dramatic Russian gesture. These jewels were put on one side and later given to Chula.

Once a year the most famous jewellers from Paris and London used to go to Siam to show their collections to the Court. These visits were always well worthwhile for them as the King, an Absolute Monarch and rich beyond dreams, would choose the finest pieces for his Queens and lesser pieces for the other wives according to their position in his favour, while other Princes would also buy jewellery for their wives. After Queen Saowabha died, her jewels were divided among her heirs and Chula's share, together with those which had belonged to his mother and which he offered to return to her (she had refused them), were kept in the bank. He now decided to take some out for Lisba and said when he took them to Cartier to be cleaned and re-set, the expression on the faces of the experts who examined them were a study of amazement and admiration.

Chula also wanted to give some to me, even though I assured him that I would not let them down in Siam as my mother had given me two necklaces - one emerald and one diamond - as her wedding present and, since her death, her other things had been divided between my brother and I. But Chula said he wanted me to have some of his jewellery as well so that he could have the pleasure of seeing it on Lisba and I, instead of just leaving it lying in the bank. So he came round to the studio one day with a packet, from which he took out a magnificent black opal and diamond set, saying only I could wear them as he knew no-one else born in October. He also brought out twenty two other pieces of jewellery from the same packet.

The weekend after the race at Berne Bira led from the start with the 8CM Maserati in the JCC 200-Mile Race at Brooklands, but the mechanics fumbled the re-fuelling and wheel-changing in the pits and he finished second to Johnny Wakefield. Then, a few days later, we were at Donington where Bira was driving in the BMW team with Dick Seaman and from there drove up north to visit the Glasgow exhibition. We went through Newcastle and, near the town of Morpeth, were going up a small rise when suddenly over the crest appeared three motorcyclists taking up the whole road and coming straight at us at a terrific speed. Bira, with his motor racing reactions, swerved right off the road and the Rolls crashed onto its side in the ditch. This lightning action was not enough to avoid them all, however, and one of the motorcyclists hit our wing and was killed outright. I was badly bruised and completely stuck in the car, but Bira forced open the door and dragged me free. The other two men were, like us, in deep shock. It was an appalling accident and I recall little of what followed except that the men admitted they had been racing each other.

We 'phoned Chula who fetched us with Calligan to go to Dublin for the next race. Chula was very gloomy as he feared that Bira, being a racing driver who had lost his licence the year before for fast and dangerous driving on the road, would be in for trouble. It was therefore a big relief when the jury returned a verdict of no blame on his part.

In Dublin the Maserati retired with piston trouble. It was altogether a most depressing period for us all with the threat of war in Europe, Chula's marriage problems, failure at the races and then our terrible accident.

We cheered up when Chula and Lisba finally announced their engagement on 14th September, and on the 17th Bira drove one of his best races, a terrific duel with Raymond Mays in the BRDC race at Brooklands - his ninth win with *Romulus*. Then a week later we were back again at Brooklands; this time with the Maserati for Dunlop's Fiftieth Jubilee Race. There were ten short events and quite a lot of continental drivers came over for the race. Everyone talked about the war scare and the reservist French drivers were expecting to be called up. Bira was only entered for one race and the German driver, Berg's, Maserati 6CM ran into the back of Bira's car when its brakes failed. Bira received a head wound and he and I were driven to hospital by Sir Malcolm Campbell's son Donald.

A week later Germany began to mobilize, the French did nothing even in the face of the threats to their allies and Chamberlain gave in to Hitler's demands on 30th September 1938, the day Chula and Lisba married. In the morning they went to the Kensington Registry Office and then on to the Siamese Legation. Lisba was with her parents and her three sisters; Chula with Bira (who was recovered from his hospital visit), Shura and me. The threat of war stopped them going abroad for their honeymoon and also prevented Mother and Hin from coming over from Paris. They went ,instead, to Devon for a few days and then returned to Chula's flat.

There were now only two more races in that season; one at the Crystal Palace, where Bira was second to George Abecassis, and one at Brooklands, the Siam Trophy, for which Chula had given a cup of Siamese silver and Bira won after an exciting fight with Arthur Dobson, bringing him the Gold Star for the third year running.

My brother announced his engagement to Ygerne before we left for Siam and my father planned to leave Evelyn Gardens and go to live with his clergyman brother and family near Roehampton.

Chula and Lisba left London before us as they wanted to stay in Paris for a few days with his mother, and we met them in Venice. Bira's eldest brother Abhas came with us and also Chula's secretary Banyen. We stayed two nights at the Bauer Grünwald Hotel in Venice before boarding the Lloyd Triestino ship, the *Conte Verde*, from where I wrote to my father and Aunts -

2nd November 1938. *Darling Poppa and the Aunts, we have now been on board the Conte Verde only two days, but already feel quite at home here and simply love the life. It's a marvellous feeling getting warmer and sunnier every day. Venice was cold but very sunny. It's a lovely place to start from, as we went to the boat in a gondola. Banyen came behind in a motor launch piled so high with luggage that there wasn't even room for him inside; he had to sit perched on top of a trunk. I have never seen so much luggage in my life. I never thought we would get on board in time. Luckily our cabin is so big that both our cabin trunks stand in corners and all the luggage goes under the beds. The people on board are of all nationalities, but nearly all middle-aged men. There is also the Maharajah of Kaputala (or something like that). Anyhow he is the third richest man in the world and has asked us all to lunch with him and eat food cooked by his own Indian chef. We get to Port Said at ten o'clock tonight and then we go ashore till about two. Chula says we mustn't go to bed tonight as we must see the canal at dawn.*
After I wrote the last letter we got to Port Said. It was terribly exciting seeing the coast of Africa. The ship went right in along-side the quay and we saw all the Arabs and Egyptians in fezzes. Chula said we ought to see a bit of the real life of the port, so we went to a little dancing place where they had a cabaret. The place was full of very drunk sailors off the Warspite. We took a car and drove to the Arab quarter; it was very hot and excruciatingly smelly; pigs and chickens were everywhere in the street. On the way out, our driver was accosted by two huge tough guys who wouldn't let us drive off. Chula was terrified and in the end made the man jump in and make a dash. He explained that all the entertainments in that quarter were run by a kind of gang and if you took tourists there, you had to ask the leader's permission and pay money. We decided to stay up and see the ship enter the Canal. It was well worth waiting for, as the dawn over the desert was simply heavenly.
Actually I am enjoying the heat but Lisba says she can't sleep because of it. The only time I felt it was at the Maharajah's lunch today. We all met him in his drawing room for drinks, he was there with his second son and his suite. Then we went into his

dining room and it was pretty hot in there, I should say about 90
degrees. I sat next to the Maharajah and he had special food
cooked in his private kitchen by his own chef and staff, with
spices from his own country. And it was all curry, so hot!!! Five
courses, and the ship was rolling a bit too! Every time the waiter
came to serve me, the Maharajah said: "More more, give the
Princess more" and every time I protested he asked if I didn't like
his food, so I had to eat everything. And then he had the electric
fan turned off because it disturbed him!!! Even so, I am proud to
say I didn't perspire, I only got very shiny, but Banyen just
melted. Anyhow the Maharajah was sweet, he wants us to go and
stay with him very badly. I expect we will on our next visit. We
would break the journey at Bombay where he would send his
private railway coach to meet us. It takes 36 hours from there. It
must be wonderful because his state is in the north where there
is always snow on the Himalayas. We talked for ages and he
showed me all the photos of his diamond jubilee last year. He's
been reigning since he was eighteen and before that, with a
regent, since he was five.
We went ashore at Aden; it's the most barren-looking place I've
ever seen. Today it's pretty rough, the captain told me it was the
beginning or the end of the monsoon. I can't remember which! I
do an hour of Siamese every day with Chula and spend the rest
of the time learning words and preparing for the next lesson.

What I didn't tell the family in my letters was the difficult situation that
was beginning to develop between Lisba and Bira, which worried me a great
deal as I could see that the fault was on both sides and felt torn between my
love and loyalty to Bira and my friendship with Lisba.

It all began on board ship with Bira being unpunctual for meals and there
I saw Lisba's point. Bira would never interrupt an exciting game on deck and
he was nearly always in the middle of one when it was time to eat. Lisba rightly
felt that as we were a party and seated at the captain's table, we should go
into meals together and on time. Chula, however, was used to Bira's ways,
so was content to wait for him in the cocktail lounge, which he much enjoyed
anyway. This inflamed Lisba's annoyance even more because it gave Chula
an excuse to drink too much, so that when Bira did at last turn up she would
give him a very sharp ticking off. Bira would take no notice at all, but later
would tell Chula that his wife was becoming stuck up now that she felt she
was royal and that it was rude of her to speak to him like that, even though
he admitted he was in the wrong, because after all he was older than she was
and *born* royal, which she most certainly had not been. Anyhow, Chula was
the only person he would take that kind of ticking off from and, of course,
Chula would never give it. He always took Bira's side and would have a row
with Lisba about it, making it quite clear to her that Bira came first with him

and she had better start to get used to it. Abhas was often Bira's partner at whatever game he had been playing, which made him late too, so he took Bira's side.

The two people most upset and embarrassed by all this were Banyen and me and we often retreated together to a quiet seat in a corner of the deck where he, who had been a schoolmaster before joining Chula's estate office, would give me extra Siamese lessons. Before leaving London, Chula had given Lisba and me dictionaries and copies of Cartwright's *Student's Manual of the Siamese Language*; at that time the best, if not the only, text book for learning the language. By working hard during the voyage I was able to pick up just enough to make a great difference to my stay in Siam and was now able to understand a word here and there, when the four men in our party spoke together.

Singapore: 18th November, 1938. *At Colombo, it was intensely hot, but I loved it. We took a car and drove right into the country, the most beautiful country I have ever seen; orchids growing wild everywhere. By the sea, it was just like the pictures of South Sea Islands with rolling waves, white sands and palms and coconut trees. I was so sorry to leave, but they all promised me that Siam is even more beautiful ... After the stop at Colombo, time just flew and then we arrived here. We were met by masses of people, Consuls and officials and when I got to the hotel, my room was a mass of baskets of orchids from different people Yesterday, we went to see a Chinese theatre, then a Malay theatre, then Chinese dancing. Today we lunched at Government house with the Governor and Lady Thomas. Terrifically smart, like Buckingham Palace, with bowing servants, soldiers saluting and tactful ADCs, but very amusing and everyone was sweet. Just like a scrap of England in the East. They even had The Times and Daily Telegraph everywhere, a retriever dog and a small private golf course.*

After lunch we were due to make a tour of the Naval Base, but we had to postpone it until our return, as we had to go to the Consul for tea, and also they were changing Commandants and it would have been a bit inconvenient. Tonight we are dining at the Siamese Consulate, then tomorrow we leave early in the morning. The Malay government have given us a private coach going straight to the country town in Siam, where we are staying for three days. It's awfully useful, as we change trains at least three times, so it means we don't have to move from our carriage; we are just shunted from one train to another. We have two nights on the train, so as tomorrow is Sunday, we arrive on Tuesday in time for breakfast. Then we go on to Bangkok about two or three days later. It's only five hours by train from there. I am sending you some cuttings from Singapore papers.

Morning Tribune 18th November, 1938:
"Prince Birabongse arrives in Singapore. A party of notable Siamese arrived by the *Conte Verde* on a four- day visit to Singapore yesterday. They will stay at Raffles until Sunday, when they leave for Bangkok".

"Royal racing motorist here without his cars. Although he intends to live indefinitely in Siam with his English wife, Prince Birabongse of Siam, who arrived yesterday, has not brought any of his racing cars with him. 'I found that when I brought out my ERA racing car to Bangkok a few months ago and shipped out a large quantity of special fuel, it was hardly worth the trouble as the lack of roads outside the city did not give me a chance to let her out' he told a *Free Press* reporter".

Chula was very worried that our visit coincided with the first return home of the young King Ananda since he came to the throne and wondered what sort of welcome we would get. He did not think there would be any official welcome for us, as the authorities would be busy organising the reception for the King's party, which was coming up by sea from Singapore to Bangkok. When our train stopped at Hard Yai, the first big station in Siam, he was pleased and surprised to find the same sort of reception he and Bira had had the year before. However, this had been ordered by the Governor of the Province and he was still worried about our reception in Bangkok.

Then he was worried about the political problems. The year before there had been a crisis and the President of the Council of Regency had committed suicide. His place had been taken by Prince Arditya, son of one of Bira's two half-sisters. The crisis had arisen because the Regency had allowed certain people to purchase Crown Lands at such low prices as to render them virtually gifts. The power was now in the hands of the military party and its leader, Luang Pibul, the Minister of Defence, which controlled the Regency and the country. Just before we arrived there had been an attempt to assassinate Luang Pibul and Chula knew he would find the political atmosphere in the country very unstable and his own position delicate.

None of this worried Bira at all. He was completely uninterested in politics and knew very little about the subject, unlike Chula who even though he had lived away from his country for many years, followed the political situation closely and was extremely well-informed. Bira knew that his reception would be warm and would have nothing to do with rank or politics but because the people, especially the young ones, hero-worshipped him. When he appeared in newsreels after winning a race somewhere the entire cinema audience would get to its feet and clap. They were also proud of his being a good sculptor, as they had seen pictures in the papers of works he had exhibited, of the Fairfield Memorial and his work for the Paris Exhibition. He had already received many commissions for portrait busts and intended to work hard while we were there, had also received invitations from motor clubs and youth movements to give talks and planned to organize a motor rally. So he had none of Chula's apprehension and was only longing to gct home and show me everything ...

CHAPTER ELEVEN

I wrote to my brother, Way -

Hua Hin 21st November 1938. *Way ,dear, well here we are in Siam!!! And it's worth the long journey. So far it's the most beautiful country imaginable. I don't know how I shall ever face England again after this!! I shall be so spoilt. You and Ygerne would love it. I've just come in from a ride on a little Siamese horse. But I shudder to think what it would cost you. Malaya especially is atrociously expensive; one dollar goes nowhere and you only get eight to the pound. Our hotel bill for six people for three days in Singapore came to over £50!!*
On the night before we left, we went to see an exhibition of Yogi. The Yogi man was amazing; swallowing snake's poison, arsenic, coconut shells and all sorts of things. The next morning we caught the train. We had an escort of police and a lot of Siamese to see us off. I'd heard the journey was like hell; so hot and everything had to be kept shut to keep the smuts out. But really it wasn't bad at all, it was hot, but I sat still with a fan on me. The country was so interesting and at every station we passed through, the platform was lined with police, and all round our carriage was roped in, so no one could get near us and we could walk about in peace. In our carriage was a shower, so I had one and dressed in a clean white suit, and Bira put on uniform, to cross the frontier.
The train we changed into was Siamese, so all the waiters and people had to kneel to talk to us, and I could air my small knowl-

edge of the language. At the station were crowds and crowds, the British Consul, rows of school children, rows of scouts and women who presented us with fruit and flowers galore. There was a band to play us in and out again and the Governor of the Province was there and all the officials. It was a terrific reception and at all the stations, people came in crowds to see us. We were all too excited to sleep much and we got up at six to see the most heavenly dawn over the sea and mountains.

I am now writing on the train to Bangkok. It is almost impossible as it shakes so much. I am so sorry to leave Hua Hin and the country house built by Chula's father. There are miles and miles of white sand and wonderful shells. The place is just a little fishing village. We were given the most tremendous reception; crowds and crowds. I am beginning to be used to being stared at. The country there is a little like Connemara in Ireland, with a touch of Biarritz; surf bathing with huge waves. Bira plays golf every day, there is a famous course and I play too, and for painting it is glorious. The house is right on the beach with a large garden and is built off the ground on white pillars, all on one storey. Round it are enormous balconies which form sitting rooms. Then at the end of the garden is another building for guests and secretaries, and two others for servants and kitchens. The food is indescribable; it has to be seen to be believed, the table is laden with marvellous delicacies at every meal. There are 24 cooks, and cooks everywhere also send us dishes as a token of respect. The people who enjoy it most are the servants, called ladies and gentlemen of the household, and the guards and secretaries, because we only pick at the dishes as there is so much, while they eat the rest. The sentries are nearly always asleep and only wake up for meals.

Among the many European royalties who had come to Bangkok in 1910 to attend King Vajiravudh's coronation had been the second son of the King of Sweden, with his wife, a Russian Grand Duchess, who had been a friend of Chula's father at St Petersburg. In order to entertain them, Prince Chakrabongse and his Russian wife had taken them to a tiger shoot in the south of the country and a camp was set up for them by the fishing village of Hua Hin. Chula's mother had been so impressed by the beauty of the place that her husband built a holiday home for them there, called a palace as it was one of his residences, and gradually other people had followed and the King had also built a palace. Later, the state built a hotel and laid out a golf course. It was on this course that Bira and I played and I was a little taken aback when told that one of the club rules was that a ball hit into the rough must be abandoned because of the tigers. However, I heard that it was rare that a tiger ventured near the course but that leopards were seen frequently.

My letter to Way continued -

When we arrived, we were thrilled to find a huge packing case from Prince Umberto. A wedding present; a bronze fountain, a copy of the little winged boy by Verrocchio which is in the cortile of Palazzo Vecchio at Florence. Bira is writing to Mr Wheeler, sending instructions for the fountain to be built in our garden and we will have it put up as soon as we get back. By the way, we are definitely staying with Prince Umberto at Naples on our way back. I only hope I shall be in time for your wedding.

We've just stopped at a station and bowed to hundreds of people who came to see us. We have to do it at every station, it is most impressive to see everyone kneeling. It is the same with servants, they can't even walk past us or stand up to speak to us. They go right down on the floor. We arrive soon at Bangkok, so I must change.

We are being met by the Regent and I expect more crowds, and tonight we attend a huge theatre and dance party, and tomorrow we lunch with the King. At Hua Hin, all the chief servants from Bira's palace came to see us. The British Minister, Sir Josiah Crosby, came to lunch yesterday. He says everyone is just longing to see us. Tonight's theatre is all sold out, even standing room, so we shall feel like the show itself in our box!! There are so many details of the life here that I long to tell you but I have no time. Anyhow so far, it's been the most marvellous holiday and experience anyone could have. So interesting and new and I love every moment of it. Show this letter to Poppa and the Aunts and give them all my very best love, and to Whiskey and everyone.

'Ta Tien, Bangkok, 7th December 1938: *Darling Aunt C, Please forgive me not writing for a week, but you simply can't imagine how difficult it is to find time, and also I wanted to wait and write you a long letter and tell you everything. First, thank you for all your letters. I loved them all and especially the photos of Popski and Uncle and Aunt Ray and Way and Ygerne. People here love to see them too and to see what you all look like!! I am sending you all a few little things because I can't bear not to send you anything for Xmas. Actually, I am so thankful to be here for my first Christmas without darling Mummy, because here in the middle of a very hot summer it won't seem like the Christmases we always had together, which I couldn't bear this year.*

I love it here, the life is marvellous and the people are so sweet to me. In fact, they have given me so many presents I am quite

embarrassed. An average of five a day, since I have been here!!
Bira is very busy doing the sculpture of a rich and important duke
and has been commissioned to do the head of the Regent next
(very good pay!), and if he has time he may be doing two enormous
statues; one of the founder of the army and one of the founder of
the navy. It would be a wonderful chance for him. I have done a
little painting but not much.

The thing one has to get used to is having no privacy. I am getting
accustomed to it. I always have two or three maids who sit on the
floor of my room all day, from the moment I wake up. Their only
duty is to dress me! One puts one stocking on, one the other, and
a third my shoes!! And then for the first time in my life, my room is
always tidy, because that is all they do. They don't even wash or
iron for me; there are other special ones for that. I only have to put
my dressing gown on to walk to the bathroom and then take it off
and it is whisked away and ironed. But the maids are sweet and
we get on terribly well. I gossip with them for hours in atrocious
Siamese which they love. Then Bira's old nurse, who is nearly
blind, comes everyday to sit in my room and brings me presents of
food, which I have to eat to please her, and she brings her servants to carry the food, and usually a friend, so that I hold quite a
levée when I dress. Lisba won't have any of it, which is a pity. They
have the most wonderful flowers here. The maids bring me
presents of them every day and the cooks send some too. I love to
watch them cook; only it's difficult for them, as they have to crawl
as their heads must never be higher than mine. They are all so
kind and so are Bira's relations. As they are older than me, I treat
them with great respect and I have learnt to greet them in the
Siamese way of holding my hands to my forehead. I always wear
Siamese clothes when Bira does and go down on my face in a
temple, because I feel in England, we would be hurt if a Siamese
remained standing in a church when everyone else knelt. The
priests were very kind and gave us an elaborate blessing on our
marriage. Then, a few days ago, we had to go and visit the old
Queen Grandmother, sister of Bira's father. We went to her palace
and after having had long practice at home, I managed to go into
her presence in the correct style and sat like a Siamese in the
same position for nearly two hours. I nearly fainted with cramp
and suffered agony, but I think she was impressed. I could see her
watching me out of the corner of her eye; just waiting for me to
give up and ask for a chair, because Siamese are trained from
childhood to sit like that and unless you are, it's very hard, but I
was determined not to be beaten and I was rewarded by a pearl
and diamond bracelet!!!

I have enclosed one or two press cuttings of our arrival. It was terrific. Quite unbelievable. Nearly all Bangkok were there; thousands and thousands. I was absolutely overwhelmed and we had so many flowers and garlands, that we had a string of people behind us, carrying them. It was ages before we could get away. Then we drove here to the palace, had lunch, unpacked and then in the evening we had to appear at the theatre. We sat in the front box and it was terrible. We had been up since six, had five hours in the train, a huge reception and a tiring day and then to sit through 3 hours of a dull play we couldn't understand, with everyone watching us and not the play. To try and not yawn was hard. After the play, we had supper and then had to dance till after three and then have another supper!!

The next day, we had lunch with the king. He is so terribly sweet. He was riding in a little electric car when we arrived and immediately he took Bira, complete with full dress uniform, spurs and sword, all round the garden. He and his brother are just like Fushki, (grandson of a friend at St Jean de Luz) and I talk French with them. After that, we spent the rest of the day calling on relations. Nearly every day, we either make calls on different people, or they come here. All the Ministers and diplomats and people. We've really only been here eleven days, but it's amazing what we've seen and done. We've been to four official tea parties given for the king by clubs and institutes. We always sit on a dais behind the king and watch entertainments or listen to speeches and things and servants hand us lovely food. And one afternoon, we had to go to the final of the interschool sports with the king. We've been to three films, a ballet, a theatre, a review, supper out every night and big dances and, last Wednesday, a trip down the river to the old palace. Lord Runciman's son Steven is here. He is terribly nice and enjoying everything thoroughly.

Today, we had the King and the Royal Entourage to tea. When you have him, he has to bring twenty people and the garden is crowded with police and they line the road. Bira took him out in the speedboat after tea. The garden is on the river, so we keep the boat at the bottom of the garden. But when the aides-de-camp saw him go, they got in an awful bother and phoned for another speed boat and crowded in - ten of them - and raced after him. Of course, they couldn't catch him and they all got very blown and drenched with spray. But the king adored the visit and wouldn't leave. He had to be dragged away. Yesterday, we lunched with the Regent (who is my nephew!!!) and today with one of Chula's uncles (Prince Rangsit), who has a lovely palace and beautiful art treasures.

Neither Chula or Bira could go back to their fathers' palaces. Chula's old home of Paruskavan Palace had been used by the state since his father died, while Bira's home, the magnificent Purapha Palace, was now closed as his sisters were married and he and his brothers, Abhas and Chirasakti, lived in England. It was decided that we would all go to stay at Ta Tien, a house by the river built in Italian style, which Chula's father had used as a landing stage for his boats and to occasionally hold parties by the river. It was furnished rather plainly in modern fashion, but Lisba found that quite a lot of the beautiful furniture from Paruskavan Palace had been stored in the cellars so had it brought up and soon made the house much more attractive.

The house was actually called a palace as it belonged to royalty. The entrance was on the big avenue near the Grand Palace, but very noisy trams ran past from early dawn, which used to wake Bira and me up as our room looked out on to that side, while Chula and Lisba's room across the corridor from us looked out on the garden at the back. Beyond the garden was the river and on the opposite side the gorgeous temple Wat Arun. Our speedboat *Romula*, which Bruno had sent out from Riva, was moored at the end of the garden where, during our stay, a small house was built for Banyen.

In the front garden by the gates, were buildings - as at Hua Hin - for secretaries, servants, and kitchens, but what surprised me was to discover that there were no bedrooms for the servants. When I slipped across one day to sit and sketch the cooks who were sitting on the floor of the kitchen balconies, each with a small charcoal fire in front of her cooking her special dish (each cook only cooked one dish), I asked them where they slept. They pointed to the wall behind them and there I saw what looked to me like raffia mats all rolled up. They indicated that when it was time to sleep, during the heat of the afternoon or at night, they just unrolled the mats and lay down where they were. Bira and Chula's valets used to sleep outside our bedroom doors; ready if they were wanted for anything in the night. Our bedroom doors, in order to allow a little air to circulate through the rooms, were like wild west bar room doors; open at the top and bottom, so really anyone could look in at any time only they never seemed to. We slept in huge, room-like tents of mosquito netting. There was no air conditioning in any of the houses in those days; only big electric fans on the ceilings; the only air conditioning I ever came across was at the cinema because of which we always took a cardigan with us, although coming out of the cinema was like walking into an oven. On our bed was a sheet, which was changed twice a day, and two long 'bolster' pillows. No pillows for our heads, as these would have made us too hot. The bolsters, Bira told me to my astonishment, were to hug. He explained (and I found he was right) that as we could not snuggle down into the bedclothes as in Europe because of the heat, we would find it easier to get to sleep hugging the bolster rather than each other in that sticky climate!

The moment Bira left the bedroom in the morning his valet would follow him into the dressing room he shared with Chula, while my girls would run giggling into me and the giggling went on all day. They were not at all like the maids we had at home; these were all girls of noble family who were only there as sort of companions and oh, they were enchanting. Always smiling and chattering and full of fun; waiting for me to return from whatever we had been doing, when they would pester me for every detail of what I had seen and what all the women had been wearing at the parties, which I mostly had to supply by little drawings. They seemed to consider it a great privilege to be there and said they were envied by their friends. One of the aides-de-camp of Chula's father, a nobleman and full colonel, had later retired to manage Prince Chakrabongse's estates, and now his son, Bisdar Chulasewok, had inherited the job. I had known Bisdar well during his visits to England and now he managed the house at Ta Tien and both Chula's and Bira's estates. He was very tall; unusually so for a Siamese, and most attractive. All the staff seemed to be his relatives: the kitchens were supervised by his mother and aunt and my girls seemed to be his cousins or nieces.

They would bring me my breakfast when Bira left to get dressed. Chula had asked Lisba and me if we wanted English or Siamese breakfast: I asked Bira what he had. He said usually a sort of rice soup with dried shrimps so I felt I had better ask for the English version. When it came, it consisted of 'Camp Coffee'; a sort of strong coffee essence from a bottle, mixed with sweetened condensed milk and a few rather stale, sweet biscuits. The request for an English breakfast had apparently caused great trouble in the kitchen, as there was no fresh milk or butter; they cooked with coconut milk and had never seen bread or jam. In the end, I had wonderful breakfasts of fruit and green tea. The variety of fruit in Siam is marvellous, most of it quite unlike any fruit I had ever come across before, and our cooks made a speciality of preparing it. I asked one evening if I could have a small bunch of grapes left by my bed for when I came in late after a dance. To my surprise that evening I found a huge bowl of them, each grape delicately peeled and the pips removed, and all still as if untouched on their bunches. When we had fruit to finish our meals, each piece was peeled and sculptured into flowers by the tiny silver knives used by the girls - whose job was to prepare fruit and do nothing else all day. The mango season had just started; I'd never eaten fruit more delicious and every mango would be carved into the shape of a rose.

Food was offered to us all day long; luckily Siamese food is not fattening as it was difficult to refuse, being simply delicious. Anyhow, one was not expected to do more than just taste it, except at meals. For lunch and dinner the main dish was always plain boiled rice; that wonderful Siamese rice, the best in the world, but difficult to find outside the country as it was nearly all exported to south China and used mainly to mix with the local rice to improve its quality. First of all, we would be served a large helping of the rice, then take a little food from all the dishes on the table and place it in a circle round the rice. In front of each place were little bowls of sauces; most of them very hot indeed as they were made with crushed peppers and spices. Siamese curry prepared with coconut milk and a squeeze of lime juice was a new experience for Lisba and me. From all the numerous meat, fish and vegetable dishes served at each meal, Bira's favourite was the sweet pork, while I loved the small slices of fresh pineapple always on the table to cool one's mouth after the spicy flavours.

Early in the morning before it became too hot, Chula would take Lisba and me sightseeing. Bira came too, whenever he could, but was usually working at his sculpture at that hour. There were over 500 monasteries in Bangkok alone and we went to the museums and the Grand Palace, which was now only used for ceremonies. Steven Runciman, who was staying at Ta Tien for a visit, would come with us; he was one of Chula's closest friends from his Cambridge days where Steven had been a brilliant, young and charmingly good-looking don. Now he was gathering information about Siam for articles he was writing for *The Times,* as a special correspondent. Sometimes, when we had spent an hour or so at one of the monasteries, Chula would have to return to carry out official duties, so they would leave me behind to paint and later send the car to fetch me.

I had been puzzled by photographs Bira had shown me of his mother, as the costumes she wore seemed strange, but now I saw that the Queen Grandmother and other elderly ladies we met all dressed that way. Their hair was cut short like a man's and instead of a skirt, they wore a 'penung', which was a male garment. It was a length of material wound round the body with the end of it brought up between the legs and tucked into a belt in the front; forming a kind of knee breeches effect. This, I discovered, was because in the past on one of the many occasions that Siam was being invaded by the Burmese, the King had ordered all the women to cut their hair and dress as men, in order to give the enemy the impression of a much larger army. Because of this, the enemy retreated and in honour of the victory the King's wives continued to dress in that manner, which, of course, all the other women copied. This fashion was only now dying out.

Another fashion of the Court, which was only followed by members of the Royal Family, was that they should all dress in the same colour when in Siamese costume; all in red on Sunday, yellow on Monday, blue on Tuesday and so on, and Bira and I always did the same. One custom on the wane, though, was the chewing of betel nut. Only the older people still did it and you could always tell them by their totally black teeth. Bira's nurse always had her betel nut set laid out on the floor in front of her on a silk handkerchief in my bedroom and chewed all day.

I don't think either Lisba or I would have enjoyed Siam so much if we had gone there alone with our husbands. It was all so strange and as we couldn't yet understand the language, we would have found the long hours we had to sit, all dressed up in that heat on platforms at official occasions, or listening to speeches or long plays, hard to bear if we hadn't sat next to each other and been able to carry on whispered conversations all the time. Happily, we had always got on very well together and shared the same sense of humour.

Bira had been longing for me to meet his two sisters, of whom he was very fond. Rambai was his full sister and was married with two children. She was very musical and had her own orchestra at the palace when she was a girl, and taught Bira to play Siamese instruments. Chalermketra was only a half-sister; daughter of Prince Bhanurangsri by his first marriage and, as her mother had been a royal princess, had been born a Royal Highness and also married a Royal Highness - a very smart marriage. It was one of her three sons who had been at Eton with Bira. Bira's mother, on the other hand, had not been of royal birth, so he and his brothers and sister were only 'Highnesses' - as was Chula by birth because his mother was a foreigner - although Chula had, however, been raised to the rank of *Royal* Highness by King Prajadhipok when the King wanted Chula to represent him in Europe on royal occasions.

Princess Chalermketra was now about 45 and a widow. When we went to visit her, what impressed me most at her palace were her orchids. It was the first time I had seen a big orchid house - and hers was full of the rarest and most gorgeous plants imaginable which had been collected from all over the country. She also sent her own servants into the jungles to search for them and it made such an impression on me that, many years later, I started a small and modest collection of my own in Italy. Princess Chalermketra loved Bira and was kindness itself to me, giving me a diamond brooch as a wedding present in the form of her and Bira's father's signatures in Siamese. Princess Rambai had also given me a brooch as a wedding present - their mother's initials in diamonds under their father's crest. I was indeed fortunate to have acquired such charming and dignified sisters-in-law. The regent's mother, who was also their sister, had died some years before.

I had been amazed at Bira's popularity at race meetings in Europe and how he was always surrounded by fans wherever he went, but that was nothing compared to his popularity here. Yet I must emphasize that it never affected him in any way - he was always modest and sweet. He just loved being back in his own country; he loved the people, he loved his family and friends, the beauty of the place and, to my joy, he loved me - so we were very happy.

We escaped whenever possible from Chula and Lisba and the much more serious life they were living - with Chula forever meeting important people and endlessly discussing the political situation. We would go off together in the speed boat up and down the river exploring the klongs, or canals, where hundreds of people lived on boats. We had to be present on all official occasions, of course, as it would have been rude and discourteous not to have been. We also went to the garden parties the British minister and the ministers of other countries gave in our honour. Everywhere we went Lisba and I were given the rank of our husbands and treated wonderfully.

Chula found he was getting on well with the leaders of the new régime, and had hopes of being offered an important job - there was even talk of allowing him to return to live in his father's palace. Bira was also very much liked by the members of the new government who said they thought he was a good example for the young people and promoted him in rank as an honorary army officer. They also talked of providing Bira with a suitable home, but Chula said that if he returned to Paruskavan Palace we could have Ta Tien, which we loved, especially as Bira had the speed boat and cabin cruiser moored at the bottom of the garden.

CHAPTER TWELVE

There was no doubt that the two people most loved by the Siamese at that time were Bira, who loved and deeply revered his King, and the young King himself, who hero-worshipped the racing driver and stuck photographs and newspaper cuttings about him into his album.

King Ananda was just 13 but seemed younger, perhaps because his constant companion was his much-loved younger brother, Prince Bhumipol, now King of Thailand, who was 10. At home with his family the King was vivacious and natural, playing games with his brother and talking with him in French. But he had to attend ceremonies, make a public profession of the Bhuddist religion, visit the Holy Shrines, pay respects to his ancestors, give away prizes at innumerable sports events, and open the Constitutional Fair. All this he did with great dignity, his only request being that whenever etiquette permitted his brother could sit beside him. Although the two boys spoke and understood a certain amount of Siamese they could not yet read or write it. All their lessons at school in Switzerland and here in the palace with their Swiss tutor, were in French, so the King's speeches had to be written out for him in roman letters and kept very short.

December 8th was the day the King opened the Constitutional Fair commemorating the signing of the Constitution which put an end to the Absolute Monarchy. In the old days the Fair had been called The Royal Winter Fair and all the important princes had stalls rather like at a charity bazaar. Now these were run by the Government departments and were really shows of their work. There was a big dancehall which, the year before, had been entirely decorated in Bira Blue and the main attraction at the Fair had been the ERA *Romulus* which had been on display.

The Fair lasted a week and was the big event of the year with people coming to see it from all over the country. My new girlfriends could talk of nothing else and their dressmakers were working overtime. Flags and bunting went up in the streets and everyone decorated their houses. Ta Tien had a racing car in lights over the gate. All smart Siam could be seen wandering round the stands during the day and visiting the Palace of Art, where Bira was among the exhibitors. At night there was dancing in the big hall attended by all the royalty.

To Aunt C I wrote -

Ta Tien, Bangkok, 15th December, 1938. *Darlingest Aunt C, I have just this moment been reading your last letter from Paris. Thank you so much. You say how very dull your letters must seem. Well you just can't imagine what pleasure it gives me to read them. You see I miss you so much and when one of your letters arrives I take it somewhere quiet and read it through lots of times. I do love it here. You can't begin to imagine how grand we are!!! I have come in for an enormous amount of admiration which of course I wallow in! My hairdresser had made his fortune as every- one now goes to him!*

This week has been a week of terrific activity here. It's the celebra- tion of the Constitution, and they have a huge fair, and a huge dance every night. It started last Friday and at four we went to the opening. About half-a-dozen princes, and Lisba and I, waited for the King in a little room, and were presented with very smart ribbons to take us everywhere, and in the Royal Box. Then the King opened the Fair and we all did a tour of the stalls, receiving presents. Among others I got a lovely fan, hand painted, with me and Bira in a racing car, with three gold stars in the sky and a moon winking! Wasn't it sweet? Then we went to the sculpture and painting exhibition and discovered Bira had won the first prize for sculpture; a silver cup. We were all very pleased. Then in the evening we went to the dance. We sat in the Royal Box and I danced with the princes. Bira and I tried to walk round the Fair to see the illuminations but the crowds collected so quickly and were so great we couldn't move.

The next evening was the Foreign Office Ball. It was like a dream. I have never been to anything like it in my life. All the women clanking with jewels and the men bowed down with orders. The Norwegian one had so many, he could hardly walk. I made friends with his wife and also with the wives of the Belgian and Dutch Ministers. About twenty people including us and the Ministers and high officials sat in a small room adjoining the ballroom, while all the rest sat in the ballroom itself. We were entertained by Siamese ballet between the dances. I danced with nearly all the Ministers, especially the small fat French one who waltzed like a dream.

112
continued on page 121

Noel Coward plays and sings after dinner at Rock in 1941.

Bira at the controls of his trains.

Ceril working at the farm during the war.

Poppa and his second wife Irene at Rock, Christmas morning, 1943.

In the train room, from left: Ceril, Lisba, Bira, Chula, Lord Herbert, a friend of the Duchess, Lady Herbert and HRH Princess Marina, Duchess of Kent.

Bira's brother Abhas and his wife Mani, widow of Bira's and Abhas's brother Chirasakti, who was killed during the war.

HRH The Duke of Kent.

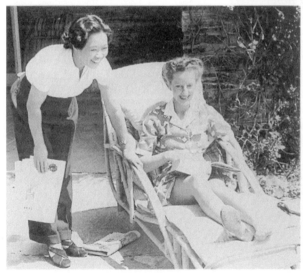

Queen Rambai - a favourite visitor - in the garden of Lynham House with Ceril.

115

Way and Ygerne with their children Dolly and Phil in 1944.

Bira and Chula in RAF and Army uniforms with Titch as a puppy.

Chula in Home Guard uniform with Ceril and Joan.

After lunch at the Rock golf club. With Ceril, Lisba and Chula are Anthony Blunt (left) and Guy Burgess during a visit to Lynham House.

Bira's bust of Lord Tredegar, which was exhibited at the 1944 Royal Academy Show.

Tredethy, 1945, taken from the air by Bira.

When Brooklands became unavailable after the war, Holgate and Bira tested the cars (here the 4CL Maserati) at a disused aerodrome.

Jersey 1947 and Chula talks to Louis Chiron. This was Chula's last race as team manager.

Bira in conversation with Count Trossi (Tipo 158 Alfetta) before the 1947 Swiss GP in which Bira retired his new 4CL Maserati with rear axle trouble.

Bira and Raymond Sommer, who was growing a moustache, hence the comment "King of Mustaches and prince of the curves - Raymond Sommer" on the photograph.

Christmas morning, 1946. Back row: Chula, Ceril, Daphne Lewis, Nan Rahm. Front row: Lisba, Shura, Phillip Martyn, Bira, Irene Quittner.

The twin-engined Miles Gemini which Bira exchanged for the Miles Messenger.

At Tredethy with Mini when just a puppy, and Titch.

120

Mummy would have been so pleased as no one could take their eyes off her emerald necklace, and Steven told me afterwards that everyone he spoke to commented on it and he told them it was Mummy's wedding present to me. The dinner was terrific. Lisba and I were the first women there so she went in on the arm of the Foreign Minister, and I went in on the arm of the Prime Minister, and sat between him and the Minister of Finance. We got on very well, I spoke French to one and German to the other. My Siamese is still not up to smart conversations!

Hua Hin, 29th December, 1938. *Aunt C darling, Thank you all so much for your Christmas cards and everything. Bira* loved *his toys; he made the model aeroplane at once. We had a lovely Christmas here. On Christmas Eve we cut down a tree in the garden which was the nearest we could get to a Christmas Tree, and then we all helped decorate it. The servants nearly went mad with excitement, they had never seen anything like it before. The tree was covered with little electric lights in all colours and deco-rated with all the things I took out with me, and I had taken masses of all coloured wrapping paper and ribbons so we all did up our presents and put them on the floor under the tree. There were 120 in all!!! And the next morning Bira was up with the dawn!!! He dragged everyone out of bed and we all rushed to the tree. Then Chula called our names out in turn and we all had to take one parcel and put it on our pile until there were none left. It took nearly two hours to open the presents; Bira got all the toys under the sun. After lunch we bathed, it's the first place I have really enjoyed bathing for a long time because the water really* is *warm, warmer even than Venice on the Lido in August, and the sea is very rough like at Biarritz, hugh waves and lovely for surf-ing. We have one whole veranda for games, we are having a New Year ping pong tournament and an all-sports competition, organ-ized by Bira of course. Chula will present cups, he's in a terrific mood of giving prizes, he even gave Lisba and me ten shillings each because we finished an enormous puzzle of the world in two days. Today Duke Anyrudh and his wife, and Prince Tongtor and Princess Laksmi, come for three days as we are having a New Year party at the hotel, with a band sent from Bangkok.
On Christmas day, Lisba and I set about to decorate everything for the Christmas dinner. A Chinese restaurant had sent us as a present an enormous Christmas cake like a wedding cake in tiers. So we put Aunt Ray's Father Christmas, which lit up, on top. Then we put ribbons from the top of the cake to the corners of the table and made long garlands of red and white flowers from the garden, and had red crackers. Aunt Ray's huge cracker we hung over the*

door and hung bunches of balloons everywhere. We turned out all
the lights except the red candles on the table and the tree lights. It
looked lovely, and as it was Sunday everyone was dressed in red.
So it all matched and we played records of carols.

The dinner was excellent, a turkey stuffed with chestnuts, and the
pudding from Harrods which travelled beautifully. The only thing
was that Lisba and I had spent hours explaining about the boiling
of the pudding, and we had cut leaves in the shape of holly ones
and sewn on red berries to stick on the top of the pudding, and
Lisba had made brandy butter and explained over and over again
about pouring the brandy over and bringing the pudding in alight.
The big moment came, and all the lights were turned out and the
Master of the Household came in holding the flaming pudding <u>still
in the basin</u> with the holly laid on top!!

After dinner all the servants, gardeners and everyone came in to
see the tree and get presents. I have never seen people enjoy
things so much. They had never seen crackers before, they
screamed with joy, just like children. The things Aunt Ray had
bought from Faudels gave more pleasure than anything I have
seen. Little babies in cradles, and toys and toy cars. But the great
thing was who should have the Father Christmas, and in the end
the caretaker's wife got it. She was so pleased, and after we had
pulled the big cracker I saw one of the gardeners whisk it away
and stick it together again to keep in his hut. But what gave more
pleasure than anything else was the silver tinsel. You see, here the
people go in a lot for garlands, and when the presents were all
taken off the tree we wondered what they were still staring at, and
then we realized, and hung tinsel round everyones neck and they
were quite overwhelmed. They had never had silver garlands
before. So it was all a great success.

Hua Hin, 1st January, 1939. *I am so sorry not to have finished
this letter but it does seem hard to find time to write. You see
there is so much to do. When we get up we rush off to the beach to
sunbathe and surf ride. Then after bathing we have lunch and I
have to learn Siamese by myself, and after tea Lisba and I have
oral lessons with Chula, and from 6-7 a private lesson with
Banyen. It's a terribly difficult language because we have to learn
to read and write as well as to speak, and there is an entirely
separate language spoken among princes which we have to learn.
There is no resemblance to other languages to help you.*

*I had a terrific Christmas card from the Maharajah and I have sent
you the stamps and also some Siamese ones. I will get lots more
for you when I get back to Bangkok. Unfortunately we have to go
back there next week as we have to go with the King and the*

Regent to a whole day review of troops in the north. We go by
special train leaving about 6 in the morning and getting back at
11.30 at night! What a day! and then a dance the next night as the
Governor of Singapore is coming and also some warships, which
means another Foreign Office Ball and all sorts of things.
Please thank Aunt Ray so much for her letter and also Daphne. I
am glad she is better; Lisba and I have been worried about her.
Bira is already making arrangements for next year. He is only
racing about 10 times but all amusing races in France and Eng-
land so we are hoping we shall be able to go to St. Jean. When we
get back this time we go straight to see Prince Umberto in Naples
for three days before coming to London. He wrote for Christmas
and it is all fixed up. I do hope we meet Mussolini! Our boat sails
from here March 30th so it does not seem long now. Bombay Duck
is very well and still singing, and the bear is here, with another
bear for company. Bira sends his love to all, he's always about to
write but it never comes off.

During the week of the Fair another attempt was made on the life of the
Minister of Defence, Luang Pibul; this time with poisoned food. He and his
wife and daughters and the people who had been dining with them were all
taken very ill indeed, and had to be rushed to hospital. Fortunately, they
recovered and as a result there was a change of Government, the charming,
elderly Phya Bahol (who had taken me in to dinner at the Foreign Office Ball)
resigned and retired from politics. Luang Pibul now became Prime Minister
and Commander-in-Chief of the army. Most of the other ministers remained
with some reshuffling. As Chula and Bira were very much in favour with
Luang Pibul he particularly wanted them to go to the review of troops at
Lopburi where the King would be inspecting the new Military Centre. Lopburi
was a small town built on the site of an ancient city where for many years there
had been an artillery training college. Now the idea was for this new Centre
to become like Aldershot and, with the new main buildings completed, the
King was to open them. When Chula and Bira had been given the invitation,
Luang Pibul had particularly said he wanted Lisba and me to accompany
them. This was obviously a great honour as the only other women invited were
the King's mother and sister and the wife of the Regent. None of the other
distinguished men who were going had been asked to bring their wives. So
Chula said whatever happened we must cut short our stay at Hua Hin as our
being present at this ceremony would show that we had been fully accepted
by the government.

Ta Tien, Bangkok, 15th January, 1939. *Way dear, You are all so*
good at writing and I love hearing from you. Tell Poppa Bira is
playing in a golf match at the Sports Club. He has a handicap of 18
which isn't bad considering he has only been playing since we

came here. He is improving every day and has only one ambition and that is to beat Poppa. This afternoon we are going to see a Siamese Bird Man fly up with wings. But the best thing of all is the amount of money Bira is earning. He is working on the Regent, and on a huge plaque of the founder of the Postal Service to go in the new post office. Both very well paid works, and yesterday he was approached with the project of doing a double life size statue of the late King in England during the summer. I don't know if it is settled or not, but if it comes off it means at least five or six hundred pounds. It is probable we will return here in October so that Bira can collect work to do for the next three or four years. Certainly now he has started it does not look as if there will be any danger of him being out of work.

It was awful having to leave Hua Hin but now I am here I love it. Especially as it is the cool season. But when we arrived from Hua Hin it was still very hot and Lisba and I felt it frightfully. The train arrived at dinner time and after dinner we tried to go to bed as we had to be up at 5.30am to go north for the opening of the Military Camp. I think I slept better than most, sleeping until 4am. Chula didn't go to bed at all and Lisba only slept until 1am and then got up, and Bira too. Anyhow we all felt pretty awful and got into the train at 6am when it was still dark. We arrived at the Camp at 10am. The whole show was the Premier's; he's armed the country more than anyone knows and started this enormous camp. All the boys are like Balillas in Italy and wear uniforms and they had a display of 2000 the other day, and sports are cultivated like in Germany. It is making Siam very important out here, and there is terrific rivalry between Japan and England for her friendship.

I would not be in the Premier's shoes though, as he has been shot at once and poisoned twice since we have been here. When we arrived at the Camp the car we were meant to have for the day would not start so the Premier at once offered his until ours was mended. Bira got in front and leapt out with a scream. He had sat on the pointed piece of a machine gun!! And the glass was nearly two inches thick, bullet-proof everywhere. The Premier never eats except in his own home. We had tea together and he just sat and watched. Everyone is petrified of him, but he and Chula seem to be hand in glove. It is also he who promoted Bira as an officer in the army, and a lot of princes are jealous because he is quite a young prince and there are many higher in rank, but they are never invited to the ceremonies and things, whereas Bira is always in front because the Premier likes him, and considers he does something for the country. By the way, keep these pages for yourself and Poppa, I only write it because I think it may interest you to know a bit more than just the social side.

We are in the midst of many intrigues, but so far on the outside. For instance going to the camp, the Premier arranged for us to travel on the King's train. Then a few days later he was poisoned and went to hospital and during that time the officials, who do not like Chula, told us to go on the ordinary train. When we arrived, someone phoned to the Premier and he dashed over to us. It had made him look a fool altering his arrangements when he was ill. He apologized profusely but Chula said it did not matter a bit. In consequence the Premier was trying to make it up to us all day and looked after us himself, and when the Royal Train left at 5pm he begged Chula to take it. But Chula said he could not possibly upset the arrangements, that there would not be enough food and someone might have to go without. So when the train left, the Premier took us back to his own house, and his wife took Lisba and me up to her bedroom. Chula then had what he had been angling for all day - and what is so difficult to get - an hour's tête-à-tête with the Premier. He altogether bettered their friendship all round. We got to know his wife and children and they are all coming to spend the evening en famille next week and see a private cinema show.

I wish I had time to write more about the happenings here, but I have not. There are so many other things I want to tell you. The big boat Macharnu has arrived. We go out in her a lot. We have two sailors, and three other men to manage the food, etc. So it's a lovely rest, not like in England! Also I have been very busy because I discovered that as well as being left money by his father, Bira was left two huge chests he had never opened, full of silver, china, and art treasures. So of course I have been through the lot. We have some _heavenly_ things. Piles of old Siamese silver, really lovely. I am bringing a few pieces back, also some china and other things as we are going to do up the studio again and have a cabinet of Siamese stuff. And there is a pile of materials over 100 years old, and little boxes and betel-nut sets in gold studded with diamonds and little pearls. Simply sweet. Really a crime not to see them on show, except of course the really valuable things which I am leaving here in the bank.

On the 12th we celebrated our first wedding anniversary. We got up at 6am and fed 47 priests according to custom. One for every year of our lives and one over. Twenty-two for me and twenty-four for Bira. Chula and Lisba gave us two beautiful Siamese finger bowls which they mean to add to every year. Bira's half sister gave me an old Siamese ring with little rubies which belonged to their grandmother Queen Debsirindra. In the afternoon we took the speedboat and explored the little canals together.

The next morning the King left. Bira and Chula in full dress uni-

form went to see him off on the warship. Then they tore back and leapt on 'Macharnu' and changed, and we all went down the river to the sea - the King kept waving to us from the Captain's bridge. The day before he had given Bira two huge model aeroplanes. Now I must stop as the Minister of Finance is coming to lunch. Please give everybody my love.

Ta Tien, Bangkok, 30th January, 1939. *Dearest Aunt C, Today there is a slight lull in activities as everyone is getting ready for the Governor of the Malay Straits' visit tomorrow.*

3rd February. *I am so sorry not to have finished this before but things have been cropping up all the time. On Tuesday we went to the big reception at the British Legation to meet the Governor and Lady Thomas, and Wednesday they came to lunch very informally here, and in the evening there was a terrific dinner again at the Legation.*
The Governor is charming; in fact they both are. Yesterday the Governor's party was taken to Ayudhya and back by river, a very long day by a very slow boat. So about 4pm, Bira and I took out the speedboat and went right up into the country to meet them, just to wave to them. But the Governor had the boat stopped and hailed us, and took off his coat and leapt in, and Lady Thomas put a scarf round her hair and she jumped in too, and we took them for a fast run. They loved it - it made a break in the journey for them. They had to go back to the big boat, but the aide-de-camp and the private secretary both insisted on coming back to Bangkok with us. The Governor has invited us all to stay at Government House on the way back and he is going to take us up in the new flying boats.
Bira is still working desperately hard. The Regent's head is finished and he is doing the Post Office work now. I have done quite a few paintings, so we are having a little show before we leave.
We really have been lucky with the weather so far as they say its been the coolest winter in years. Tonight we have a dinner here for the American and Dutch Ministers. Both their wives have been sweet to me and I have been to see them informally and sit in their gardens. Tomorrow a ballet is being held for us - the ballet here has to be seen to be believed, it is so beautiful. The colours of the costumes are fantastic and the music and dancing are wonderful, but quite indescribable. The show goes on for hours and hours and people talk all the way through, and eat sweets and little chestnuts, and then have a huge supper afterwards.
Poppa darling, I am awfully sorry to hear you had the 'flu. I hope you are quite all right now. Since I wrote to Way, a lot has been

happening. A huge plot to kill the Premier was discovered and hundreds of people have been arrested. An enormous purge; quite a lot of Princes among them. I hope you were not worried if you read about it in the papers. Wild rumours fly about all the time and everyone seems worried about their relations, but it is hard to know what is true and what is not. Anyhow, most of the people arrested were very anti-Chula, and jealous of him. He himself has always supported the present government in every way. I only hope it blows over soon.

Ta Tien, Bangkok, 10th February, 1939. *Dearest Aunt Ray, You do all write so much and so well. Thank you. Please tell Way I loved his letter, he writes wonderful long ones, also thank Aunt C too, and for Bira's letter. He was very grateful to her for forwarding his letter to Raymond Mays. We go off to Angkor tomorrow at 6.30 in the morning; we shall be there three days. The Commander-in-Chief of the French navy in the Far East is here and yesterday there was a reception and dance at the French Legation. Bira is sick of dinners and receptions - he loathes them - and the night before last there was a particularly boring one so we wriggled out of it, and took Bira's brother and four Siamese friends and went to the cinema. Then had supper, and took a sort of gondola, only much bigger, on the river. We took masses of cushions and drinks and went all down one of the small canals. It was full moon like daylight and we passed all the Siamese sleeping in their house-boats, and the Chinese cooking and eating and seeing theatres. We stopped and ate some of the Chinese food - it was delicious, like spaghetti, very highly flavoured. We did not get back until 4.30.*
Every Sunday we take the big yacht and go right up the river into the country and anchor. Then we bathe, and Bira has had sails put on the dinghy, so he sails up and down, and we lie on the deck.'

Ta Tien, Bangkok, 15th February, 1938. *Darling Aunt C, Thank you so much for your letter which I got on returning from Indo China. We went there on Saturday; we left at 7 in the morning feeling very tired after a lot of late nights. The train arrived at the frontier at 3.30 and then we had a car sent by the government to take us to Siemrap where we were staying - about 100 miles. A very dull drive over flat land relieved by the most heavenly birds everywhere. Then as we got near the jungle and the hills, we arrived. It was an amazing sensation to find a typically French hotel in the middle of this wilderness. I pity the manager who lives there year in and year out. We went to bed early as we had to be* up at dawn next day. Angkor was about five miles away; I don't know how to describe it. In the 11th century the country was inhabited by a very strong and highly civilized nation, the Khmers, or Cambodians as they are called now. The Siamese were their slaves - they had several times been beaten by them in battle - and had to pay homage and every year bring gallons and gallons of water by ox cart from Siam as they hadn't an adequate water supply. Many died like this or were killed for spilling the water en route.

The Khmers had built the most amazing city and masses of temples. Unfortunately only the temples were of stone, and the houses and palaces were of wood, so only the temples remain. All the temples were built to the God Vishnu, and then in the 12th century they were converted to Buddhism so there are many beautiful Buddhas to be seen. In the 13th century the Siamese became sick of being slaves and twice sent an army, and sacked the city on each occasion. So the Khmers decided to leave the city altogether as it was too near the Siamese, and built another capital further away. They left and never came back. Bit-by-bit it was all covered by jungle and forgotten, then about 1840 a Frenchman was hunting lions and came on this dense jungle. He was told by the local people it was haunted and that no one ever went there. So he went to have a look out of curiosity and stumbled on these huge temples.

At that time the country was Siamese, but later the French took it, and they began to excavate. Altogether they discovered about 100 temples in a radius of 10km. In the morning, on Sunday, we started by looking at a wonderful artificial lake, and carved steps and sculptures, and then we saw some of the smaller temples. The way the trees had grown over them was amazing; the roots clutched the walls like huge fingers. We walked miles with the guide and it was alright until about 10am when it began to get really hot and we melted. We staggered round until noon, and it was only the wonder of this marvellous place, and these amazing sculptures in the depth of the jungle, which kept us going!!

We had some lunch and slept until three when we went out again; this time to the big temple called Angkor Wat. It has two moats and innumerable bridges. Again the sculptures were like a dream, but the bats!!! Bon Dieu the smell!!! Centuries of bats had made messes and we staggered through with hankies to our noses, and me holding a parasol up in the darkest tower and with my head wrapped in a scarf, while they flapped and squeaked up above us. You can imagine how lovely Angkor must be that we still enjoyed it in spite of them, and to add to that we had to pick our way among the big snakes coiled up and sleeping on the ground.

We got to our hotel again about 6pm, dead beat, and I wrote postcards until dinner when we ate and then went back to Angkor to see Cambodian dancing, which was like Siamese, only not so good. And there were hundreds of small boys who were even more terrifying than the bats as they carried reed torches, and pressed round us asking for money and I honestly thought they would set us all alight! That night Bira and I were too tired to sleep and the beds were hard beyond belief. The next morning we started off to see more ruins, but what I loved more than anything else were the little monkeys with their babies in the trees. They were adorable. After lunch we went on elephants up the hills into the jungle. The real thing! Not like at the Zoo!! Only we were a bit scared as they weren't too well trained and kept making awful noises and stamping about, and Chula kept telling us stories about how he had seen elephants run amok when he was young!!

We collected our luggage at about 4.30pm and started in the car for the frontier. We had an old Cambodian driver who drove so badly we almost died of fright, and after he had nearly driven off the road several times Bira insisted on taking his place. There was no hotel so we had to stay at a sort of rest house. We caught the train at 9.30 next morning and arrived back here at 5.30. This morning Steven Runciman came back by air from a tour of Indo China. Weren't his Times articles good?

Hua Hin, 28th February, 1939. It is heaven to be here again as it is cool and windy. We were all dead beat when we arrived but are already feeling quite different. Bira had a bad cold and cough for a week, and Steven a rash from the heat, but both are all right now. Bira has finished the Post Office work, a fish fountain, and now has a Chinese millionaire who said money didn't count as long as Bira did his head, and he could charge anything. He also has a large statue for the Orphans' Home to do, and to design a badge for them, and do a statue of Chula's grandmother for an institute. He has been guaranteed £2000 in copies alone the moment he does the Premier's head and the Premier has promised to sit for him, but he is ill at the moment.

After we came back from Angkor we all had to go into full mourning because the old duchess who supplied us with extra cooks died, also Chula's aunt, also the Second Regent, and also the Pope was being cremated (The Buddhist Pope). There have been masses of ceremonies. In a way it was a saving for us as we had so many parties and things we would have collapsed if they hadn't all been cancelled.

Chula decided we ought to visit Ayudhya, the old capital, while Steven was here. We left Bangkok by boat at 7.30am so as to sightsee in the cool, but the boat broke down and we didn't arrive until 1.30. The Governor of the province met us and took us everywhere. Having thought we would just do a little sightseeing before the sun was hot and then spend the rest of the day on the boat bathing etc. we had no hats or parasols, and the sun was at its height and the temperature was 130 degrees in the sun and 112 in the shade! I can't describe it to you. We were in the sun for two hours walking round ruins! Steven and Lisba are terrific sightseers but even they admitted they didn't see anything. Our clothes were just wet rags and we had to keep smiling for the photographers. How we didn't all get sunstroke I can't think! Anyhow we didn't. We stopped at Bang-Pa-In for dinner and had fireworks, and then the boat broke down completely and we had to be towed to Bangkok. Steven told hair-raising ghost stories all the way and we didn't get back until 4am. The next night was the dinner at the Belgian Legation and we dozed all the evening, not knowing how to keep awake. One thing that was sweet at Ayudhya was that I saw lovely wild parrots flying about! Just like your Cosy, up in the trees.

I hardly like to bother you again but the Siamese New Year is the first of April and I want to give the Regent's wife and others some little gift and all the things in Bangkok they know so well. I would like something extra nice as they have been so good to me. Please could you go to Harrods, first to the lace counter and get some collars, the pretty sort you pin or tack on dresses or blouses. They have nothing like that here. I suggest lace ones, and pastel coloured chiffons, perhaps embroidered ones. The Siamese love anything dainty but a bit more elaborate in taste than we do. They have organdy here but no chiffon or laces. If there was one in gold it would be perfect. Then could you go to the handkerchief department and get me three evening hankies, Lisba's mother sent me one for Christmas and it has been so admired. Hers was chiffon with a wide net border. And also some smart men's hankies with the initial T, for Prince Tongtor. We leave Hua Hin on 16 March and go back to Bangkok for just over a week. We have parties every night though of course we can't dance as we will be in half mourning. We then go to Penang and take a boat for Singapore arriving 28 March. Isn't it near now! I _am_ longing to see you again.

CHAPTER THIRTEEN

I was sad to say goodbye to my new family and friends but would be seeing them again in a few months. I was convinced I would be happy to make Siam my home; returning to Europe every summer for Bira to race. Lisba and I had picked up a certain amount of the language by now although it was difficult; the letters being written rather like Sanskrit with 48 consonants and 24 vowels, as well as 5 sound tones. We also had to learn Court Siamese, which was used all the time by the Royal family among themselves, and which Chula and Bira spoke together and Banyen and Bisdar used to address them.

Sir Josiah Crosby, the British minister, told me that when he first came to Siam some 40 years previously he had learnt to speak Siamese well, but knew nothing of Court language. Once, when on an official occasion King Chulalongkorn (who had heard that he knew Siamese) came up to him and addressed him in that language, Sir Josiah did not know what to do. To reply would mean doing the unthinkable; talking to the King in the 'common' language, but the King smiled and said he understood the difficulty and that he could reply in what Sir Josiah called his 'market' Siamese.

He had known Bira's father who, he said was royalty personified; the old school of royalty, and most popular with the European community, so I knew from where Bira had inherited his charm. Sir Josiah said it was sad the new government people had never known the old palace life, with its exquisite manners and traditions, and that the old way of life was, regrettably being replaced by the worst of the European and American ways of life. He said he missed the 'old Siam' very much.

Lloyd Triestino *Victoria*, 2nd April 1939. *Darling Poppa and the Aunts, this is the most lovely ship, smaller than the* Conte Verde, *but more beautifully fitted out inside. In Singapore, Bira bought a complete set of printing and enlarging apparatus and spends his time shut in the bathroom, developing his films. He got on well with the governor in Singapore, as he too is mad on photography. He and Lady Thomas are the most delightful people; we loved them and had a wonderful time. They adored Bira and he and the governor teased each other all the time. The governor took him off to play golf with him and the Head of the Naval Forces and the Air Commodore. They evidently had a grand time together. We had two nights there. We arrived after lunch when everyone was resting, so I went off and had my hair washed. I felt very smart; driving everywhere in an immense Daimler with a flag in front and a huge red crown.*

When I got back, everyone except Sir Shenton had had tea, so we had it together, and he took me in the garden - oh the smell of the gardenia bushes in flower! - and then he showed me round everywhere. The next morning, we went over the Naval Base. It's the most amazing place I have ever seen; so immense. There are already ten thousand people living there and work goes on day and night. That evening there was a dinner party; all army people, and after dinner Sir Shenton and Bira both showed films. Then at about eleven, the ADCs took the younger people and Abhas, Bira and me, to Raffles to dance, and then we went to all the other people's houses for drinks and things until 4.30.

It is lovely now to be resting on the ship. When we got back to Bangkok from Hua Hin, there was a big Motor Rally and Trial. Bira was Chief Marshal and I entered the baby Fiat for fun. I was absolutely thrilled with the things Aunt C got for me. They were an <u>enormous</u> success; <u>exactly</u> what I wanted and everyone loved them. They arrived in perfect condition. When we left Bangkok, crowds came to see us off and the flowers were unbelievable. Bira has some very good photos I will show you. There were many tears, especially my special maid who had wept all the day before. We arrived the next day at Penang and stayed the night, before taking the boat to Singapore. It was such fun at Penang, as we went to the cinema and I saw Uncle in the news, at a pony show. It was so unexpected and I was thrilled. Loads and loads of love to you all and to the Bridegroom!!! and see you all soon.

Lloyd Triestino Victoria, 13th April 1939, at Port Said. *On the boat, we get very little news as it is Italian, but we gather the situation in Europe is pretty bad. Chula, Lisba and Abhas got off the ship at about 11 o'clock last night and drove to Cairo. They want to get news there, and are joining the ship again here at Port Said. I have got very friendly with old Countess Apponya, King Zog's wife's aunt, and also with a Spanish millionaire, who lives at*

St Jean de Luz and knows everyone and is a friend of King
Alphonso. Both of them are kept in touch with news by cable and
that is how I know what is going on! We have cabled to Prince
Umberto to know if his plans have changed at all.

Prince Umberto's plans had changed. We heard the news that Italy had
occupied Albania when we reached Aden and, as we saw the coast of that
country in the distance, I stood on deck leaning on the rail with Queen
Geraldine's aunt, who told me of her great anxiety for her niece's future. When
we got to Naples an *aide-de-camp* came on board with huge bouquets for
Lisba and me from Prince Umberto, and the news that the Prince could not
spend the day with us as planned and dinner and the opera that night had
been cancelled. He had been called to Rome to meet the Albanian Delegation
who had come to 'offer' the throne to King Victor Emmanuel. He lent us his
boat to go to Capri, accompanied by his ADC, and when he returned from
Rome two days later Chula and Bira went to stay with him at the palace for
a few days.

Lisba and I had chosen not to wait. I wanted to get home well before Way's
wedding and, as Lisba's mother and sister Janie had come to meet the ship,
we four travelled back to England together. Bira returned just in time to film
the wedding in Essex.

The racing season was about to begin and there were a lot of changes in
the air. The most important one for us was that Bira could no longer compete
for the British Racing Drivers' Club Gold Star as he was no longer an honorary
British driver; he was a Siamese one. The Royal Automobile Association of
Siam had joined the *Association Internationale des Automobiles Réconnues*
and could now issue international competition licences and had to choose a
national racing colour. As all the main colours were already taken, it was
decided to have the body of the cars Bira Blue, with the chassis and wheels
the yellow of Siam's highest order; the Chakri.

Then there were rumoured changes in the Grand Prix formula for 1941
onwards which was perhaps to be altered to 11/2-litres supercharged:
Mercedes (W165) and Alfa Romeo (*Tipo* 158) were already building racing
cars of that engine capacity for their *voiturette* team. Only Maserati had
new, 11/2-litre 'customer cars' (the 4CL) for sale, but Chula and Bira did not
think they were reliable yet. They therefore decided to continue with their two
ERAs, Romulus and Hanuman, together with the 8CM Maserati, and to have
them all very well prepared, as they believed the only way an amateur could
hope to be successful was to have his cars even better prepared than the
works cars if possible. To try and do this for the coming season, they planned
to go to fewer races than before; giving Holgate and their new young mechanic
Carlo Silva more time for preparation.

Another reason they decided to race less in 1939 was that Bira would need
more time to work in our studio, as he wanted to complete as many orders
as possible before we returned to Siam in the autumn. They chose five races

at the Crystal Palace, three at Brooklands, one at Donington and Le Mans, Rheims and Albi abroad.

At the ERA works there were changes too. While we were in Siam Humphrey Cook had announced he could not go on financing the factory alone: he was hoping help might be forthcoming from some sort of public subscription, but it never materialised and the ERA company virtually closed down.

Bira was very happy to win his first race - the JCC International Trophy on 6th May at Brooklands - in the new Siamese colours driving the Maserati. The weather was appalling, but Bira invariably drove well in the rain. As always, the Private View at the Royal Academy had been the day before, but this year Bira had submitted nothing as all his new work was in Siam.

Banyen had stayed behind in Bangkok to look after everything there with Bisdar whilst Bien Chulindra came back with us. When not busy typing the text of Chula's historical books in Siamese, he was to help Shura with the *White Mouse Garage* accounts.

Chula was to devote a great deal of his time, and that of Shura and Bien, to the organising of a Grand Prix race to be held in Siam that winter. He had talked it over with Prime Minister Luang Pibul and suggested that, as the Siamese people had become very interested in motor racing because of Bira's successes, would it not be a good idea for them to see a race for themselves? Also, as a Grand Prix had never been held in the East before, would it not be appropriate for the only Eastern country which had a successful racing driver to be the first to organise one? He had suggested that the government put up a large sum of money, and well-known drivers from as many different countries as possible be invited; giving them handsome starting money and paying their expenses and those of their wives and mechanics, as well as giving generous cash prizes. The only stipulation he made was that he must be in sole charge of the organisation. He didn't want to have to deal with committees in Siam made up of people who had no idea about motor racing. It was after Bira won the Sydenham Trophy, and *The Times* wrote "Bira must be regarded as the undisputed champion of the Crystal Palace Circuit" that Chula got Luang Pibul's cable giving him the 'go ahead.'

Bira had chosen the circuit while we were there and designed it so that at one point it went right round the Grand Palace. It had to be a town circuit like Monte Carlo as there were no roads leading out of Bangkok in those days. Twelve drivers were to be invited including Bira. Luang Pibul fixed 10th December 1939 as the race day, since it was Constitution Day and the week of the big Fair. In that way, all the people he expected would come to see the race from the surrounding countries would be able to visit the fair as well. The race would be for 1500cc cars and only independent drivers were to be invited. The official reason given for this was that ,as works teams raced to advertise their cars (and Siam had no car factories) they didn't see why they should help to advertise the factories of other countries. Of course, it was also to give their own driver a fairer chance!

Among those invited were Raymond Mays with his ERA, Percy Maclure with his Riley, Raymond Sommer from France, Johnny Lurani and Piero Taruffi from Italy and Toulo de Graffenreid from Switzerland with Maseratis plus drivers from Germany and Holland. George Abecassis was invited with his Alta but refused as he could not leave his work for the long journey.

We went up to Donington for the Nuffield Trophy race and as it was a scratch race, the new Mercedes, Alfa Romeo and Maserati 1 1/2-litre works cars were eagerly expected though, in the end, none of them turned up, to the great disappointment of the organisers and public. So it became another duel between Mays and Bira, with their Zoller-blown ERAs, which Bira won. The *Bystander* wrote "Bira is a superb driver. All honour to the men who make racing in this country worthwhile". This successful start to the season, with four wins in a row, made the people in Siam look forward even more eagerly to seeing a race. I couldn't help feeling it would be awful if Bira won in Bangkok as everyone would think the whole thing had been arranged to that end which, I suppose, was the reason Chula was doing it, yet if Bira failed to win I thought the country would go into mourning. At that moment he was designing a most attractive poster for it.

Yet another change. It was announced that, henceforth, Siam would be known as *Thailand* and we were now *Thais*. It took some getting used to ...

In fact, the Siamese had always called themselves Thai; it was foreigners who had given the country the name of Siam. Now they wanted to use their real name - meaning Land of the Free or Independent - the name of the ancient tribe from which were descended.

The next event in our programme was Le Mans, where Bira had always wanted to race. Sommer had written, saying he had an offer of a works Alfa and asked if Bira would share it. So Bira drove Chula and me there, while Shura and Abhas followed with the box of signals. We stayed at the Hotel de Paris and, after dinner, Sommer and Bira went to see their car. To their disappointment it was not the 2.9-litre, 8-cylinder supercharged type they had expected and knew would be one of the fastest cars in the race, but a new, unblown 2 1/2-litre 6C coupé, which Alfa had built for sports races. It had been a misunderstanding on Sommer's part.

The 24-hour race ran from 4 o'clock on Saturday, and the space behind the pits was always full of caravans and tents for people to rest in or use to entertain their friends. Not to be outdone, Chula arranged with the hotel for us to have a big caravan, but all they produced was a rather nasty-smelling marquee; the sort you put up on lawns for weddings, with a couple of brass beds in it. It was not a success. During the night, while Sommer was taking his turn at the wheel, Chula suggested Bira and I get a little sleep, but it was quite impossible to stay in there. It had been put up on the edge of the road, and every time a car came roaring past it gave the impression of coming straight at the beds and we jumped up in fear!

I was equally frightened when Sommer took me round the course and was shaking when I got out of the car, only to be comforted when Bira said that when he went out with Sommer he was terrified; certain that he could never brake so late for corners or drive so fast. Yet the first time he went out he clocked even faster times. The car broke down and was retired but we felt it had been a marvellous experience.

Just before the next race at the Crystal Palace, we heard that Dick Seaman had been killed in the Belgian Grand Prix. Bira felt it deeply, having lost a great friend, and a few years later, Chula was to write his *Dick Seaman-Racing Motorist*. (G.T. Foulis).

The next weekend Chula, Bira and I went to Rheims, and from there were going on to Albi for the race on the following Sunday, 16th July. It was the first time Rheims was holding a 1500cc race before the French Grand Prix, and the event would have given a foretaste of the likely 1941 Grand Prix Formula. Three of the new Alfa Romeo *Tipo* 158s had been entered but were then withdrawn for political reasons arising from Franco-Italian tension. It was decreed that no Italian car or driver could race in France, except Nuvolari as he was driving a German car, the Auto Union. Shades of the approaching war ... Bira was to drive Hanuman, which Chula and he felt should be as fast as any car, so we set off with high hopes in Bira's Rolls and stayed at the *Lyon d'Or*. On the first practice day Bira did the second fastest time after Dobson, who was driving Humphrey Cook's new E-type ERA, GP1.

Chula said he didn't see why I should get up again at dawn next morning for the practice, so I slept on only to be woken by Chula shaking me. I saw the look on his face and was dressed in a moment. Chula, shocked, just managed to whisper "He's in the hospital".

Bira had crashed badly, but had been able to pick himself up and a French driver had stopped and given him a lift back to the pits. Chula had realised something had happened when he saw from his stopwatch that Bira was overdue, and then he heard the loud speakers call for an ambulance. The *Motor* wrote "We waited, Prince Chula and his staff exercised an admirable calm, although their anxiety must have been appalling". When Bira arrived at the pits, his overalls were torn and it could be seen that he had a great wound on one hip. Bira said it had been his own fault, really. He had seen from Chula's signals that he had done the second fastest time (to Dobson) and thought he would do just one more really fast lap, before coming in to try and get the pole position on the starting grid the next day. Then he got into a bad skid on some loose gravel at the side of the road, missed a tree, hit a bank and was thrown out. It was a miracle that he had escaped so lightly: there was only severe bruising and the leg wound to show for the accident.

Chula phoned to Lisba who flew to join us. The Auto Union and Mercedes teams always travelled with their own doctor and they sent him at once to examine Bira; he came each day to dress the wound himself. After a couple of days Bira wanted to leave the hospital because he wanted badly to race at Albi. He talked this over with the German doctor who, as his job was to look after the German drivers, was an expert on the subject. He thought that physically Bira should be able to drive, if he could manage the heavy gear pedal on the ERA, but he wasn't sure whether his nerves would have had time to recover by then. Bira, on the other hand, felt it was absolutely essential for him to drive again at once after such a frightening crash: he was afraid that if he didn't he might never have the nerve to race again ...

The one thing everyone agreed on was that Bira needed a couple of days' absolute quiet. As Chula and Lisba had already left to go and stay with Chula's mother and step-father, we got Shura to drive us there to join them as I still felt too shaken to drive myself. Holgate and Silva had taken poor, wrecked *Hanuman* to Calais (where they had left *Romulus*, just in case), picked up *Romulus*, and were now back in France on their way to Albi. They stopped first at Mother's house at Rambouillet and put the car on the road. Bira hopped and limped over and drove it up and down, to the surprise of the villagers; changing gear a lot to try his leg on the gear pedal. He decided he could manage, so Holgate put the car back in the van and he and Silva drove on to Albi, with Shura driving Chula and Lisba behind them.

Bira and I stayed on until the Friday afternoon, when I drove the Rolls to Paris and we left it there, continuing by train, hoping to get a good rest in our sleeper. Instead, we had a dreadful night. No sooner had we got into bed than Bira broke out in a rash all over his body; that same rash he had suffered from for years but which we had thought cured. It had been brought on again by the anti-tetanus injection he had been given in hospital. He became swollen all over and we were awake all night. In the morning we had to change to a local train at Toulouse which was hot and crowded and we sat with our luggage on our knees. When Bira got out of the train he could hardly see because his face was so swollen. He was exhausted, skipped lunch and went straight to bed - poor Bira; it was his 25th birthday! The hotel sent for a doctor, who gave him an injection against the swelling and he rested for an hour or two. Then he got into his overalls and went out to practice.

That night it was absolutely essential for Bira to sleep well and the doctor, a wise man, said the best thing to stop the itching and bring down the swelling was vinegar. So Bira went to sleep naked on our bath towels, with the windows closed in case of a draught, and I sat up gently sponging him. I still can't mix a salad dressing without thinking of that hot July night ... When Chula put his head round the door in the morning, the vinegar fumes sent him reeling out again, but it had produced good results. Bira had been able to sleep, the rash had gone down, and he finished the race third. He had not felt well enough to do battle with anyone, but at least he had proved to himself that his nerves had not been affected by the crash. *Motor Sport* wrote "One can only stand in respectful admiration of Bira's courage in racing again the following weekend at Albi. Of such stuff are heroes made".

At Brooklands Bank Holiday Meeting in August Bira drove the 3-litre Maserati 8CM in the Campbell Trophy Race. But Mays was there with the 2-litre ERA which was faster than the Maserati, added to which, Mays made one of his famously-good starts and beat Bira into second place. Bira was due to race on 26th August for the Imperial Trophy at the Crystal Palace, but withdrew as he said he just didn't feel like driving.

Great Britain and France declared war on Germany on 3rd September 1939.

CHAPTER FOURTEEN

Chula, Lisba, Bira, Shura and I went to stay in a hotel near London. Chula wanted us all to be together to think carefully about our futures. The Bangkok race was, of course, cancelled, so Chula suggested that as we no longer had to hurry home to prepare for it, we might take a house somewhere in the country for a few months, while he settled up his affairs in England. This would give Lisba and me time to say goodbye to our family and friends, because if the war went on for some years, it could be a long time before we saw them again. We found a house in Cornwall belonging to a business friend of Lisba's father and Chula took it for six months. In the end we stayed there six years.

We all set off for the Cornish village of Rock and were told afterwards that our arrival had seemed rather like a circus coming to town. Bira and Chula led the way in the Rolls; taking Joan and Romeo, Bira's bulldog pup (Popski was now living with Uncle Harry) and towing *Romulus*, which Bira would not leave behind. Bien followed with Abhas' dog, while Lisba, who had now learned to drive, brought the birds - Bombay Duck and Josiah, a rare Malayan grackle the size of a blackbird, that Chula had brought back from Thailand. It used to puff out its chest and bow, and I fear we had named it after the British minister to Thailand. Then came Shura driving the *White Mouse* van, filled with any luggage that would not fit into the cars and Chula's desk and files, together with the radiogram and all our records. Mrs Healey and I brought up the rear in the baby Fiat with the cats Whiskey and Tiger on her knees. They had protested so violently when we tried to put them in baskets that we had to take them out again. Of course, we couldn't stop on the way for fear of them escaping and, as it was a long drive to Cornwall, it was a rather smelly foursome that got out of the car at Rock. Ives and his family came by train, also Mrs Healey's niece Mrs Wells with her young daughter Jean. Mrs Healey reigned supreme in the kitchen and carried on a perpetual feud with Ives.

Bira and I went back to London to stay with the Aunts, while Bira dismantled his train room and packed the racing cups for Shura to fetch with the van, together with the Maserati and *Hanuman*; still in oiled pieces after the crash at Rheims. Chula and Bira wanted them away from the danger of bombs and ready to use again as soon as the war ended.

My father joined the Home Guard and commanded the Barnes Company; drilling them on the golf course at Roehampton Club, and lived with his clergyman brother and wife, whose son was a regular officer in the RAF. Another of his nephews, a doctor, was to receive an MC in the Libyan desert, as when taken prisoner by the Germans he stole an ambulance and brought his wounded back to their lines. Yet a third nephew (his favourite) was later badly wounded at Calais during the invasion of Europe.

Way was training in Scotland before being sent abroad for most of the war, while Chula's and Bira's friends were all now in one uniform or another. The two felt very frustrated, especially Bira, who longed to join the RAF like so many of his racing friends. Because Chula and Bira were princes of a neutral country with diplomatic status, they were not allowed to take part in any war effort whatsoever, and it was only after lengthy discussions with the Foreign Office that they were at last allowed to join the Home Guard in Cornwall.

After a short while at Rock we arranged to go back to Thailand via Canada and Japan, but the British ship on which we were due to sail was requisitioned at the last moment as it was needed for troop carrying. So we tried to find a Japanese ship, but they had decided not to call any more at British ports. Then Chula got a cable from Luang Pibul asking him to remain in Europe and represent Thailand at the League of Nations in Geneva, so he asked the owner of the house to extend our lease for a year. However, the League of Nations collapsed soon after.

Chula then settled down again to his writing. He had finished the life of Camillo Cavour and began to research his next book on Hannibal. He was also planning to write an autobiography when Dick Seaman's mother wrote and asked him to write about Dick's life. Bira also wrote a book. Chula had given him a little Bira Blue typewriter and he sat cross-legged on the floor at once to learn to use it. When Bira announced that he, too, would write a book we all laughed and asked him what it would be about. "Oh, bits and pieces" was his reply. That became the title and several editions of the book were published.

We received news from Banyen and Bisdar's letters and the newspapers they sent. Thailand had always been on friendly terms with her neighbours; the British in Malaya and Burma and the French in Indo-China - often playing one country off against the other, but maintaining good diplomatic relations with both. Now, things began to change with the fall of France in 1940. The Japanese made much propaganda in Thailand about *East for the Easterners*;

trying to take France's place as friend, and then after Dunkirk the place of Britain, too.

Luang Pibul took advantage of the collapse of France to send troops to take some of its territory near the Thai border, but thought it wiser to go on being friends with the British as they were backed by America. Also, the naval base at Singapore was considered to be impregnable and everyone thought it would ensure Malaya and Burma would never fall to the Japanese. He intended to remain strictly neutral but events on December 7th and 8th 1941 forced him to change his policy.

Simultaneously with the attack on Pearl Harbour, Japanese troops landed in Southern Thailand, and the Japanese ambassador went to see Luang Pibul (Japan was the first country to send an ambassador to Bangkok; other countries had only sent ministers). The ambassador asked for free passage through Thailand for Japanese troops to enable them to attack Malaya and Burma. The Thai government were not in a position to refuse so Luang Pibul issued a communiqué saying that resistance to the Japanese on Thai territory would only lead to great loss of life and bring no advantages. In exchange for this, the Japanese said they would respect Thai independence and on 21st December 1941 a Pact of Alliance was drawn up in the sacred temple of the Emerald Buddha. On 25th January 1942 the Thai government declared war on Britain and the United States and we found ourselves enemy aliens in Britain ...

Like all Thai subjects, I later received a letter of instructions -

No. 404/2485
The Thai Legation, 23, Ashburn Place, London SW7

The Thai Minister has received a telegram from Mr Arthakit Banomyong, Thai Chargé d'affaires at Bern, asking him in effect to communicate to all Thais in England and Eire, that by HE the Premier's order, they are all instructed to return to Thailand on the first exchange vessel. Anyone refusing to do so will lose Thai nationality and be barred for ever from entering Thailand. In the case of officials, the penalty includes instant dismissal from the service.
The Thai Minister has therefore the honour to bring the above to your notice.

London, 13th July 1942.
Princess Birabongse Bhanubandh, Lynham, Rock, Nr. Wadebridge.

In the interval between the Thai declaration of war on Britain and the United States and our receiving these orders, we had endless discussions about what to do. To refuse Luang Pibul's order was a serious decision, yet to return to Thailand occupied by the Japanese was unthinkable. The exchange vessel sailed without us.

After we became enemy aliens the local police came and removed all our wireless sets. Bira loved his wireless, so without saying anything to us he rang up Anthony Eden and, very surprisingly, got through to him. The next day the sets were returned and because of our diplomatic status we were left alone thereafter. Some time after we became 'Free Thais': the Thai Minister in Washington, who had also refused to return home, wrote that he was forming an official Free Thai movement.

We decided to stay where we were and choose our own war work. Chula had some money in England and, as no more funds would be coming from Thailand, told Bira to hand over all his, and asked Lisba and I to do the same. He felt we could manage if we pooled our resources and let him administer them, but he could not give us any 'spending money' at all. If we wanted some we must earn it. Shura was better placed than any of us to do this as his photography was of professional standard. He was soon kept busy providing photographs of young evacuees, which their society mothers sent to their husbands away at war. He became a regular contributor to the *Tatler* and *Sketch* and a few years later married the prettiest of the mothers, a young widow staying at Rock with her little boy. I made enough for my needs from portrait painting, and Bira began to make excellent wooden toys which he sent to Hamleys where they sold well.

Lisba and I had been helping at the Red Cross Centre since we came to Rock and she decided to stay on there, while I preferred to work on the land. Chula used to go on night duty in the Home Guard with the son of Mr Marshall, who owned the farm just below our house and the fields we could see from our windows on the headland sloping down to the estuary where the river met the sea. These fields were now cut off from the beach by thick barbed wire as part of the defence against German invasion.

Chula and Irving Marshall kept each other awake during the long night watches by telling stories of their lives and soon Irving became a family friend. Bira, who had joined the Signals Section, went on night duty with young Ronnie Potts, who also became a friend and, years later, one of Chula's secretaries. I asked Mr Marshall if I could come and lend a hand and went to the farm until the end of the war. I was extremely happy there.

Chula's mother and Hin got out of France through Spain and then to Portugal; eventually reaching America to spend the war years in Portland, Oregon, with Hin's family.

During the spring of 1940 Bira did a head of one of Lisba's cousins, which was shown at the Academy that year. He was sculpting still; mostly portrait heads to keep his hand in. He did an excellent head of Shura and one of Aunt Ray.

Our spare rooms were always full of friends, as Rock was a beautiful place near the sea. Before going on service overseas Way came with Ygerne when she was expecting their first child, Philip; born in 1941. Their second, Elaine;

always known as Dolly, was born in 1943. My father came, also my dear French governess Maddy, and of course Daphne Lewis, when she got leave from the WAAF. Her elder sister, Irene Quittner, came too; she was working at a fire station in London and with Henry Maxwell was one of our best loved guests. Another favourite guest was ex-Queen Rambai.

In May 1941 King Prajadhipok died at home at Virginia Water. He and Chula had not been on speaking terms for many years because of a row over Bira. When Bira as a boy had first come to England it had been reported back to the King by the Siamese minister in London that Chula was becoming too fond of him, and that instead of Bira going to the Legation in the holidays he was being taken away by Chula. The King wrote a furious letter commanding Chula to leave the boy alone, saying that he considered his influence on him a very bad thing. Chula was equally furious as he was already deeply fond of Bira, and anyhow hated being thwarted in anything. But he had to be extremely careful as his uncle was still an Absolute Monarch. Although in Thailand the ordinary people received justice in the law courts, the King had complete power over members of the Royal Family. The King had the power to recall Chula and imprison him for life in the Grand Palace and confiscate all his property. Chula stopped seeing Bira for a short time but sent the King a letter Bira's father had written to him while he was at Harrow, thanking him for being friends with Abhas and telling him that he was soon going to send his next son to England and hoped Chula would keep an eye on him. To this the King replied that keeping an eye on him was one thing; taking him away every holiday was another and it had to stop. The minister in London was told that Chula was not to be allowed to see Bira and the house master at Eton told the same thing. So Chula could only manage to see him now and then in secret, but he bombarded the King with letters of protest until he finally got sick of receiving them and said he washed his hands of the whole thing. However, Chula had been very fond of his uncle, as had Bira, and they both went up to London for the cremation.

King Prajadhipok's widow, Queen Rambai, stayed on in their house. Her brother, Prince Svasti, lived nearby with his family; he had gone into exile with the King and managed all his affairs.

It was to the Svastis I went to convalesce after having my appendix removed. I had been staying with the Aunts at Cadogan Place when I felt ill and Dr Pettivel sent me to the London Clinic. Chula and Bira left Cornwall at once; Bira dropped Chula at Claridges so that he could be near the Clinic, while he went to stay at Virginia Water. He hated seeing anyone he loved ill and either became panic-stricken or else very bored, but Chula and Aunt C sat with me every day.

Bira was having a wonderful time. Because of the quarrel he had not seen Prince Svasti for some years, but had heard rumours about his model trains. Now they found each other ideal companions; they played golf at Wentworth every day and with the trains in the evening. Svasti had an even bigger, better and more elaborate train room than Bira's!

I loved being at Virginia Water and got to know Queen Rambai, who was absolutely sweet and very lovely. I was a little surprised the first time she took me into her bedroom to find her husband's ashes in an urn on her dressing table, but she explained that she was going to keep them there until the day came that she could return to Thailand and place them with his ancestors.

Now that Bira was a 'Free Thai', he tried to pull every string he knew to join the RAF or the Royal Naval Air Service or, failing that, the Air Transport Auxiliary. Unfortunately, he was unable to pass the eye tests, having contracted measles at school and worn glasses afterwards, with lensed goggles for racing. He was bitterly disappointed as his younger brother Chirasakti had joined the ATA to ferry planes from factories to airfields. Sadly he was killed, leaving a young Thai widow and two little sons.

So Bira went into the Air Training Corps instead and from then on we saw very little of him. He became a gliding instructor with the rank of Flight Lieutenant, eventually becoming gliding instructor for the South West of England with his own school in North Cornwall. Gliding became a passion, and after the war he was to become as well known in the gliding world as in that of motor racing, and almost as successful. He was the third man in England to get a 'Gold C'.

Chula now joined the Army Cadet Force, whose officers received commissions from the Territorial Army Reserve. He continued with Cadet work after the war; becoming Adjutant and Training Officer to the 4th Cadet Battalion, The Duke of Cornwall's Light Infantry and later their Commanding Officer, while Lisba became the County Superintendent of the St John's Ambulance Brigade Nursing Division in Cornwall.

We received many visitors, amongst which were Bira's gliding friends and also Mr Bassett-Lowke, whose Northampton factory made so many of his models and trains. David Milford Haven (the 3rd Marquess) who was stationed in Cornwall visited frequently, and after he had been repatriated Sir Josiah Crosby arrived to tell us what had happened during the Japanese occupation of Bangkok. When Noel Coward was staying nearby he came to dinner and spent the evening singing to us. Princess Marina, whom Chula had met on several occasions, stayed in Rock with her children soon after her husband the Duke of Kent was killed in an air accident. The children came to play with Bira's toys and trains.

Then there was Anthony Blunt, much later revealed as a spy, who came to ask whether Chula thought Thailand would remain neutral, to which Chula replied that he was sure it would. Sir Josiah, too, had been quite certain until the last moment. Blunt had not been among Chula's group of friends at Cambridge, but they had met once or twice. He rang and asked if he could come again and this time bring his friend Guy Burgess with him. Guy had been at Eton with Bira, but when they visited Bira was away gliding. What I remember most about their visit was the amount of drink that was consumed, and that Guy Burgess was the only guest we ever had who never washed the whole time he was there. Lisba showed me his towels after they left, still folded and unused, but I was not surprised. I had noticed his grubby, sweat-stained sports jacket and creased flannels.

Chula loved having people to stay, preferably his friends; failing that, anyone would do as he wanted to be surrounded by people and have an audience. No one was bored if Bira was at home; he invented games, planned parties and outings and kept everyone amused. Being one of Chula's guests was exhausting as he expected them to sit up talking most of the night; when there were several people staying they tried to arrange this by taking it in turns. Chula often told people how he wished he had been King for one main reason - no-one could go to bed before him. There again, Bira and I were the exceptions; we could go off to bed whenever we wanted; still spoiled and indulged in everything.

Several honeymooning couples came to stay with us - my father and step-mother were one such pair. They had met in London where Irene was living alone, having been divorced from her second husband for many years. Her first husband was killed in action in 1915, leaving her with one son, Hal Hudson, a contemporary of Way and Bira at Eton. My father had asked me if I minded him marrying again and I told him I couldn't be happier about it, as now he could have a home again with a nice person. Abhas came too, after marrying the widow of his and Bira's brother Chirasakti and Paul, brother of Raymond Mays' friend, Peter Berthon, also came after his wedding.

My dear Whiskey died at Rock aged 19, as did Bira's young bulldog, Romeo. For Bira's thirtieth birthday Chula gave him a West Highland puppy he called Titch, while Bira, the year after, gave Chula a bulldog called Hercules or Herk.

Eventually the war in Europe came to an end, whereupon our landlord gave us three months' notice to quit!

CHAPTER FIFTEEN

We left Lynham with much regret, deciding that, whatever happened, we four would stay together. Chula said he could not bear the thought that Bira and I would go back to London and leave him. We all loved Cornwall and an estate agent sent us to see a house near Bodmin called Tredethy. Lisba disliked it at once, saying it was too big and ugly and would be impossible to run, but Chula fell in love at first sight - the high ceilinged rooms reminding him of palaces. It was going cheaply as there was no mains water or electricity and it was very isolated. Nevertheless, Chula insisted he must have the place and was to love it for the rest of his life. The price was £5000 but Chula hadn't got that amount. Lisba's father came to the rescue, saying he would lend the money to Chula on condition Tredethy was put in Lisba's name. Using the motor racing van, we all now moved to Lisba's new house.

Part of Tredethy had been converted into a flat for the matron during the war, when the house had been a children's hospital, and Chula said this was to be Bira's and my home. While Bira went to get his pilot's licence, I painted the rooms and sent for our furniture, which had been stored when the studios were bombed. Mrs Healey and Ives returned to London and, as it was not easy at first to get staff, we all helped out.

Chula put himself in charge of the washing-up. Pots and pans, which Chula called 'the black washing up', were done by Lisba and me - often helped by Bien - far away down long corridors at the back of the house. 'The white washing up', consisting of plates, silver, and glass, was done in the butler's pantry next to the dining room, where Shura washed and Chula dried, helped by our guests; this was greatly enjoyed by Chula, as lots of amusing chat went on.

One day shortly after our arrival we could see, as he ground his teeth and glared at everyone in silence, that Chula was in one of his bad moods. This had gone on all day and had came to a head during the washing-up: it seemed Shura handed Chula a plate to dry with a tiny smear of mustard still on it. So it began. Shura was "inefficient, unreliable, a danger to our health, unable to do even the simplest things well" ... and this the same Shura who was more efficient than anyone. Chula wasn't even able to tie his shoe laces properly, but Shura never minded being shouted at and never answered back. With his Russian blood he seemed to understand Chula's character and his love and loyalty were so deep that nothing upset him. Anyhow, from that day until we found a butler and his wife, Chula put on an apron and did the washing-up himself, although not nearly as well as Shura, who was down-graded to putting the clean things back in the cupboards. I never saw Bira around when the washing-up was being done; he was always already upstairs telephoning to arrange the next day's activities.

We received no news from Thailand as the war continued in the East. Then the Japanese surrender was at last signed on the US Battleship *Missouri* in Tokyo Bay on 2nd September 1945, although it was not until that winter that Banyen and Bisdar contacted us, and Chula was able to hear with relief that his property had not been confiscated as he had feared, and his estate office had gone on collecting the rents. His and Bira's incomes had accumulated over the last years and now amounted to very large sums of money, but during the war the Thai currency had been badly devalued and was now only worth about a sixth of its pre-war value. Still, there was enough for financial problems to be at an end. Unfortunately, there were now severe exchange control regulations in force to prevent money from being sent out of the country. Gradually, Banyen was able to ship funds out but it took time and it was not until early spring 1946 that Chula and Bira felt it possible to think about a racing season again.

During the winter of 1945 Bira had gone to Marshall's Flying School at Cambridge, and in January 1946 was the first pupil to pass out with an 'A' licence since the war. Now money was coming through he bought an Auster, a light, two-seater plane made by Taylorcraft and with this, no longer felt cut-off living far away in Cornwall. The little plane became, as far as petrol rationing would allow, his main means of transport, and one of our fields was turned into a landing strip. Aunt Ray was one of the first people he took up; although she had never flown before when he invited her to accompany him she put on her hat and gloves at once and stepped into the plane.

Bira also bought a glider, a boat he moored at Fowey and a large American station wagon to carry his gliding and sailing equipment. It seated nine people in comfort and took us all to the cinema, hunt balls and picnics on Bodmin Moor. I bought a cow! Having learned to milk at the farm I thought it a good idea to help our rations with a little extra butter and cream. Ygerne's brother, Arthur Harris, owned a fine herd of Jersey cows so said he would send me one of his the following Saturday. Aunt C said it was a pity as trains were crowded at the weekend: however, Tessa didn't step out of a full carriage but travelled in solitary splendour in a cattle truck, met by me at Bodmin Road Station.

Bira had put in a lot of gliding hours during the war, thereby qualifying for his 'A', 'B', & 'C' certificates, and was now keen to get his 'Silver C'. His enthusiasm increased all the time, his ambition being to get the coveted 'Gold C'. Philip Wills was his hero. To get the 'Silver C', Bira had to pass three tests: duration, distance and height. For the duration he had to stay in the air for over five hours, and did this quite soon at Long Mynd in Wales, flying round and round in the moonlight while I sat in the clubhouse below with a thermos of hot chocolate ready for him.

I soon discovered there were various ways of getting a sailplane into the air. One was aero-towing, another was to place the plane on the edge of a hill or mountain and get hefty helpers to push it into space. Alternatively, it was possible to be winched off the ground at gliding clubs by a sort of catapult affair called a 'bungy', or else I could drive the car along the runway of a disused aerodrome in Cornwall, towing the sailplane at exactly the speed Bira told me and keeping it steady until the glider left the ground. When overhead Bira would release the towing cable and disappear into the clouds, watching his variometers and hoping for thermal lifts.

Busy flying, gliding, sailing and making plans to race again, the trains remained in their packing cases and sculpture was neglected. *The White Mouse Garage* was, miraculously, still standing, although buildings all round had disappeared and were just bomb sites. Stanley Holgate had stayed on working in the garage doing sub-contract engineering work for the war. Now Shura drove the two ERAs and the Maserati back there in the van.

Motor racing started up very slowly indeed. Before the war the International Calendar was published each November and the races listed could practically always be counted on to take place. Now, the 1946 calendar listed only two races in Britain which would be held 'if possible' in the autumn. Brooklands was a war casualty, Donington a dump for disused army vehicles and it was doubtful if the Crystal Palace could be used again. Some speed trials were being organised on empty aerodromes, but they were to be national events which a Thai driver could not enter; it looked as if Bira would have to race abroad. It would mean that the sport would become much more expensive than before the war when the professional drivers could count on bonuses from oil, tyre and other manufacturers, and the supply of free fuel. Now, not only would they have to buy their own fuel, they would have to get the formula, the additives and mix it themselves, a complicated process but essential for small, highly-stressed supercharged racing cars like the ERA. Fortunately, they had Shura, not the inefficient man unable to do the washing-up properly, but the scientifically-minded technician who was to do all the fuel blending for them at the *White Mouse Garage*.

The first invitation Bira had to race abroad came from Charles Faroux to attend the Nice Grand Prix on 22nd April 1946. At this time, though, nothing was anywhere like back to normal, and they were told that racing cars could not yet be transported across the Channel. In any case, Bira could not have gone for another reason. When Chula sent their passports to the French Embassy for visas (as one had to do with Diplomatic Passports) together with *laissez-passers,* they were refused and told that France was still at war with Thailand. The French now wanted back the territory in Indo-China taken by the Thais in 1940 and, until they got it, would not sign a Peace Treaty ...

Grand Prix races were now for 1.5-litre supercharged and up to 4.5-litre unsupercharged cars. France was planning to hold several events in 1946 but as Bira couldn't enter the country his first race was to be at Chimay in Belgium. Permission was obtained to test the Maserati on a disused aerodrome at Fairlop near London but Chula refused to fly there with Bira, having never been up in a plane and swearing that he never would. The six years in storage had done the Maserati no good and, despite all-night work by Shura and Holgate before the race, Bira trailed in last after numerous pit stops. This was not a very happy start to the season and was followed by a great shock. Before leaving Belgium they saw in the papers that the young King Ananda had been shot dead in an accident which was never really explained. He was succeeded by his brother Prince Bhumipol.

As the next race for Bira was the Grand Prix des Nations in Geneva on 21st July, followed by the Ulster Trophy on 10th August, we went to Long Mynd for the Cambridge University Gliding Club meeting. There Bira qualified for his 'Silver C' long distance test, flying 183 miles to Aldeburgh on the Suffolk coast where I went to fetch him with the trailer. He then flew his sailplane up to 14,000 feet and obtained not only the altitude qualification for his 'Silver C' but also for the 'Gold C'. Now he had his 'Silver C' and only needed duration and distance tests for the Gold. Titch, his beloved dog, always went up with Bira for they were inseparable.

The only thing I regretted was that we missed Shura's wedding. Ever since meeting her at Rock, he had been in love with Nancy Martyn. Chula was very put out at the thought of them getting married and having to share Shura's love and loyalty with someone else, but Shura was happy, and Nan made their flat at the back of Tredethy into a delightful home for him and her schoolboy son. Shura was an extremely kind step-father to Phillip Martyn, who would one day become a world class backgammon player and marry Nina, the widow of Jochen Rindt, the well-known Austrian racing driver killed at Monza, by whom he had a daughter, Tamara. Alexander and Nancy de Rahm, or Shura and Nan Rahm as they liked to be called in England, only had a short honeymoon because Shura was leaving for Geneva with Holgate a week later, looking forward to seeing his family again after so many years.

Chula, Lisba, Bira and I left London on the *Golden Arrow* and, as it seemed that France was nearing a solution with Thailand over the occupied territories, we were granted transit visas to cross Paris from the Gare du Nord to the Gare de Lyon for the night train to Geneva. Chula's Russian first cousins Michael and Ivan Desnitsky came to meet us in Paris; the younger just beginning his successful film career as Ivan Desny.

The Alfa Romeo *Tipo 158 Alfettas* ,which had beaten everyone before the war and were now to again dominate racing, were to be driven at Geneva by Farina, Trossi, Varzi and Wimille and the Maserati opposition was led by Nuvolari, Villoresi and Sommer. 'Toulo' de Graffenried was there with his new Maserati, Parnell with a pre-war model, and Raymond Mays with the Zoller-blown ERA, R4D. We met Bob and Joan Gerard at Geneva for the first time, and Brooke, fresh from his victory at Chimay. It was depressing for Mays and Bira, the fastest of the ERAs in practice, to see that the Italian cars were in a class of their own and to know it would be a long time before British cars would be competitive ... Bira came sixth behind the Alfas and Maseratis, and his *Romulus* was the only British car to finish. It must be remembered that the Italian factories had been able to work on their cars during most of the war, while all the British cars had been laid up, and there were, as yet, no new ones.

If he hadn't won in Ulster Bira might have given up racing altogether and concentrated on gliding and sculpture instead, which could, in the end, have brought him more satisfaction. They decided to take *Hanuman*, which Holgate had completely rebuilt after the crash at Rheims. Chula got to know Group Captain (later Air Commodore) John McIntyre and his glamorous wife Betty during the war, and as John was working at the Air Ministry he managed to get seats for himself, Betty and Bira to fly to Ireland, while Chula went by car and boat with Bien, taking Titch. Lisba and I stayed at home because travelling seemed still too complicated for us all to go. I took advantage of this to have Way, now working at the BBC, to stay with Ygerne, Phil and Dolly, as Chula didn't really like children.

No entries came from abroad for the Tourist Trophy as there was no starting money to attract them, and anyway the Italians might perhaps have not felt welcome so soon after the war. There were six cars in the scratch race and there was an exciting duel between Reg Parnell's 16-valve 4CL Maserati and Bira's ERA. The other entries were the Bobs Gerard and Cowell with ERAs, David Hampshire with a Maserati and Leslie Johnson with an ex-White Mouse Delage. Bob Gerard made the best start, but Bira and Parnell chased him hard and Bira quickly took the lead, which he kept until the end.

The two races in England listed on the 1946 calendar never took place, and Bira could not go to race at Turin, Milan or the Bois de Boulogne or Barcelona because of the French-Thai question which was not then com-pletely settled. So, apart from two domestic sprint events (Brighton and Shelsley Walsh) that was all there was to the first postwar season.

We had very much hoped to return to Thailand in the autumn. One of Chula's uncles, Prince Rangsit, was now sole Regent. He had been in prison throughout the war, having been arrested for involvement in the 'coup' against the Premier while we were there, but had now been completely rehabilitated. Luang Pibul had been tried as a war criminal, then pardoned, and was now living in retirement. Chula thought it would be safe to go back, but we were advised against it by his friends who said Luang Pibul might soon return to power. Indeed, a year later he was Prime Minister again.

We stayed in England and Bira changed his small plane for a larger one, a Miles Messenger, and we went gliding a great deal. Chula was writing his last motor racing book *Blue and Yellow*, (G.T. Foulis) about the 1939 and 1946 seasons which he sweetly dedicated to 'Wife of Driver, friend of Author'.

About this time Bira developed shingles and I caught chicken pox from him. He recovered first and went skiing at Scheidegg with John and Betty McIntyre, telling me to hurry up and get well and join them. Lisba was also away, skiing at St Moritz, and normally Chula would have been very happy for us to spend some time together on our own at Tredethy, but he was frightened of getting chicken pox himself. All we could do was chat endlessly on the phone and when he wanted to see how I looked, hoping I hadn't scratched my spots and left scars, his plan was to have the gardener put a long ladder against the front of the house so he could climb up to my balcony and look in. He never managed it, however, as he had no head for heights.

Neither had Bira. By the time I joined him the McIntyres had left, also Evelyn Haccius. Bira had tired of the ski school and Evelyn and Charles Ramus, both expert skiers, had taken him out with them. One day they all put skins on their skis and walked up to the Männlichen Pass, when suddenly Bira called out that he felt terribly dizzy and couldn't look down. They managed to get him to the top for a picnic, where Bira told them he had never been able to climb even the Eiffel Tower. They asked about his flying and gliding, which he said was quite different: he never felt giddy when aloft. Later, they skied down to Grindelwald with Bira, as Evelyn told me afterwards, looking just like a little snowman, falling, rolling over, up again and skiing downhill at terrific speed!

At home we discussed what to do for the 1947 racing season. Chula and Bira felt that to remain competitive at all they must sell the big 3-litre Maserati and the ERA *Hanuman*, keep *Romulus* for sentimental reasons and buy one of the new, 1.5-litre 4CL Maseratis. Such a 'customer' car would never be able to compete with the works Maserati but would be faster than *Hanuman*. They called the new car *Romeo* after Bira's beloved bulldog, and it won that year at Chimay. Then Bira decided to turn semi-professional. Chula realised he simply could no longer afford the great expense and when Bira had an offer to drive in the Simca-Gordini team with Sommer and Wimille, Chula advised him to accept. Amedée Gordini, of Italian extraction but French nationality, was an engineer who had evolved a team of single-seat racing cars with modified Simca engines and financial backing from the Simca Car Company. Bira won that year at Rheims, the Isle of Man and Lausanne, and there was good companionship between the team drivers. We had always liked Sommer and his wife, visiting them at their villa on the Riviera, and got on well with the Wimilles.

So Chula, very sad indeed, soon retired from motor racing. He hated ending the Chula-Bira team because it had filled his life for such a long time and brought him satisfaction and a name in motor racing as an outstandingly good team manager. He was to miss it all terribly, hated us being away all the time and found it hard to get the same amusement from anything else. He handed his stopwatches and charts over to me, and the Maserati and its van to Bira.

There was another reason apart from the cost which had made Chula realise the time had come for him to leave the racing scene. It was because he saw that Bira was gradually changing; was becoming very independent, no longer wanted to take advice and be told what to do. The last remnants of Bira the boy had disappeared and he was now Bira the man, who wanted to plan and choose his own way of life and fly to all the races. Bira retained Holgate and they came to an agreement where, when Holgate was not preparing the Maserati or coming to races with us, he could take on other work. Bira wanted to do the season with the Gordini Works Team, and just a few extra races with the Maserati.

I always went up to London to see the Aunts, and while there had been dining at the Savoy Grill with Chula one evening when Rex Harrison came over and joined us. He was taking the part of King Mongkut in the film *The King and I*; years later remade as a musical film with Yul Brynner in that part. He wanted to talk to Chula about costumes and customs at the Court, which did not please Chula at all as he felt the story of Anna and the King of Siam was not true to life. However, when Bira and I saw the play with Herbert Lom and Valerie Hobson playing the leading roles, we had enjoyed it, Bira whispering to me when the royal children came on to ask which I thought was meant to be his father!

Chula's mother and Hin came back from America in 1947, bringing mother-in-law trouble for Lisba. All had gone smoothly before Lisba and Chula married, but the first signs of trouble began on their honeymoon when they were staying at the Crillon. They had lunch at Mother's flat one day, and she commented on a particularly lovely brooch Lisba was wearing. Lisba said she had put it on as they were going from there to visit the Duke and Duchess of Windsor, to which Mother replied acidly that "she had never supposed it had been put on for her's and Hin's benefit ..." Then when Chula and Lisba had gone to stay at *Le Mesle* after Bira crashed at Rheims and Lisba was wearing a simple cotton dress, Mother said she saw Lisba was "suitably dressed for staying with humble and poor relations". Chula was rightly angry - poor they most certainly weren't, because Chula gave his mother a quite enormous allowance, but he tried to avoid having a row with her if possible as, apart from the respect he certainly had for her, when it came to rowing she completely outclassed him.

So the long separation had in a way been a relief. Now here they were again and we hoped for the best and, apart from one dinner party, before which mother and son had argued fiercely and she had held forth all through the meal about the admiration she had for Russian Emperors who had had the courage and good sense to have their sons put to death, all went well ...

Poor Hin, that tall, well-meaning American; he somehow always seemed to put his foot in things. Chula told his mother he wanted to give her a car

continued on page 161

André Eglevsky and Rosella Hightower, who were dancing at Monte Carlo with the American Ballet Company, with Bira and the Simca Gordini.

Bariloche, the Argentine, 1949. From left: Jean-Pierre Wimille, Nicole Wimille, Dora Green, Luigi Villoresi and Reg Parnell. Seated in front is Alberto Ascari.

Buenos Aires 1949. Left to right: Ascari, Parnell, Bira, Villoresi, Farina.

Bira in gliding outfit.

Bira talks with Lofty England (left) and 'Wally' Hassan of Jaguar during practice at Silverstone.

After spinning off when a rear tyre burst whilst leading the production car race at Silverstone in his Jaguar XK120, Bira valiantly - but unsuccessfully - tried to change the wheel.

Bira in his Maserati 4CLT/48 at the 1949 British Grand Prix. This picture shows the famous White Mouse emblem on the car and the dedication to Bruno.

Drivers' wives in the pit before the race. Left to right: Didi Chiron, Alda Platé, Elsa de Graffenried, Ceril.

155

*Bira being congratulated
by Fangio.*

*Farina in conversation
with Roy Salvadori, Ceril
and Luigi Villoresi.*

Bira with one of the 'Whites'.

Bira and Ceril at Chula's 40th birthday dance in 1949. Behind are Ronnie Potts and his fianceé.

Bruno and Ceril at Madonna di Campiglio, January 1950.

Bruno and Ceril in the garden at the villa in 1950.

Bruno building the landing stage in front of the villa in 1953.

After the regatta at Riva in 1956. Bira and Bruno are in dark suits; in the background are Salee - who became Bira's third wife - and Ceril.

Bruno at Campagnola, winter 1965.

Ceril at Campagnola, looking out over the lake, summer 1980.

Ceril, 1990.

and she must choose anything she liked. When he went over to see it and started to get in the back the door came off its hinges as he grasped the handle. Grinding his teeth with fury, he asked the name of the dealer so as to complain, only to hear that Hin had got the car direct from the factory through a friend in order to save money. Chula was nearly beside himself with rage at his step-father's interference with his gift to his mother.

CHAPTER SIXTEEN

We went to Riva to see Bruno Tomasoni and found him just the same - charming, friendly and delighted to see us again. He had known we were coming, as I had written to him the moment the war ended to get news, and we had exchanged letters regularly since then. Bira rediscovered his love of Lake Garda - such a heavenly place for sailing - and said he would like to buy a house there to have a home of our own; a place to go between races on the Continent, as he was getting tired of flying to and from Cornwall all the time. He also wanted to have our dogs with us. By now I, too, had a West Highland terrier, which Chula had given me as a wife for Titch.

Our last race of the 1947 season had been at Monza and Bruno had come with us, but Bira only completed one lap. He was driving that race with the *Scuderia Milano* team, as were Sommer and Ruggeri.

When we flew home Chula suggested it would be fun to visit America - a new experience for all four of us. We sailed on the *Queen Mary* on 20th November and Banyen, another friend whom we had not seen since before the war, came with us. We wanted this trip to be a small sign of gratitude to him for undoubtedly saving Chula and Bira from ruin by looking after their interests during the conflict.

We were met at the dock by our great friend, Daphne Lewis, who was living in New York. We stayed at the Waldorf-Astoria and our first night went to see Ethel Morman in *Annie Get Your Gun* at the Imperial Theatre. The next day Bira and I lunched with Miss Hadley, a friend of Aunt Ray's who always stayed with the Aunts when visiting London.

We wanted to fit as much as possible into a short time: Thanksgiving Day we lunched at the Ritz-Carlton, visited the Planetarium, saw *Madame Butterfly* in the evening at the Metropolitan and danced at the St Regis! It was great fun and we felt as if we were living in an American film, especially when we went by train to Washington where we were met by Prince Wan Waitayakom (the Thai Ambassador) and his staff and were shown around the FBI and its museum. We saw the Senate from the Diplomats' Gallery, lunched in their restaurant, saw the Lincoln and Jefferson museums, Mount Vernon and Washington's tomb, then went back to New York for the world heavyweight fight at Madison Square between Joe Louis and Jersey Joe Walcott. Joe Louis was knocked down twice but retained his title on points after a split decision. We returned to the Garden a few nights later to see the New York Rangers versus the Detroit Red Wings ice hockey match, having supper afterwards at Joe Dempsey's Broadway Restaurant where Bira asked for an autograph as a change from giving one.

We took a night train to Buffalo to see Niagara Falls and went on to stay with one of Chula's Cambridge friends, Mark Stevens and his wife Betsy, at Grosse Pointe Farms from where we were taken around the Ford factory and given lunch by the directors at the Dearborn Inn.

Lisba and I were intrigued to see television sets in all the rooms at the Stevens' as well as an internal circuit which enabled them to see their children in the nursery from other rooms. Bira was the only person I knew who had owned a television set before the war - I had watched him on it when he did a talk about racing with Lord Howe. Up until then I had not seen television again as it had not yet reached Cornwall. Lisba and I were also amazed when Betsy took us to a Frozen Food Market as we had never seen frozen food in England.

Returning to New York Bira took me to see Midget Car Races at the Bronx and, on our last night, we saw *Oklahoma* at the St James Theatre, going on afterwards to supper and dancing at the El Morocco. We sailed for home on the *Mauretania*, Bira winning the table tennis tournament on board and receiving, together with a card saying "To the victor the spoils", a bottle of champagne which he gave to Chula. We arrived home at Tredethy just in time for Christmas 1947.

The first race in 1948 was at Pau. Chula and Bira went on ahead by car while Lisba and I followed in the train, as she had an important St John's Ambulance meeting to attend before leaving. We were staying at the Continental, as were the Duke and Duchess of Richmond and Gordon, who had come to see the race. We took tables in the dining room next to each other, so that racing talk could be exchanged. Bira, Wimille and José Scaron were driving Simcas for Gordini; Sommer, de Graffenreid and Nello Pagani, the famous motorcycle champion were with Maseratis, and Chiron, Rosier and Pozzi with Talbots. For Bira, who had had that good run of luck with the Simcas the year before, it was to be one unfinished race after another.

We then went to Jersey for Chula's farewell to racing, so made it a big party. My father and step-mother were living there; they had a charming house just outside St Helier where the race was to take place - and as Aunt Ray had never seen a race, she stayed with them. Shura brought Nan and

Phillip Martyn and Aubrey and Rosemary Essen-Scott came too; Aubrey and Shura were to help Holgate in the pit, as they were racing with the 4CL Maserati. Irving Marshall came with another Cornish man, Jack Bunt, and Bien with the Thai Ambassador. Bira and I flew there with Titch and my dog Mini. Bira put up the fastest time in practice; he and Villoresi were the favourites but both had to retire and Gerard won with his ERA.

We left Titch and Mini to go back to Cornwall with Chula and Lisba and flew straight on to Geneva for two races on the following Sunday 30th April. We were joined by Prince Bertil of Sweden and his friend Lilian Craig. Bira retired his *Équipe Gordini* 1100cc Simca in the Geneva Cup race and the *Grand Prix des Nations* which followed in the afternoon was won by Nino Farina with his new, two-stage supercharged 4CLT Maserati. Bira's 1430cc Simca again proved unreliable. We flew home to Cornwall.

Flying to races may have seemed very dashing, but there were a lot of drawbacks - like not having a car of our own when we arrived, and we could take very few things with us. The only luggage space we had was on the back seat; where there was just room for one suitcase with Bira's racing equipment and one small one for our clothes. The only way we could manage was to travel in suits; taking off our jackets and spreading them on the suitcases, together with Bira's crash helmet, our macks and my lap chart board. In the suitcase we put spare shirts and blouses, cardigans and an old skirt for me to wear in the pits.

Now we were off to Monte Carlo in the new, twin-engined Miles Gemini Bira had exchanged for the Messenger. When we touched down at Nice we taxied to the parking space and found another private plane next to ours. Two Italian brothers were just getting out; they had flown from Egypt to see the race and, as they had a car, gave us a lift to the Hotel de Paris - our honeymoon hotel. The next morning they turned up again, saying they had dined with Gianni Agnelli of the Fiat founding family who very much wanted to meet Bira. He sent a message asking if we would dine with him that evening at his hotel, La Réserve, at Beaulieu. If so, they would pick us up and take us there. At first we said we were terribly sorry; we would have to refuse as practice was at six in the morning and we didn't want a late night. They assured us dinner would be early and they would bring us back directly after; so we accepted. I said they must warn our host we had no evening clothes of any sort with us. explaining our luggage problems. They replied that, owning a small plane themselves, they quite understood.

When we arrived at Beaulieu Agnelli was waiting and we sat and had drinks while endless talk of racing went on. They wanted to know all about Bira's career and how it started and there seemed no sign of us eating. Indeed, it wasn't until we were joined very much later by a beautiful woman in full evening dress that we went into dinner - well after nine. Our hopes of an early night vanished but we enjoyed it - Agnelli was charming, and the brothers drove us around during our stay. So did Nuvolari who, staying in our hotel, would drive us to the practice sessions. He and Bira were very much the same size and joked that they could have exchanged overalls. They would discuss racing together; in French, of course - it was the universal language in Continental racing circles at that time.

The race was the first to be held at Monte Carlo for ten years, and everyone felt it was a symbol of the return to normality after the war. A lot of cars failed to finish, as did Bira, and the race was won by Farina (Maserati 4CLT) from Chiron's Talbot.

Two of our friends were at Monte Carlo; both Andrés. Lt Colonel André Melin, *Aviateur de Réserve, Commandeur de la Légion d'Honneur*, had come to London with de Gaulle. Maddy had gone to Carlton Gardens to offer her services and they asked her to teach the Colonel English. She failed but they became friends. He was now about to leave for New Caledonia as Governor of the big leper colony there. The other was André Eglevski at Monte Carlo with the American Ballet Company; where the prima ballerina was the red indian dancer Rosella Hightower. We went to see them dance and both the Andrés came to watch the race from our pit.

We flew back to Tredethy to repack our suitcase with warmer clothes and left for Stockholm on 26th May. We lunched and dined with Bertil and Lilian, and were driven about by an old friend of Chula and Bira; Baron Babel Rudbeck. Bira did some gliding, failed again to finish the race, and on our way home we stayed in Copenhagen, where the members of the Royal Danish Automobile Club gave a big dinner in Bira's honour. We also visited the famous amusement park and gardens at Tivoli, which Bira adored.

Bira won various prizes in gliding competitions that year (in 1947 he received the Wakefield Trophy for the longest cross-country flight). We also went to air rallies between races, and at Versailles met Pierre and Youyou Genin from Lyons, who both owned Geminis like ours and had flown one of them out to Bangkok on their honeymoon. Of course, this gave Bira the idea to do the same thing himself one day.

David Milford Haven, with his very attractive Australian girlfriend Robin Spencer, came to join us at San Remo for the race on 27th June. Ascari and Villoresi were there with the new works 4CLT/ 48 Maseratis - known afterwards as the *Tipo San Remo* - were fastest in practice and won the race in that order. Bira also was very fast in practice in his Maserati 4CL but could do no better than 5th behind Sommer in one of the new 2-litre Ferraris. We went on to Berne for the *Grand Prix de l'Europe*, staying at the Bellevue as usual, and visited my great friend Evelyn; seeing the Haccius' lovely garden and her mother's cages of budgerigars. Evelyn came on 4th July to see the race with us in which Bira was fourth in his Simca.

Then we had to hurry home as, on the 8th of that month, we were going to the royal garden party! We had received the invitation the month before, which read "The Lord Chamberlain has received the King's commands to invite their Highnesses Prince and Princess Birabongse to an afternoon party to be held in the garden of Buckingham Palace on Thursday 8th July 1948, at 4.00pm.

A Carriage Card is enclosed, which will admit to Buckingham Palace by the Garden Gate, where they should meet their Majesties at 4.00 pm."

David Milford Haven had also been invited and as he was a relative - being one of Queen Victoria's many descendants - he, like us, was asked to be a member of the King and Queen's party. Later, he was to be best man to his first cousin Prince Phillip Mountbatten when he married Princess Elizabeth. We went up in the lift with Chula and Lisba to wait with the royal entourage for their Majesties to come in, and then followed them out into the garden. There they separated and walked in different directions to allow as many of their guests as possible to see them. We walked with the Queen and Princess Margaret, and David and Bira - neither of whom much enjoyed these sort of occasions -stuck together all the afternoon to talk about racing. In the Royal Tea Tent they were joined by King George VI, who had always taken an interest in Bira's racing career. Bira and I were staying with the Aunts and the following day went to the Eton and Harrow match at Lords. I had always enjoyed going with my parents as a child and Bira liked meeting old school friends. He was also rather fond of cricket.

Rheims was next for the *Coupe des Petites Cylindrées* preceding the French Grand Prix on 18th July, where we visited the Champagne Pommery et Greno cellars who gave a *vin d'honneur* for the drivers. Another breakdown and Bira was relieved when Ruggeri, manager of the Maserati-equipped *Scuderia Milano*, asked him to drive the next race with them in France at Comminges. We got a telegram at Tredethy saying the car wasn't ready but would Bira drive for them at Albi on 29th August? So we went instead to Holland with Holgate and Bira's Maserati 4CL for the first Dutch Grand Prix held at Zandvoort among the sand dunes.

The organizers put us in a hotel at Bloemendaal, where Billy Butlin and his wife were staying. Billy had not known there was to be a race - he had come to see if the place would be suitable for a new holiday camp - and when we dined together he told us all about his plans for new camps in the future. They came to the race and were as thrilled as we were when Bira won both his heat and the final: he needed the win after so many failures with the Gordini-Simca.

Then came Albi. When we arrived and went into the hotel restaurant to join the *Scuderia Milano* team at a big table in the middle of the room, who did we see sitting at a small table in a corner but Maddy and her artist friend Celia Bedford. We were as surprised as they were. We never talked to Maddy at all about racing, so she had no idea we would be there - in fact, she and Celia thought it was a big cycle race that was to be run - and though I knew Maddy was on holiday in France, I hadn't known where. Of course, we went to eat with them. Celia Bedford was well known, exhibiting her work a great deal, and went to France every summer with Maddy where she would sit outside cafés producing sketches of people which she would work into pictures at her studio.

Bira gave them grandstand tickets for the race which they were too polite to refuse, and we four went to the Toulouse-Lautrec museum together. They were, however, quite thankful when we all left and quiet returned to the hotel again, although Maddy did tell me afterwards that they got much better service; their status had risen considerably.

I sent a wire to Chula - "BIRA DROVE FOR RUGGERI **STOP** CAR PAINTED BLUE AND YELLOW **STOP** BLEW UP WHEN LEADING **STOP** RECEIVED SEVENTY POUNDS **STOP** GOING BERTIL VILLA MIRAGE ST MAXIME TOMORROW **STOP** MAY DRIVE FERRARI TURIN **STOP**".

I had to keep Bira's accounts very carefully; writing down every item we spent - even if we each had an ice cream at a café out came the little notebook and it was jotted down. Back at Tredethy I gave the book, together with all the bills - even the tickets to the Albi museum - to Shura, who would put it all in order and the finished result then went to Chula. I would sit beside him at his desk to go through it, as even though Bira was now on his own, Chula tried through me to keep him solvent. If it had been left to Bira, the money would have gone out far quicker than it came in. Although the Simca had broken down such a lot and results were poor; in terms of money gained, the season had been quite satisfactory.

Team managers got very good starting money; especially with a driver like Bira whose name could still draw the crowds, and also from various other sources - while the drivers were given a portion of the starting money and could keep any prize money. On top of that, all our hotel and often travel expenses were paid for by the organizers. So soon after the war it meant a way of life that we could not have otherwise had when, as British residents, we were allowed to take only £30 out of the country.

We went on to stay with Bertil and Lilian in their fascinating house by the sea; with bedrooms on a level with the road and the kitchen leading on to the beach, from where Bertil, a keen snorkler, would swim underwater to spear large fish to cook for us. He was a *Cordon Bleu* chef, as was Louis Chiron. When one went to the Chirons for a meal, the elegant Didi did the entertaining, while Chiron put his head round the kitchen door from time to time to join in the talk, and then, when he was ready, served a delicious meal.

We flew from Cannes to Milan, while Bertil and Lilian followed by car. Bruno joined us there and I kept my lap chart at Monza standing next to the *Scuderia Ferrari* pit manager, who told us Enzo Ferrari would very much like to talk to Bira before he raced the new Grand Prix car for them at Turin the following weekend. We said we would fly to Modena on Thursday.

Bira then decided that he would spend his accumulated prize money at once. He wanted to keep a boat on Lake Garda to sail between motor races, and for me to crew him in the local regattas. Bruno took us to Sirmione to the boat builder Bisoli; advised Bira to order a *Snipe* class yacht and promised it would be ready waiting at the Fraglia at Riva when we returned in the spring. Bira also ordered a Maserati A6G-1500 *Coupé* he had fallen in love with in Turin, and urged Bruno to find a house for him to buy near Riva - if possible, right on the lake. It would mean that with a house, car and boat in

Italy we would be away from Tredethy all the following summer. I wondered what Chula would say; what we would do about our dogs and also where all the money was coming from. Bira said airily that he had a great deal of money in Thailand (which was true), and that Banyen must just find a way to send it to Italy. Small details like that never worried him.

On Thursday Bruno came to Trento to see us off in the plane and Enzo Ferrari was waiting at Modena airport. He drove us straight into the centre of the city to his favourite *Ristorante Boninsegna*. Bira ordered spaghetti bolognese - he hardly ever ate anything else in Italy - while I said I'd have whatever Ferrari ordered. I was a bit dismayed when a plate piled high with small fried octopus arrived as I'd never eaten them before. I hardly joined in the conversation at all as the octopus were difficult to chew and my knowledge of cars limited. It was fortunate, then, that when later I was left alone with Ferrari at the factory while Bira tried out a car, we hit on a subject of conversation interesting to us both - pigs. It seemed that Enzo Ferrari was very interested in farming, especially pig farming; and owned two farms himself. We got on to the subject when he asked where we had been and what we had done during the war. To his obvious amazement and amusement I told him how I had loved helping on a farm. We were deep in all this when Bira came back and the conversation changed to cars and contracts.

When Ferrari drove us back to the airport his young son Dino came too. Ferrari adored the boy - who climbed into the Gemini with Bira at once. His father explained to me how delicate his son was and that on no account must Bira take him up in the plane; which Dino was begging him to do. I quietly conveyed this message to Bira in Thai, so he just showed the boy all his gadgets (Bira had gadgets on everything), and explained how the plane worked and said he would take him up another time. Ferrari and I stood by talking and he told me how much he admired Bira's style of driving; he thought him brilliant, calm and regular -what he called 'clean driving'. He would like Bira to drive for him but there were two things that worried him. Would Bira always obey pit signals at once? - and there I reassured him as Bira had never disobeyed a pit signal in his entire career and in that he was absolutely disciplined; but when Ferrari asked if I was sure he would turn up always for car tests when he was ordered to, I hesitated. I wondered whether if clouds were right and thermals looked probable, Bira would just leave the testing to others and go gliding. I felt Ferrari had the same doubts. He and Dino waved us goodbye and we flew on to Turin for Bira to drive the new *Tipo 125 monoposto* for him in the Italian Grand Prix on 5th September; joined by Bertil and Lilian. Bira retired after driving strongly in the rain.

Soon we were back at Tredethy but preparing to leave almost immediately for the Florence Grand Prix on 26th September - a Formula 2 race in which Bira was entered by Gordini and took fifth place.

On the morning when we left for a race abroad the routine was always the same. As soon as he awoke, Bira reached for the phone to get a weather report, dressed at speed, called for me to follow him to the plane as quickly as possible and was off. I dressed, closed the suitcases, kissed the dogs and shut them in the flat. Down to the kitchen to make sandwiches and fill a thermos, look for Shura or Bien to drive me up to the airfield, begging them to take the dogs out as soon as we took off and be sweet to them.

Meanwhile, Bira would have pushed the plane out of the hangar with the help of one of the gardeners, and be warming up the engines and sorting the maps when I arrived. However, this day (the only time it happened), he left one of the maps behind.

My job was the map reading; looking down to try and identify railway lines, rivers, towns and roads - and when late that afternoon we were flying along the coast past La Spezia, about to turn inland towards Florence, I discovered the map page I needed was missing. To add to that, Bira said we were very low on petrol and it was getting dark. He said that as the sea wasn't tidal there I must look out for a long empty stretch of beach and we must go down - there was not enough petrol left to circle round to try to find Florence without the map. It was now really dark; little lights flickered in the houses below us when, suddenly to our relief and joy, we saw an illuminated runway with planes on it. An aerodrome! Bira called up the tower to ask where we were and say we were out of petrol and coming down. We were told we were at Pisa, that it was an American army airfield and we were absolutely forbidden to land. We landed ...

A jeep roared over and two military policemen with revolvers arrested us. We tried to explain to them it was an emergency; we tried to use diplomatic status; said Bira was a racing driver on his way to a race - we tried everything, but to no avail. They said we would be locked up for the night and could take absolutely nothing out of the plane. However, it took more than an armed MP to part me from my beauty case, and fortunately our prison was a hotel in the centre of Pisa, taken over as the US military headquarters. We were told our crime would be looked into by 'high ups' in the morning and put in the back of the jeep. My first view ever of the Leaning Tower was in full moonlight and I begged them to drive past it very slowly.

The following morning calls went out to embassies and we were eventually released with a stiff lecture. Bira gave autographs, had a free fill up for the plane and we flew on to Florence using a US military map - a parting gift.

Chula, kind and precise as always, had given me a list of what sights I was to see; in what order I was to see them; how long I was to stay looking at each and where I should take a guide. Obedient as usual, I was standing outside the *Duomo* with a guide book in one hand and Chula's instructions in the other while Bira was at the Gordini garage, when the Sommers and Villoresi passed by in an open carriage. They stopped and told me to get in and see Florence more comfortably on this hot day and then lunch with them at Fiesole. It was tempting but the thought of returning to Tredethy without having followed Chula's list was too daunting. They drove off, teasing me for being a typical English tourist.

From Florence we flew to Bologna, where Bira received a wire from Shura, asking him to bring back spares from the Maserati works - "STANLEY REPORTED ALL FOUR CONRODS CRACKED ALSO VALVES AND VALVE SPRINGS POOR STATE ESPECIALLY INLET **STOP** PLEASE GET THESE OTHERWISE NO SILVERSTONE ALSO TRY THIRD GEAR CONSTANT MESH WHICH WAS FOUND DAMAGED BUT SPARE AVAILABLE HERE".

Bira said there was just time for a quick trip to Venice as an early birthday treat for me before Silverstone. When he walked back from the Bologna control tower with his flight plan, the young member of the airport staff who accompanied him said, rather sadly that even though he lived so near Venice he had never been there so we invited him as our guest. He couldn't at first believe we meant it, then raced off to get a colleague to replace him while Bira unloaded the racing suitcase and Maserati parts to make room for him. It was a perfect visit to Venice and while we were there, the young man - Corrado Ruffini - revealed that he was really a sculptor and only working at the airport to earn money to live. On our return to Bologna, while Bira was reloading the plane and getting a new flight plan, Corrado went off on his Vespa and returned with a big parcel, which he said was his birthday present to me. It was an exquisite Madonna with Bambino in terracotta (done while he was serving in Abyssinia) and now one of my most precious possessions.

We were back in time for Silverstone - the day before my 32nd birthday on 3rd October 1948.

Bill Boddy, editor of *Motor Sport,* wrote "Great as is the debt of gratitude which we owe to the RAC and to voluntary officials and helpers too numerous to mention, for giving us today at the new Silverstone track, Britain's first Grand Prix since the war, quite naturally it is the drivers of the competing cars who will be most in the public eye". He went on "B Bira shouldn't need any introduction. Entered by his cousin Prince Chula of Siam, Bira has been one of the most popular drivers in the game. He has driven Maserati, Austin, Talbot, BMW, Simca and many other cars, and had the great honour of being allowed to handle a Ferrari in the recent Italian Grand Prix. Today, he drives a 16-valve Maserati; on which so many of his victories have been obtained, and he can be relied upon to give a polished exhibition no matter where he finishes. His epic victory in the Maserati at Zandvoort will be in everyone's memory".

Ten cars finished the race and seventeen retired. The race was won by Villoresi, Ascari was second and the magnificent Bob Gerard in his ERA third. Fourth was Rosier on a Talbot, followed by Bira in a new 4CLT/48 Maserati. Enrico Platé was ninth, many laps behind, and after that gave up racing. He had never been very successful but loved the sport, and his idea now was to start a fresh career as team owner and manager. He was to buy two Maseratis, keep on his own mechanics Felice and Scatuzzi, and wanted to engage well-known drivers who would bring good starting money. He invited Toulo de Graffenried and Bira to join him.

Bira received several tentative offers for the 1949 season - apart from the Ferrari one - but felt this would suit him best. We liked Toulo and Elsa more than anyone in the racing circle, Bira got on very well with Platé - who had great respect and admiration for him - and thought he would be free and happy in that entourage - which he was.

After going to the *Coupe du Salon* at Montlhéry, again with Bertil and Lilian, we only had one more race that season; the Grand Prix of Penya Rhin at Barcelona on 31st October. As there was a good gap between the races, Bira thought it would make a change for us to drive slowly through France to Spain in the Rolls. Also, he wanted to spend less time at Tredethy now as there had been a bit of the old trouble between him and Lisba, which Chula was devastated about.

We reached the Hotel Majestic at Barcelona two or three days before practice started. Toulo had a friend there who had been at school with him at Lausanne - José Vilá Marsans - who took us everywhere: to the yacht club for Bira to sail; to the *Plaza de Toros* to see Luis Miguel Dominquin (but bull fights were not for Bira and me) - and to the gypsy caves to see the Flamenco dancing. One night, he said he would take us to the best restaurant, but as we were driving along the wide avenue Toulo told him to stop; he must be making a mistake. When we asked what he meant, he said he had just seen Chiron's car outside a restaurant, so that must have even better food!

After our usual Christmas and New Year house party at Tredethy, Bira and I left to race in the Argentine, together with Reg Parnell - the only driver from England. Holgate and Reg's mechanics were going by sea with the Maseratis - and Eric Greene, the Rolls Royce representative in Buenos Aires, had offered to let us use his garage.

CHAPTER SEVENTEEN

We left on 12th January on our eleventh wedding anniversary, and Aunt C and Maddy came to see us off at the Buckingham Palace airport bus terminal. Betty Parnell was there to say goodbye to Reg.

We planned to sleep one night in Rio de Janiero and then fly on the next day to Buenos Aires. I thought how glamorous it sounded - to be seeing Rio by night in the company of two famous racing drivers. It made one think of Copacabana beach - exotic night spots in a carnival atmosphere of rumbas and cha-cha-chas - only it wasn't like that. We were tired after the long flight - we had left London at 10 o'clock in the morning, refuelling at Dakar in Senegal during the night and landing at Natal, Brazil, late the morning after - finally reaching Rio for dinner in the evening after two days and one night on the plane. We three dined quietly in our hotel, walked to look at the sea, bought some postcards, ate ice creams in a café; talking about racing all the time. We might have been at Brighton! We were called at six the next morning and taken to the airport. All we saw of Rio was when the pilot, as usual inviting Bira to sit with him, flew us over the bay - and very lovely it was. We followed the coast to Uruguay, landed at Montevideo and then over to Buenos Aires to a warm welcome from the Argentinian Automobile Club; flowers for me, and interviews and photographers.

There were to be four *Formula Libre* races - two Buenos Aires Grands Prix on 30th January and 6th February, the Rosario Grand Prix on 13th February and another at Mar del Plata on 27th February. We were due to fly back to England on 7th March.

The other drivers from Europe soon arrived - Ascari and Villoresi with Maseratis, Farina with a supercharged 2-litre *monoposto* Ferrari and Wimille with his little Simca. The rest of the cars were driven by South Americans headed by Juan Manuel Fangio. Parnell and Bira's Maseratis were already in Eric Greene's garage, and the race atmosphere in the city was electric. As soon as we reached the Alvear Palace Hotel people started to call and leave cards; among them the representative of *The Motor*, Henry Tyszka - and a young Viennese doctor, Harold von Beck, who had raced and sailplaned in Europe before the war.

Henry and Harold, together with Paul Pinsent and his wife, were the people who took care of me while Bira went gliding, for which the conditions were excellent; summer weather, long distances, the right cumulus in the sky and heat from the earth to create those hoped-for thermals. The members of the Gliding Club - the *Club Argentino de Planeadores* - welcomed Bira at once as a fellow spirit. He made a great friend there, Joe Ortner, who came to Tredethy later in the year to glide with him in England.

The organisers of the races arranged to send the European drivers on an excursion to Baliloche in the high mountains down south on the borders of Chile. It was a place about to be opened up as a summer and winter resort - and our being taken there was obviously to advertise it. Bira and I were given two tickets on the charter plane and a voucher for a room at the big hotel (only just finished). However, the evening before Bira said he was going gliding instead - the weather reports looked too good to miss. So I rang up Eric Greene's wife Dora and asked if she would come with me instead.

It was a spectacular place with stupendous views, but after we had been taken in a bus for a drive, and a trip on the lake the drivers were very bored and longed to get back to their cars and the race. The hotel was empty but for us - there was no village to go to and simply nothing to do. Nicole Wimille discovered a hairdresser and disappeared, Dora and I found a shop selling locally-made jerseys - and the men just sat about; talking the usual shop, doing their best in English for Reg Parnell.

Bira returned from his gliding glowing with success - and practice for the race in Buenos Aires began. As at all town circuits we had to be out before six, as it was only then the roads could be closed. I climbed on to the pit counter, stopwatch in hand, and waved to Nicole doing the same thing a few pits away. We were the only two wives who had come from Europe.

Holgate watched over my shoulder, joined by Bira when he had finished his laps - they had to see what time he was clocking in comparison with the other drivers. Wimille went out and I timed his standing lap and the first warming-up laps, waiting for the fast one. Then I realised he hadn't come round and later, looking along the counters, saw a driver draw up at Wimille's pit and Nicole leave suddenly. I hoped and prayed and went on with the timing.

When we got back to the hotel they told us the news. Wimille had crashed and died before they got him to hospital. They told us Nicole had been brought back to the hotel and was alone in their room. Bira took my hand and rushed upstairs - their room was next to ours - and when Bira opened the door and ran to put his arms round Nicole I couldn't move. I thought it was our room

- the furnishings were identical, the coffee tray still on the bed with the pyjamas - all as we had left it not much more than an hour before. It could have been me sitting there, white and staring - not tears, just deep shock - and if it **had** been me, what could anyone have said to help? Ascari and Villoresi ran in, and I was to see in the hours that followed the real understanding and kindness of Italian men. They never left Nicole alone - one of them was always there, arranging all the bureaucratic details that were necessary - before putting her on the plane taking Jean-Pierre's body back to France.

The race was held on the Sunday: we were a show that went on.

The last race in the Argentine series was at Mar del Plata. On the morning we were to leave in the special train taking the drivers, Bira went to the Gliding Club first with tickets for the race to give his friends. I packed, very worried that if Bira didn't return soon we would miss the train. Then the friends 'phoned to say that he had found perfect sailplaning conditions and had already left to glide to Mar del Plata instead - but with our train tickets and all our money in his pocket - and by now the train would have left.

Henry Tyszka burst into the room - he had been to the station to see us off and, not finding us there, had come to see what had happened. When I told him he seized the suitcases, rushed me into a taxi, saying that though the drivers' train had left the mechanics' train was still in the station as they hadn't finished loading the racing cars. We flew down the platform as the train, full of shouting, yelling men rather like football supporters, was about to start, and I didn't much fancy the idea of squeezing into a crowded carriage with them for a long journey. Then suddenly there was Holgate, leaning out of a window. In a second, he and Reg's mechanic had me and my luggage in and the train drew out. Their carriage was empty - they explained that they knew all about noisy Latins and, wanting a quiet journey and a nap, had stood guard at their door so that no one had been able to get by. They dozed; I read; they took me to lunch with them in the restaurant car and I thanked heaven for British mechanics - nothing ever fussed Holgate or upset him and no-one asked for my ticket.

Before unloading the two Maseratis when we reached Mar del Plata and without knowing a word of Spanish, they found out which hotel I was to go to, put me in a taxi, paid the fare and Holgate said as soon as he had sorted everything out he would be round to report and see what had happened to Bira. Bira turned up late in the evening, very pleased with life, saying he had landed in the middle of a ranch somewhere, phoned the Mar del Plata Gliding Club who'd fetched him by plane and taken charge of the glider. He said "Do you know darling, I think I must be the only driver who has sailplaned to a race!"

The garage owner where Holgate had put the Maserati took us and the car to practice sessions in his lorry. On race day when he came to our hotel Holgate, who was up in front, could only shrug his shoulders and laugh as we thought of Chula and the *White Mouse* days. A vehicle with a sticker on

174

the windscreen and a driver inside could get into the pit area, with no rule as to how many people were in that vehicle. As a result the garage owner had not only invited his wife and family, but all their cousins and friends, to see the race from our pit. There was no room for them all inside the lorry so the younger ones clung on outside!

Fangio beat Bira into second place by 90 seconds. Upon returning to our room afterwards we found a bunch of flowers with a note saying "Prince Bira, congratulations for the race you nearly won. The boys of the Royal Hotel, Mar del Plata 1949"

There were wonderful farewell parties in Buenos Aires - the final one lasting all night until our friends put us on the plane in the morning.

When we returned to Tredethy we found Chula deeply depressed but delighted to have us back - only the depression worsened when Bira flew away almost at once to plan the coming season with Platé. On 16th March he wired to me from Modena "CONCLUDING BUSINESS END WEEK LOVE TERRIBLY BIRA". When he came home he went either gliding or out in the boat.

Chula felt very sorry for himself indeed as, while we had been away, Lisba had gone skiing at St Moritz as usual - leaving him at Tredethy on his own - and now she was back was immersed in her St John's work which she enjoyed and excelled at. He felt he was being deserted by us all, and asked me if I would consider, as he loved me, going away to live with him in America. I said he knew well I would never leave Bira - so he said would I if Bira left me? I pointed out that for fifteen years Bira had never shown the slightest sign of not wanting to be with me. Chula then asked if I couldn't see how Bira was changing; had left him, wanting only movement, new experiences, new friends. He warned me I would lose him, too.

Chula cheered up a little for his fortieth birthday, enjoying the house party and dance we gave. His cousin Ivan Desny was with us - he was making quite a name for himself in the French and German film world - and the Rank organisation had given him a part in a British film called *Madeleine* being made at Pinewood Studios. The film was directed by David Lean and based on a famous Scottish murder trial in 1854. Ann Todd (who later married David Lean) played Madeleine, and Ivan the French lover she was accused of murdering. Some of the outdoor scenes were shot at Polzeath, near Rock, so when Ivan was free he stayed with us and Bira would fly him back to Denham airport when the producer, Stanley Haynes, needed him.

Platé wanted to make as much money as he could from race organizers, so planned to enter his cars for as many races as possible. It often meant there was no time to prepare the cars perfectly but, even so, Bira enjoyed some successes.

We left Tredethy three weeks after our return from the Argentine, starting the 1949 season on 3rd April at San Remo. A stone broke Bira's goggles and glass went into his eyes as it had done in a previous accident, causing great pain. He was advised to take a short rest and we returned to Cornwall. There were flowers in my room from Chula and a note saying "Welcome home - with lots of love from your two mice". Underneath were drawn a large white mouse and a small one - himself and my little dog, whom he called Mini Mouse.

We flew to Jersey for the race there on 28th April, staying with my father and step-mother; joined by Platé and Toulo - and the following weekend were all at Perpignan in France for the Grand Prix du Roussillon where Bira came second (on aggregate after two heats) to Fangio by a few seconds. He won the Swedish Grand Prix a few weeks later, followed in second place by de Graffenried, which was all very profitable for Platé.

We had a gap before going to Berne for the Swiss Grand Prix and stayed first with Bertil and Lilian at St Maxime, and then at the *Beau Rivage* at La Napoule, which we liked so much that the following year Bira bought a villa there. The race at Berne was on 3rd July and Chula wired "TOO DEPRESSED FOR LETTERS **STOP** WISH BIRA GOOD DRIVE **STOP** WRITING ALBI LOVE CHULA". From Albi we went to Rheims and celebrated Bira's 35th birthday at the *Lyon d'Or*, where we were staying. Then to Holland, where Bira came in third in the Final behind Villoresi and de Graffenried at Zandvoort on 30th July.

Home at last for two weeks and our great friends Delia and Lindsay Sowerby and the gliding enthusiast we met in Argentina, Joe Ortner, came to stay. I spent a lot of time sunbathing in the garden with Chula and Lisba, which we loved, and catching up on all our news as we would soon be going away for another two months' racing. Bira planned to stay at Riva on Lake Garda and sail his new boat between the races at Lausanne, Monza and Czechoslovakia. He bought a car for the trip, as neither the Rolls or station wagon were suitable. Bira loved the new Morris Minor which had just appeared, in the same way that he had loved the baby Fiat *Topolino* years before. They were like toys, he said, and the Morris was sprayed Bira Blue. We set off on 16th August for Silverstone, staying with Lisba's old nanny, Jessie Woodman, and taking the dogs. They returned to Cornwall after the race with Shura when we left for Switzerland.

Someone must have been taking photos during the practice at Silverstone, as one of me talking to Toulo and Bira appeared in *Illustrated* and Chula sent it to me with a little note saying "I am proud of my loved pupil". It was with an article headed *"Wives of the race pits."* in which I was amused to read "Acknowledged as perhaps the most accomplished scorer amongst the wives is Princess Birabongse, whose husband, Prince Birabongse of Siam is one of the best known drivers. In racing circles they tell a story about English born Princess Ceril, which emphasizes her ability. At a meeting in South America, even the race track officials lost count of the lap scores and had to check the 'official' results upon the Princess's chart". The article was signed by Jack Ensill. I wish it were true but, to be honest, I don't remember any such incident. I was certainly no Madame Hoffmann.

After Lausanne we had nearly two weeks to wait before the Grand Prix of Europe at Monza. On our way to Riva, we stopped in Berne to invite Evelyn Haccius to come with us. She protested, saying she couldn't drop everything and come on the spur of the moment - and anyhow had no clothes ready. We told her she knew us well enough to know clothes didn't matter to us (we never went anywhere smart if we could help it) and to just throw a couple of cotton dresses and a bathing suit in a case and come.

We had wonderful hot blue days on Lake Garda - Evelyn getting darker and darker as she paddled one of the sailing club's canoes about - as did Bira; out sailing all day. In fact, I had not seen him that colour since Hua Hin where I called him *Dumdum - dum* being Thai for black, and so I started calling him that again. I raced with Bira in several local regattas - and the rest of the time swam and sketched; watched often by Bruno. Every evening, the four of us drove to different villages on the lake to have ices.

Evelyn went back to Berne and we had to think of Monza. Bruno took me to Rovereto to fetch Bira's overalls from the cleaners, and on the way back we stopped to look at little Lake Loppio. Bruno suddenly turned to me and apologised for what he was about to say: he had never meant to talk to me about it but simply couldn't stop himself telling me what he felt for me. I think I had guessed it for a long time, understanding that because of Bira he preferred to keep quiet. What I had not been prepared for (and which had taken me completely by surprise this visit) was that I felt the same for him ...

We said we would not let this make any difference to our long friendship. Bruno had always thought Bira's and my marriage a wonderful one - he said few marriages were so happy and nothing would make him do anything to harm ours. He loved Bira, and we were only happy to know we would see quite a lot of each other in the future. Bruno thought he had at last found the perfect house for us and would know for certain when we returned in February. Bira had told him we would go skiing at Madonna di Campiglio (not far from Riva) as soon as we got back from the Argentine. Bruno was to book our room and join us every weekend.

Bira also asked Bruno to sell his Snipe class boat because he had now tried his Star class one; *Mimosa* - with which Bruno had won the Swiss championship at Zürich in 1947. Bira also wanted to race in that class and asked Bruno to look out for a Star for him for next year.

We left for Monza (Bruno came to watch the Grand Prix from the pit); returning to Riva together for two more weeks before leaving for Czechoslovakia.

This was the first time a race was being held behind what was now the Iron Curtain, and we were all a bit apprehensive about it and decided to go there in a column of cars, with the lorries going on in convoy from Milan. The starting place for our group was Riva - and Enrico and Alda Platé in one car, Toulo de Graffenried and Elsa in another, 'Nino' Farina with his mechanic and Chiron with a friend, all reached Riva in time for an early lunch. Then we set off, soon running into thick fog, with the drivers taking it in turn to lead the others. We spent the night in Udine and reached Brno the day after where I found a telegram from Chula "HOPE ALL WELL AND BIRA REMEMBERS DIFFICULT CIRCUIT **STOP** MISSING YOU **STOP** AFTER RACE PLEASE

WIRE NEWS INCLUDING ABOUT RETURN BEST LOVE".

On 26th September The *Daily Mail* wrote "Three racing cars run into crowd. Four die, fifty-four hurt at same corner. Three racing drivers; one of them British, left the track one after another and ploughed through screaming spectators packed beside a hairpin bend. The tragedy occurred in the first lap of the race. Half a million spectators had stormed the track; overwhelming marshals and fighting each other to see the first race in Brno for ten years. The Italian racing ace, Giuseppe Farina, came roaring up to a masked hairpin bend in his heavy Maserati. As he began to corner, the car skidded; smashing through the concrete posts guarding the bend. A Maserati driven by Britain's Parnell plunged through the gap. Order was restored and the victims were taken away in all the available ambulances in the city - when Prince Bira, the Siamese ace, reached the bend. He skidded, knocked down five concrete posts and hurtled towards the remnants of the crowd and the rescue workers. He too pulled up - after avoiding a score of spectators. Prince Bira is in hospital with a cut leg".

I sent a wire to Chula "BIRA CRASHED WHILE LEADING **STOP** PAINFUL LEG INJURIES STITCHED IN HOSPITAL **STOP** WILL ATTEMPT RETURN AS SOON AS POSSIBLE **STOP**".

I had never seen Bira so frightened - he was really terrified and clutched my hand in the ambulance. "Promise me darling, you won't leave me for a moment? Even if they have to operate, you must be there all the time. Promise! Don't you see - they are taking me to a Communist hospital, and I am a prince - think what they did to royalty during the revolution!" He was quite obsessed by this. I stayed with him all the time holding his hand, hoping I wouldn't faint. The doctors had tried to get me to wait outside, but Bira wouldn't hear of it, and when they said he must stay a few days in hospital, he absolutely refused. Nothing would have kept him in what he thought of as a *Red Hospital*; his only desire was to get out of the country as soon as possible. After signing a paper absolving the hospital of responsibility, we went to the hotel. He said "Wound or no wound - you must drive me through the Iron Curtain the next morning".

He was in great pain all night - even after taking the pills they had given him - but struggled up in the morning - and somehow I got him into the car and drove towards the frontier. We were late starting; it had taken a long time to get him dressed and I would much rather have waited one more day. Still, it was only about 50 miles to the frontier and the same distance on to Vienna, where I hoped we could rest.

It was nearly midday when we reached the customs post and as I went to take our passports and car papers out of Bira's briefcase he put his hand to his forehead. "I've left them behind in the hotel" he said. He told me he had hidden all the documents and money before the race behind a picture - and with all he had been through afterwards had quite forgotten about them. So there we were, with nothing for it but to turn round and go back for the papers and return again to the frontier. When we eventually approached Vienna it was already getting dark and Bira was pale and in pain. I was out of my mind with worry - and then a new fear struck him. We knew Vienna was divided into four Zones of occupation - Russian, French, American and British. How on earth, he said, could we be sure we didn't go into the Russian one by mistake? New panic, new thoughts of the Russian Revolution and all the stories Bira had heard ever since he was a boy from Mother and her refugee friends.

Suddenly I told him he was saved; I saw American soldiers standing on the pavement - we were in the American zone. So I asked the GIs where we could get a bed for the night. It was getting late - all we wanted was for Bira to be able to lie down; we didn't want food, just for him to take his painkillers and try to sleep. The soldiers pointed across the road to what seemed a rather modest hotel, but they said we'd be OK there, and we were thankful for anything. I went in and asked for a room - they said they had one, but I must pay in advance. We left everything (except a small overnight case) in the car, hoping the American military police would be patrolling the streets and, despite the hotel being very noisy, Bira slept. We were both dead beat by then.

In the morning I rang for coffee and breakfast - but got no answer. There was no-one about as I gradually got Bira down the stairs, only one or two girls in dressing gowns who looked round doors -and then I realised we had spent the night in a brothel!

We were thankful when we reached Zürich and found a lovely hotel on the lake and a good Swiss doctor who took charge of Bira and dressed his wounds, which he said had been extremely well attended to by the Czech doctors. He made Bira stay in bed for a few days and we eventually got back to Tredethy on 3rd October - my 33rd birthday.

CHAPTER EIGHTEEN

Bira's leg wounds healed quickly, and although not able to go gliding at first he was soon out in his boat. When I was busy, the wife of an Eton friend who farmed fairly near us sometimes went with him. I was stunned when Bira told me he was having an affair with her - and anyhow he felt he now wanted to be free to have affairs with anyone he liked, and to bring the girls to stay and even go racing with us. I pointed out that this might create difficulties, so he said in that case, would I give him a divorce? It was completely unexpected, as although during the last year for the first time in our marriage I knew he had had a couple of brief affairs, I had no idea he felt this way. Chula, as always, had proved to be much wiser than I. I told Bira if a divorce was what he wanted, then of course I would agree.

Bira went on to say that he didn't really want to leave me at all - he wanted to go on being married but I must agree to this new arrangement. I said that to have his cake and eat it like that wouldn't, in my opinion, make anyone happy. I thought if freedom was what he wanted it would be far better for us to have a complete break and each go our own way   and do it now while we loved each other and there was no bitterness or ill-feeling. Like that, we could remain friends and look back on our years together with happiness. Bira said he saw my point, insisting again that he must in future feel free. We decided the best thing was for him to go to the Argentine alone, think the whole thing over carefully and give me his reply on his return: either to continue our marriage as it had been before, or for us both to start a new life.

Bira exchanged the air tickets to Buenos Aires for a sea passage so as to have time on the voyage to think over his future. I went to Paris with Daphne Lewis for a week while he packed his things.

Chula wrote to me in Paris -

*As I have not heard anything to the contrary, I presume you and
Daphne arrived safely in Paris. Bira has confined himself to the
flat with a very bad cold and has had all his meals there. The talk
has not been too depressing, as he is more keen on the future
than being sad about the past. He has agreed that as long as you
make Tredethy your home, he will not come back here unless you
are reconciled and return as man and wife. Love to Daphne. Lots
and lots of love for yourself, darling.*

Waiting in the flat when I returned was a letter from Bira -

14th November 1949. *My darling, this is it. I have to leave now on
my way alone. I feel it is the best for me to have two complete
months to settle down alone, without making any definite decision
on anything. Through many circumstances we came to where we
are now, but I do feel that life has not ended for either of us. I have
had a really happy time with you - what with racing and travels
and so forth. You have been more tolerant and forgiving than
anyone I know - and I love you for that. I am what I am today and
deserve anything that comes along and fate will deal with me as
she wants - but I should like to tell you and you believe it, that I
have never loved anyone like you before or will ever again. Take
care of our sweet memories. Yours always, Bira.*

He wrote to Chula saying that he had enjoyed the voyage; having an affair
on board. When Chula told me the girl's name I felt it was a small world - she
had been in my class at Spaldings.

A few days after reaching Buenos Aires Bira 'phoned to say "Please come
and join me, I've thought things over and am lonely here without you. I miss
you terribly". I asked if this meant he had decided he wanted to continue our
marriage as before - in which case I would come. He said no - he wanted to
remain married, but must be free to have other girls when he wanted to - and
for me to agree for them to come and live with us. Shades of his polygamous
ancestors were appearing and so I said again it must be our old marriage, or
a new life for us both. A week later he 'phoned again - a repetition of the first
call, saying he had already sent me an air ticket. I didn't use it ...

Chula was of the opinion that there was little chance of a reconciliation
and began to talk about my future. On no account was I to leave Tredethy -
it was always to be my home and he couldn't bear me to go. I said he must
understand that it would be absolutely impossible for me to go on living there
without Bira. To live together as two couples (as we had done for the last ten
years) making one family was one thing - but to stay on alone would be unfair
to Lisba. Now at last, they would have their home to themselves - something
I knew she had wanted for a long time - and **I** wanted at last to have a house
of my own. Chula said yes, he could understand that, and would therefore

build a house for me in their grounds - or else buy me a house nearby. If none of that suited me and I wanted to live in London near the Aunts, then he would buy me a flat. It would be his *pied-à-terre* when he came to London.

There were signs of better relations between Chula and Luang Pibul's government at last, and rumours were circulating in Bangkok that although Chula had not been back to Thailand for eleven years, he might be asked to be the new Thai Ambassador in London. In the end, however, it came to nothing. I told Chula we would talk about it all when Bira returned and I knew his answer. I didn't tell him that none of his proposals would suit me at all.

All this time Bruno and I had been writing to each other as we had (apart from the war years) since 1938 - only of course the tone of our letters had changed considerably. In fact, it was his very loving letters that kept me going during this sad parting from Bira although, in my replies, I never said anything to him about what had happened between Bira and I. I didn't feel it fair to give him any hope that we might some day have a future together until I was quite sure. I just told him I had decided not to go to the Argentine.

Christmas was quiet compared to former years - Tredethy was very dull without Bira. I told Chula and Lisba I would be going to Italy in January and wrote to Bruno saying I would be coming to *Campiglio* just as Bira and I had planned and maybe Bira would join me on his return from the Argentine, but that I wasn't sure. I needed the quiet to think things over carefully. Bruno came at the weekends; he had had to give up skiing after the accident to his leg but we went for long walks and were very happy together.

After three weeks Chula wrote that Bira was back. It seems he had an accident in Buenos Aires, and while in hospital for a few days had been visited by his gliding friends who had taken along a very pretty Argentinian girl called Chelita. Bira had gone quite mad about her and she moved into the hotel with him. Now he had brought her back to England, fetched the station wagon, the plane and the glider and they were living in a caravan on an airfield near Folkestone. Chula said he feared it was Bira's reply to me and I felt he was right.

Chula advised me to get a divorce. If I agreed, he would see our solicitor, John Stanton ,about it. I told him I agreed. When Bruno came at the weekend I told him the whole story and he was terribly shocked and surprised. He said I must not do anything drastic; not to break up my marriage without a lot of thought. He was very sad for Bira who, he thought, was making a great mistake. I told Bruno I had really thought the whole thing over carefully - even if Bira and I were to be reconciled, our marriage couldn't go on much longer. The end was inevitable and I wanted it to finish in a friendly way and not to have it drag on and end in bitterness. "In that case", Bruno said, "remember, if you want it, I will always be there to love you and look after you for as long as I live" - which he did.

I decided to return to England, so when Bruno left I wrote to my father, Way, Uncle Harry and the Aunts, also Maddy, telling them what had happened, emphasizing that Bira was in no way to blame - our marriage had quite simply come to an end.

I had to stay one night in Riva in order to get the early bus the following day to Milan and catch an afternoon plane to London. I went to Riva in the morning, and after lunch Bruno suggested I might like to go and see the house he had found for Bira and me, even if now we would not want it. It was a glorious day - blue sky and lake, with snow on the far mountains. When we arrived I knew at once that it was paradise, which was the word all my family and friends used on first seeing it. I found a small villa in a large olive grove, the grass full of early violets and smelling of herbs. It reminded me of Hua Hin, with a low wall running along the edge of the beach, broken by a gate leading down to the lake. On the other side was a cypress hedge hiding the garden from the road which led to the village of Malcesine a few miles away. In front of the main gate there was a garage with a little logia looking over the lake housing the pump which drew water for the villa from a well: municipal water was not to reach us for many years. Behind the garage was a washhouse, which was never used at all because my maid (like all the locals) did our laundry in the lake. In the winter we were privileged because, as we took our olives to be milled opposite the garage (and in those days extracting oil was done by boiling water which ran down the outside of a drum containing the stone-crushed olives), we could, like all who used that mill, wash in front of it where the hot water ran into the lake.

The piece of land was part of a point which jutted out into the lake - hence the name *Punta Campagnola*. There were only two houses - mine and a large one further along the beach, which we could not see from our garden. Both had been taken over by the Germans during the war; mine as a field hospital. The house had not been used, but the garden had been completely destroyed. In the far distance were mountains (as at Hua Hin) - not the mountains of Burma, but the beautiful Dolomites. The other side of the point was a natural harbour with fishing boats.

Bruno could see I was enchanted by it all, so asked why didn't I buy it for myself and come and live near him? It was a great temptation, the solution to my problem of where to go now - but how could I find the money to pay for it? To use capital would reduce my income, which I couldn't afford to do. Then I thought of my mother's wedding present to me; the necklace that was lying in the bank and which I would never wear again. I asked Bruno to buy the house.

I stayed a few days with the Aunts before going to Cornwall and, from there, wrote to tell Chula about Bruno and my decision to buy the villa, saying that I had no intention of ever marrying again. I also told or wrote the same thing to family and friends. From Chula I got a terrible letter; not of anger, but of great sorrow. The theme was one of "I have been stabbed in the back", which he wrote in capital letters and underlined so strongly all the way down the page that it tore. Anyway, I went back to face him and pack up everything. Lisba had written a sweet and understanding letter, wishing me much happiness in the future, obviously glad I would make a new life far away ...

Mini was waiting. Titch had gone with Bira, who had left a message saying I could have the Morris, for which I was most grateful as I needed a car badly. He also said I could have all the furniture from our flat, as he intended to find a house in the South of France for him and Chelita and would buy furniture out there. Bruno wrote that he had made a down payment on the villa and the removal van arrived.

I didn't stay long at Tredethy - there was no point. Chula was very kind; never referred again to my plans and on the morning I left arranged to be out on Army Cadet duty to avoid seeing me go. I found an envelope under my door containing a letter which read "Darling Ceril, I had hoped to leave you a note telling you of my feelings on your leaving this morning, but it is late and I am too sleepy to do justice to my feelings. So will just say that I will miss you more than words can say".

Before going out, he came up to my room in uniform - he didn't speak at all, just took me in his arms, hugged me for a long time and went out of the room with tears streaming down his face. In some ways it was worse than leaving Bira, but there had been no alternative.

I had already said goodbye to Shura and Nan, also to Bien - so only Lisba stood on the steps to see Mini and me drive away.

Bira came to Cadogan Place to see me. He asked if I would return to him - in which case he would send Chelita back to the Argentine. He said he had made a big mistake. I said it was too late - we couldn't turn back now. Our marriage would never be the same again - even if he said it would be the old way of marriage - which I didn't now think he would stick to. We would just have to go through all this again, which I didn't want. He agreed and went away very sad indeed.

Daphne drove out to Italy with me, the car piled to the roof and Mini on her knees. We stayed a night with Mother and Hin, and Mother wept saying Bira and I parting reminded her so much of when she had left Chula's father to go to Shanghai. She hoped I would be as happy with Bruno as she had been with Hin.

Daphne returned to England after two weeks. May 1st was a national holiday in Italy and Bruno and I went off to sail in a regatta, returning late that evening. I found a telegram - "PLEASE MEET ME TRENTO NOON. WOULD LIKE TO TALK WITH YOU ALONE. LOVE DUMDUM". I was sad to think Bira would have waited that day at the airport at Trento, thinking I didn't want to see him. Of course, if I had not been away when the wire came I would have gone.

Then came his letter:

Trento, 1st May 1950. *I was down in Cannes alone to buy a house and I became very depressed. During the last weeks, I had terrible sad dreams about you. Each morning when I woke up, I felt like writing to tell you all about it, but thought I had better not spoil your peace any more. I have been very wrong as a husband* to you and now I shall suffer for the rest of my life. What urged me to come here today was just to have a personal contact with you and find out for myself whether you still love me a bit. However, fate seems to have dealt me another blow by not bringing you here to the airport.

Well darlingest Ceril, before I leave Trento for Cannes, I want you to know that my love for you is engraved so deep in my heart that I shan't feel the same with anyone else - even Chelita. She has been much sweeter since those quarrels we had last month, but in every one of them you were the centre of interest. I don't know what she will say when I get back to England after my attempt to see you this time, but I don't really care. All I wanted to do today was just to see you in person and talk things over with you.

Well darling, I shan't be a nuisance any longer and will leave you to your future happiness - but please Ceril darling, <u>think</u> and <u>believe</u> that you have been and still are the only one I really love. I know now how important a person you are in my life and I take all the blame for what happened to our lives. All my love darling, Dumdum.

CHAPTER NINETEEN

Family and friends came to stay at *Campagnola* all through the summer. They, fortunately, seemed to like Bruno. He was then forty, a bachelor and we always spoke French together. Apart from sailing and photography and, of course his work, the main interest in his life now was helping me restore the house and garden.

In June Bira again flew to Trento and Bruno and I went there to meet him at the airport. He asked if we were now divorced as he had heard nothing. I said I had been to London the month before and had obtained the divorce in the Law Courts, as we had been married legally in England, and that it was automatically recognized in Thailand. He leaned over to kiss me, saying sadly "So this really is the end". He told us he had just bought a small villa in the hills above La Napoule, where we had stayed the previous summer.

9th June Chula wrote -

I hope truly and with all my heart all is well with you, and Bruno is making you sufficiently happy to justify the funtastic mad thing you have done. I miss darling Mini so much and hope she is well. With very much love now and forever more.

Bira wrote from Albi, 15th July 1950 -

Your birthday card arrived here on the breakfast tray this morning, just when I was thinking of you. I felt very sentimental and sad that this year is the first year you are not with me on my birthday, with your sweet little presents under the pillow and under the bedclothes! I couldn't help crying a little which upset

Chelita, but explained what those days meant to me. I miss you so much darling, but life is life - you can't have your cake and eat it!! However, it is a little consolation to think that at least we can still be friends and that I could see you whenever possible - even though I couldn't live with you. The heat is terrific like last year, so I hope I will finish the race alright.

My racing luck has completely deserted me and I don't expect to complete any more races. Now just to win some money from the 'prime' and hope for the best. I hope to see you soon, darling. Right now I feel too sad to write more, so you'll understand. Titch sends his love to his wife. Lots of kisses for Mini. My love, Dumdum.

P.S. I rang your father four times, but no reply. He must have been away from Jersey.

15th August 1950. *I came here at 11.00 to see you, but you've already left for Como. Titch was very pleased to see Mini! I brought you your favourite scent and Titch a present for darling Mini! Well, I'm destined to miss seeing you once again. All my love, Dumdum.*

From Venice, 17th August 1950. *I am here for a short holiday. I miss you very much and thought of many happy moments we had together. I hope to have some 'new project' for Monza, so you and Bruno must come for it. Love as always, Dumdum.*

Les Faunes, Mandelieu, 20th August 1950. *I hope you received my card from Venice. I really missed you so much. I am looking forward to seeing you and Bruno at Monza in a fortnight's time. I was hoping to have a new car for that event; the new OSCA 4 .5-litre unsupercharged engine built by Maserati brothers - but I haven't found the source of supply to pay for it yet. I think the King of Siam might be interested in buying it for me, as I know it is useless to count on any further help from Chula. I am quite friendly with the king and his wife, who is <u>charming</u> and so pretty. Platé was talking about you the other day and I told him you might be coming for the race. The Scuderia is carrying on in the most amazing way; void of any hope of doing well! Still, it brings home some little extra money for me, so I have to be content with that. Darling, be sweet and write to me here. Lots of love to you and Mini. Your Dumdum.*

Tredethy, 28th August 1950. *Ceril darling, Bira came alone for two days. I think he seems restless and unhappy, so he tries to be forcedly gay and irresponsible. He is very disillusioned about his* racing and has become a 'hack' for starting-money. With lots of love, Chula.

Les Faunes, Mandelieu, 23rd December 1950. *My darling Ceril, two more days to go and then I can open your parcel! I am so excited at the very thought and feel you are close to me once again. I can't help comparing things Chelita does for me, with you. Well, I suppose that's life - one thinks one will improve situations by changing - but rarely one succeeds.*

I have grown up tremendously and have learned many things. Do you see, you and I have never lived together properly. After we were married, we just began to get settled in our little studio for a few months - when war broke out. Then we all moved off to Cornwall, where we shared a house with another family. We have never lived alone to solve out our very own problems, you and I. If we had lived alone together, I think we would have had the opportunity to thrash things out and get to the basic understanding. I can see it very clearly now that the two things which terminated our married life were my selfishness and your pride. Of course, if we had the chance to act all over again, we probably would have done the same thing.

In myself, I have learned that I could never find another companion to suit me as well as you darling, and so I won't even try to. With this new life I lead, I am more independent - but I can't say I am ecstatic. I miss the feeling that my companion knows art and literature, and when I see a piece of sculpture now, I have to admire it in silence. Motor racing too is a lonely business, though I receive the companionship of a beautiful woman. Not to be compared with the perfect chart keeper and aftermath discussions! Well darling, don't think I am trying to dig up the past life. I only wish that I could make up to you for all the things I hurt you and wronged you. I am a spoilt child and know it, and if I could gain real happiness further than I have received from you, I am a lucky man!

Here's some news. I have given up driving in Platé's team. The new Osca hasn't materialized yet - the king doesn't want to give it to Platé to manage. There is some talk of the Australian Club paying £3000 for de Graffenried and me to appear in Sydney, so we may troop out there shortly. If we go, I shall try and sell the Maserati. I also hope to fly the Gemini out to Bangkok; taking three weeks over the journey. Rather a mad venture, but it's me - what can I lose? I would like to pay you another visit. Is it possible? Are you marrying Bruno? Is he jealous and minds your friendship with me?

You will be interested to know that I collected my first diamond for the 'Gold C' a month ago, when I climbed in a helm wind at Fayence to a height of 18000 feet; without oxygen or warm clothing! I nearly perished with the cold. I am the second diamond in GB beating Wills, who still holds British height record of 16000 feet. The first diamond is a fellow who made 300 kilometres a declared goal. I hope to compete with this honour with 500 kilometres next spring. I have the Weihe in France now and have called it 'Willie', so I hope 'Willie' Weihe and I will go places next year! The dear Gemini is now at Hugh Kennard for C of A, and I hope to fetch her back next month. All these things have drained a large hole in my already reduced pocket, so if I sneak along, dressed as an Italian peasant to Punta Campagnola to cut some wood for you, will you throw me a few crumbs and the remainings of your spaghettis?

Les Faunes, Mandelieu, 3rd January 1951. *Thank you so much for your terribly sweet Xmas parcel. I have read your letter through twice and quite understand your sentiments and resolutions. I think you are most wise and sensible as ever. The only wish I have is that you should look back on our 12 years as something beautiful and sacred, as I do myself. I too realise that it is no use looking backwards and the only way is to go forward smartly, but very* important *not to go through life without profiting by your experience. As for my life at the present, things have not worked out as well as I had expected.*
I should like to write to Aunt Ray, but I suppose it's not time yet. Keep well my darling and don't break your leg skiing. I'll write again soon. My love always, Dumdum, and a kiss from Titch.

Tredethy 2nd February 1951. *Darling Ceril, the Christmas party went off well, although for me personally without the Biras, it was more like an ordinary party with Christmas as an excuse. Unfortunately on the 27th, the day before they were due to leave, Mother had an open row with Lisba over food which was very bad indeed. It was the worst row since the one she had with Bira at Neuilly after an Easter party. Fortunately, the dance we gave on the 28th without them was a tremendous success - as good as that famous one in 1946 - do you remember? It was the first dance we had here since your departure, and it was odd for me not to have to keep an eye on you, so I could have as many dances with you as possible!*

Tredethy, 20th February 1951. *I heard from Bira about his visit to you with Chelita. He said you received them most kindly and sweetly. Sat 17th, we took the* Golden Arrow *to Paris with Henry and stayed at the George V. We all went to see Mother for tea the* next day. Lisba had written to apologize for shouting and it had been accepted. I had also written to say that although Lisba had been wrong to shout, Mother had been wrong to start the trouble. She had arranged a tea party for us, as I expect she thought it would be less awkward. She was deadly cold with Lisba. We saw a play every day; Henry does so love it in Paris. Jahns, the Americans, gave a big lunch party at the Ritz, to which both Mother and Hin were invited. Jahn put Lisba on his right and Mother on his left which was a complete disaster and she sulked right through lunch.

Tredethy, 11th April 1951. *We had a gay Easter with Henry and Daphne. I was glad to know that the second volume of my Thai autobiography (which is due out on the 12th) has already sold 1700 copies. I wonder if you read the first volume. It is pity to give up any language one has taken the trouble to learn. Very much love to you and darling little Mini Mouse.*

Ecurie Royale, Siam, 18th April 1951. *You probably have heard and read all about the new OSCA which won at Goodwood. I have also been invited to drive the BRM. I feel this year will open a new phase to my racing and I hope my bad luck will gradually go off. Poor old Platé is still struggling again this year with de Graffenried and Harry Schell. I have done so far 3 races, tomorrow I start practising for San Remo. I shall miss you there. Love as always darling, Dumdum.*

Villa les Faunes, 27th June 1951. *I have been to Italy several times to see Platé and the OSCA. I thought of bursting in to see you again like the last time, but remembering that you did not like it, I refrained from doing so. The fact is I do miss you a lot, darling. I expect you are at your busiest with visitors, and therefore if I had burst in à la Bira fashion, it might have been awkward.*
Darling, are you happy? I wish I was in a position to help you financially, but I have to struggle along the best I can, as you know Chula is tightening up the belt all round. My racing season has been a flop and financially I have lost, so I am far worse than you imagine. I have been out of racing now for over a month and I feel it terribly. I don't know when I will be able to start again. Breaking a car doesn't pay what ever. I have to go to Milan again sometime next month before my birthday and thought it would be nice if I could see you. I wish I could come and have some more sailing on the lake -I love it so.

Tredethy, 16th August 1951. *The Siamese Civil war was alarm-*

ing. My house at Ta Tien was occupied for 30 hours by government troops and suffered damage from the fighting. I am sending you a copy of a letter I sent to Bira, which will give you all the news. I have not seen Bira, as all his races in England have been cancelled owing to lack of a car and he cannot afford to come here without being paid. I was glad to hear from him that he had sailing successes at Riva, but I would not find it possible to be with you while you had someone else. He and Chelita seem to be getting on better and the situation has calmed down a great deal.

Lisba and I are going to spend a week at La Napoule from 1st to 8th September and expect to see something of them.

CHAPTER TWENTY

I received many letters from my friends in Bangkok, sad that Bira and I had parted. They went on writing to me and some I saw in London like Bisdar and his wife Peungpit and Lady Chalow Anyrudh (widow of Duke Anyrudh) and some friends came to Italy. A part of me would always feel Thai - I had so loved the country, my kind relations and my many friends. The Thais are a lovely people and had welcomed me as one of them. I still had my Thai diplomatic passport, but by now I also had a British one again. A new law had been passed after the war that all British-born women who married foreigners could have dual nationality. I gradually began to use my British passport more than my Thai , because then I didn't have to apply for a visa each time I travelled - which I did either with Bruno, or going alone to England to see the Aunts and my father (while they came out every summer to stay with me). Through the years, I became a 'regular' on the *Orient Express* and *Golden Arrow*; travelling on them several times a year.

Bira had greatly enjoyed sailing at Riva during the summer. Chelita was now more relaxed - she said she had been afraid Bira would return to me, but I assured her that I loved Bruno and my life was now with him. She complained a lot about Bira, saying he was difficult to live with and wasn't showing any sign of marrying her and that he was being unfaithful. I said I was sad about that, but if he had promised to marry her I was sure he would. In fact; Bira said he was going to marry Chelita as she wanted - after all, he could always get divorced again if it didn't work out!

Bruno and I, on the other hand, had no intention of marrying. We were very happy as we were, and the more I was with him the more I realized how lucky I was. We had started as friends before the war, then had fallen in love two years ago - perhaps more physically at the start - but real love grew with

192

continued on page 201

Author's Note

While looking through old boxes in 1995, I came across some rolls of film and had them developed. To my surprise they were photographs taken by Bira which had never been printed. The earliest were from September 1933, soon after we met and he began taking me out in his MG Magnette. Another roll was of the beginning of Chula and Bira's trip to Spain and Portugal in the spring of 1935. The last photographs were taken on the way to and from the Czechoslovakian Grand Prix at Brno in 1949.

Three photographs of Bira's road-going MG Magnette, taken in September 1933. Note the very sporty front cycle wings, external exhaust system and cushion which supported the diminutive Bira at the wheel.

This page & opposite, top: In spring 1935, Chula and Bira embarked on a motoring holiday in Spain and Portugal in Bira's sporting Bentley. With aero-screens and folded windscreen, the car is refuelled at Dover before embarkation.

To honour his royal visitors, the Dover harbour master turns out in full uniform and chats with Chula as Bira wields the Leica.

The cross-Channel Steamer SS Canterbury approaches the quay astern.

In the days before RoRo ferries, cars were winched aboard with a cradle under each wheel and bolsters to protect the bodywork.

'Toulo' and Elsa de Graffenried, Ceril and Elda Platé.

Enrico Platé entered two of the latest Maserati Tipo 4CLT/48 San Remo Grand Prix cars (for Bira and de Graffenried) in the 1949 Czechoslovakian Grand Prix at Brno, a notoriously difficult and dangerous circuit. Here, (clockwise) mechanic Scatuzzi, the Swiss Baron 'Toulo' de Graffenried and his wife Elsa, Ceril and Bira, Elda and Enrico Platé and mechanic Felice, take lunch alfresco on the way to Udine.

197

Travelling in convoy with the Platé team was the irrepressible Dr Giuseppe 'Nino' Farina; by preference an Alfa man, but in this year when Alfa Corse was resting on its laurels, grateful for a Maserati - also of the Tipo 4CLT/48 variety. Little did this merry group realise that tragedy lay ahead ...

Armed with flasks of Chianti, mechanics Scatuzzi and Felice prepare to lead the Platé team into Austria on the long haul to Brno; de Graffenfied and Ceril waiting at the Italian border while bureaucracy takes its measured course. The two Platé Maseratis are loaded on a double-decker truck and accompanied by a huge drum of alcohol fuel.

The Issigonis-designed Morris Minor in its special colour scheme halted for an overnight stay in the Austrian Tyrol as Ceril drove towards Switzerland and more medical assistance for the injured Bira.

Overleaf, top: In the horrendous accident at the 1949 Czechoslovakian Grand Prix, Farina and Parnell lost control of their cars and plunged into the virtually uncontrolled crowds of spectators, causing four deaths and severe injuries. Bira, then race leader, also left the road at this point, fortunately without injury to the public, but with some damage to himself. Ceril drove Bira on the homeward journey in the 'Bira Blue' sidevalve Morris Minor seen here before Hitler's 'Eagles Nest' at Berchtesgaden, Bavaria, shortly before it was razed to the ground.

This poignant portrait is the last photograph of Ceril taken by Bira before they parted three weeks later. Sitting by the lake at Zürich, Ceril is checking the route before they set out for the long drive home to Tredethy.

each year that passed. He said marrying couldn't make us any happier than we were - he had never wanted to be married and I didn't want to risk another happy marriage failing. Yet we were both free - there was no one else for either of us and never would be. I began to paint again, enjoyed having my friends to stay and planning my garden.

I was still receiving regular letters from both Bira and Chula -

Tredethy, 30th October 1951.*Darling Ceril, early in September, Lisba and I spent a week with Bira at his little villa. Both he and Chelita looked after us well. I think she is a good, kind hearted girl - but you know my views. One can afford to marry for romance once, but if that fails, the second must be a sensible marriage. if I were Bira, I would not marry again at all. Not even a sensible one!*

Les Faunes, 9th December 1951. *It is just nine days before I get married to Chelita, so I am writing to let you know our plans. I am leaving here with Chelita and Titch for Milan; seeing the OSCA people and to find a mechanic to go to Uruguay. I then leave for Paris to wed Chelita at the Siamese Embassy on the morning of the 18th. Chula and Lisba are coming over for it. We go to South America at the end of January. I am hoping to sell the OSCA over there and take it easy with Formula 2 racing with Gordini or Platé 2-litre Maserati, for the next season of 1952. I don't think Formula 1 racing is right for a private concern. One loses too much money.'I have bought a yacht of 10 tons and 11.30 metres in length. It is to replace Marie Anne which we enjoyed very much this summer. She wasn't quite up to my requirements, so I hope to have as much fun, if not more, on this bigger yacht this summer. I will come to Riva to race my Snipe as usual.*

Tredethy, 14th January 1952. *Thank you for the water colour, which is charming and is being framed. We had to go over to Paris for Bira's wedding, but made it as short as possible. We are leaving here for London tomorrow and leave Rome by KLM the 21st for Bangkok. I have thought over the whole thing very carefully and feel I must go back unless I wish to be a self-confessed exile. I admit I am very nervous about flying.*

Motonave *Augusta*, 9th March 1952. *Well, here we are - off again to SA to do two races at Montevideo. The OSCA is going better now and I hope I will be able to sell it out there! My love, Dumdum.*

Buenos Aires, 7th April 1952. *Again broken down in both races. Have signed up with Gordini for Formula 2 this year. Hope luck will change.*

Tredethy, 12th April 1952. *The trip to Siam was a great success. I was surprised to find I did not mind the flight at all. The only effect it had on me was to make me feel very sleepy. Henry came to see us off as far as Rome. At Baghdad, we were invited to lunch by the Prince Regent, whom I know slightly. The house was English suburban. From Baghdad, we flew direct to Karachi for dinner, left about midnight and had a non-stop flight to Bangkok. We were received a few days after our arrival by the king and queen and given tea. It was all very formal and dull. We only saw them alone once again before we left, when we went to say goodbye. Life in Bangkok is very expensive. Bira wants to go with Chelita next autumn by the Gemini, having flown the whole way. I think it is very frightening.*

Les Faunes, 26th October 1952. *We have been away in England to get the Gemini done up for the trip to Bangkok. I am rather excited with the idea of flying back under our own steam, as it will establish a record of being the first Siamese to have flown himself home. Apart from this, it is the cheapest way to go back for two people. I expect to be away for about 3-4 months; depending on how we like it out there. I have had the most unsuccessful racing season of my whole career and it has made me less keen on the sport, so unless I could find a new financier, I'll probably give it up.*

Tredethy, 1st November 1952. *It was sweet of you to think of Lisba and me on our wedding anniversary. Fourteen years certainly seems a long time - and that our marriage has lasted this long is at least 65% to Lisba's credit for her forbearance. I wonder when you will actually be in London. I think I may be able to brace myself up to go and see you, so write and let me know soon.*

Tredethy, 19th May 1953. *We had a lovely time in Thailand. Bira and Chelita were unexpectedly living at Ta Tien the whole time, as he was trying to work for Thai Airways as a pilot. They are now back at Les Faunes and he is racing again. I represent my king at the Coronation. We are given a suite at the Mayfair Hotel from 30th May to 7th June. The third volume of my Thai autobiography is out and has sold 4000 copies! I am sending you a copy, as there is lots and lots about you.*

Ecurie Royale, 15th July 1953. *My darling Ceril, it was really sweet of you to have sent me a book on my birthday. I am taking a Comet to Bangkok this Monday to arrange a Siamese ballet company to go to New York. If it comes off, it will be fun as well as*

*profitable for me. Sol Hirsch, the famous American impresario, has
approached me to do this, and as far as I can see, it may catch on
like Anna and the King of Siam. Please tell Bruno I am mad about
Fiadolin (his new Star Class boat). I am hoping to sail her at
Naples for the World Championship. With lots of love as always,
Dumdum.*

Les Faunes, 27th February 1954. *We are off to Genoa to watch
the last day of Star racing. Fiadolin is being sailed by the Com-
mandant du Port de Monaco. Maybe the club will buy her.
'Titciboo' arrives here from New York on the eighth morning and
she's plunged into her first race from the 8th to 13th in the Regatta Royale. I am thrilled to try her out and hope Lippincott has
made her as well as the others. My motor racing in South America
was so- so and I finished 7th and 6th in the two races with a
Maserati. This year, I am driving for Gordini once again. Maybe
with the new motor he is building, it will be quite good. Anyhow,
we can only wait and see. I want to go to the International World
Championship for gliding in Derbyshire this summer with the
Weihe. Have been practising at Fayence and got up to 5,000
metres diamond altitude yesterday. It will be the first time if I can
do all the three - sea, land and air world championships this year!
Love as always, Dumdum.*

At the end of the 1954 season Bira gave up racing. He had come to sail
during the summer at Riva, and as Bruno took his Star *Chérie IV* to many of
the same regattas in Italy and France as Bira, we met him and Chelita quite
often. Things were not going too smoothly between them, as during a lone visit
to Thailand Bira had met a very pretty Siamese air hostess called Salee (who
later became his third wife) and had brought her back to Europe with him to
live at the villa. With someone of Chelita's Latin temperament, sparks
inevitably flew. I saw this when he came with them both to see me at
Campagnola.

When we went to race at Nice the following spring Chelita was alone with
Bira. As usual, she was most attractive and vivacious and seemed happy - but
when Bira came to Riva in the summer, only Salee was with him. Then we met
him at Luino on Lake Maggiore, where both he and Bruno were racing their
Stars, and he was with Chelita. A group of their friends from Cannes had come
to watch the racing and Bira pointed one of them out to me as Chelita's San
Dominican lover. It all seemed very complicated and involved. When Bruno
was sailing at Livorno, Bira turned up on his own with just the crew of his new
73rd foot schooner *Lelanta*; his latest toy which he had brought to show
Bruno. Bira took me out to watch the racing in a little Bira Blue speed boat
he kept on board, and at the prize giving at the Naval Academy we three sat
together and talked all evening - but not about his private life. He just told

me that Chelita was expecting a baby, hoping to save their marriage, and that Salee was at the villa looking after Titch.

Bira had just come into a great deal of money unexpectedly, as his father's palace had been sold and his handicapped brother had died; the estate being divided among the remaining brothers and sisters. Chula told me about it in one of his letters, saying that, of course, the money should be left in Bangkok to be invested by Banyen and Bisdar, and only the income sent out to Bira. Instead, he had asked for it all and it was disappearing very fast. He made improvements to the villa, bought a large open Buick and now this new yacht. He also had to make big payments to the French government - he had never realized that if one owns a property taxes need to be paid!. Then he crashed and wrecked the Buick in Paris, and being uninsured, had to pay the damages of the other car involved - on top of losing his own car! Then came the disaster with the boat. Chelita had had the baby a month before - a little boy called Biradej - and Bira took mother and child with a large group of friends on a cruise. A storm blew up and the boat sank. It, too, was uninsured. The incident was reported in the papers -

The Daily Telegraph, 1st October 1955. "Leghorn, Friday. Prince Bira, 41, wealthy Siamese racing driver and sportsman, his wife, their 40-day old son and 20 guests escaped, when the prince's yacht *Lelanta* was wrecked off the small Italian island of Capraia at midnight last night. All were thrown into the sea. When they were near the island, a storm gathered and they ran for shelter in the island's little port - but were unable to reach it. The first waves hit the yacht just outside the harbour and sent it crashing against the pier.

The prince, who is a powerful swimmer, was reported to have caught the child and held its head above water for an hour. All able-bodied men of Capraia's 500 population left their beds. They manned the fishing boats on the beach and rowed out to where the prince and his friends were struggling in the water".

The letters continued -

Tredethy, 21st January 1956. *Darling Ceril, I do hope you received the postcards which I sent you from Thailand and on the way. I now have some very important news for you. It is that Lisba is expecting a baby, which by calculation should appear round about 8th August. Bira, Chelita and Titch came to meet us at Naples on 6th January. Although I found them looking quite well, I was sad to see Bira looking very miserable - as he had a serious financial setback, owing to his yacht accident. Fortunately, he inherited a reasonable sum from his crippled brother, who died recently, and was paying for the repairs out of that for, needless to say, it was typical of Bira that the yacht was not insured. Very much love always, Chula.*

Tredethy, 1st April 1956. *I cannot remember whether I told you* *or not that Queen Grandmother who died last December, will be cremated on 22nd April. I am flying back especially for it, not to please the king or anybody else, but for her great kindness to me in the past. I remember especially her whole-hearted reception of Lisba and yourself; following our marriages. Lisba and I fly to Holland on Saturday, 7th April. We are to stay the weekend at Soestdijk Palace with Queen Juliana and Prince Bernhard. I fly on to Bangkok by KLM and Lisba flies back to London. I am happy to say she has been keeping well the whole time, and her gynaecologist, Sir William Gilliatt, is fully satisfied with her. While in Thailand, I may see Bira who has gone there since February. The idea was to start some business and earn some money, as without motor racing and very high starting money, he finds the allowance from me insufficient. Chelita followed him out there on 5th March, but was back at Les Faunes by the 18th. She says she cannot stand life in Thailand and finds Bira very difficult there - while Bira says he must be there to work for at least four years. What the future holds, I do not know. The situation fills me and Bira's friends with anxiety. With much love, Chula.*

Tredethy, 1st October 1956.*In case you have not heard from Bira himself about it, I regret to inform you that Bira and Chelita were divorced according to Thai law by mutual consent at the Thai Embassy in Paris on 29th September. Bira is shortly returning to Thailand - I do not know for how long. Chelita, who has been given custody of Biradej, is shortly going to marry a South American man they have both known for sometime. The property near Cannes known as 'Villa les Faunes', has been made over to Biradej, and will therefore be under Chelita's control until Biradej is 21 - but Bira will remove all effects therein. It is all very sad but inevitable. The other news you should know is that Shura has ceased working for me.*

Bira Sport, **Siphya Road, Bangkok, 20th August 1957.** *My dearest Ceril, it is nice to feel when one gets older, one is still remembered by so many people - especially by the loved ones. I'm desolated that I'm not able to be present at Riva for the regatta as usual, but here I am working very hard trying to establish Bira Sport. I sell Neckar cars which come from Germany, which are really 1100cc Fiats. Also I am agent of other makes of cars. The business is going slowly and gradually building up our goodwill. I daresay it will take a few years before we make a good profit. It is a funny feeling to be sitting at a desk working everyday from 8.00 am till 5.00 pm, after so many years living in Europe as a free agent. However, I'm settling down in Bangkok quite nicely and* *taking my coming old age philosophically. Titch is getting very old. He is really a link between my past life and now, and sometimes he makes me think back on the wonderful times I had with him during those years. I expect you'll have fun at Riva as usual in the regatta, and I hope Bruno will succeed in winning some prizes. Do let me have some of your news when you can. I send you my love, as always.*

Bira Sport, Bangkok, 3rd April 1959. *My dearest Ceril, I am planning to make a trip to Europe this year about July and hope to have my new 'Star' which I ordered from Eichenlaub to sail on the Italian lakes. Please ask Bruno to send me a full list of regattas in Italy for 'Star' boats. I am so out of practice, and if I don't want to disgrace myself at Naples Olympic Games next year, I must work hard this summer. How is your life in Italy, darling? I hope to see something of you this year. Chelita is now separated from her husband and I wish I could have Biradej back.*

In the *Daily Mail* in 1959 Paul Tanfield wrote "Gilbert Benitez-Rexach, who married the former Princess Bira of Siam, said to his wife, Celia (Chelita): "I'm going out for a box of matches, dear." That was on 12th February. She hasn't seen him since. Gilbert explained his absence to me: "Our marriage was dissolved in Puerto Rico last month. It's embarrassing that my ex-wife and I should both now live in Cannes." Celia's other ex-husband, Prince Bira, the former racing car driver, sailed into nearby Monte Carlo harbour. After their divorce in 1956, the prince removed his boy and put him in the care of the King of Siam. Later, Bira agreed to let Celia have him until he is seven. "The prince", said Celia last night, "made a gentleman's agreement about Chiquito. Gilbert said he would pay for his upbringing. But since he has walked out, he hasn't paid a penny. I have to foot all the bills myself - and look now what has happened. I was so astonished to get Gilbert's telegram saying we were divorced, that I lost a child!" Her second husband is living at the home of his step-mother, the famous former singer 'La Mineau' and probably the wealthiest woman on the Cote d'Azur. "I have an excellent understanding with Bira", said Celia. "He loves to play with his son - Chiquito is everyone's favourite, but it isn't possible for a Latin girl to live with an Oriental husband. There are too many differences. Our minds don't work the same." But she is a lonely woman, with one ex-husband living just up the road. And another 20 miles along the coast in his yacht."

The *Bira Sport* business closed and Bira started up a new enterprise. Salee had gone back to Bangkok with him and they married but when Bira brought another girl, Lom, to live with them, Salee divorced him.

Bira Commerce Co. Ltd, Bangkok, 18th January 1960. *Darling Ceril, thank you for your sweet card. I am desolated that I had not*

touched a 'Star' boat for a full year. I hope I can do so in June,
prior to Naples. I send you my love as always.

When I next saw Bira, he had brought Lom to Geneva and continued his finance business there. He sailed for Thailand in the 1960 Olympics.

CHAPTER TWENTY ONE

In 1954 my aunts gave up the house in Cadogan Place: they were both well over seventy and it was too big for them. Aunt C went to live in Devon near Uncle Harry and his second wife Olive, while Aunt Ray moved into a service flat in Pont Street, which became my London home. My father died in Jersey in 1955. Fortunately, my brother and I were with him.

In August 1956 Chula and Lisba's daughter Narisa was born, named after Prince Naris, the member of the Thai Royal Family Chula most revered. Then Shura and Nan came to live in London, where Shura started a photographic business called *Trans-Globe*. It was a great sorrow for him to leave Chula after 20 years but the household at Tredethy had never been an easy one for him and Nan to live in (mostly due to Chula's mercurial moods), and it was only their patience and Shura's great loyalty that had made their long stay there possible. They came out to stay with me and I saw a lot of them in London.

I received a letter from Chula's mother who was not at all well -

Neuilly, 20th December 1958. *Darling Ceril, you do not know how happy I am to feel that you haven't forgotten me. I love you, and your photo with Mini is always on my desk. When I heard that she died, I wanted to write to you, as I knew how sad you felt, but since September 1956 when I got this rotten asthma in a place near Lake Annecy, I am not what I like to be. At the end of October, Nou came here with Narisa, her nurse Miss Thomas (a lovely woman), Lisba and Ronnie. They stayed at George V, but came every day here. Just four days they were. Narisa is a very bright, good looking and well behaved child. I am so sad that on account of my state of health, I can't go to England and stay with Nou and*

Lisba and see more of Narisa, but I am now absolutely neurasthemique and stay in all the time.

I was extremely sad to receive the following note from Shura -

32 The Little Boltons, 6th January 1960. *Darlingest Ceril, a short notice in today's Times reads: "Deaths. STONE. On 3rd January 1960, at Neuilly-sur-Seine, France, Mrs Catherine Stone (née Desnitsky), mother of HRH Prince Chula of Thailand, GCVO". Loving you, Shura.*

Lisba wrote -

Tredethy, 7th January 1960. *We had a very nice Xmas all together, and of course dear Narisa enjoyed it exceedingly. I am now returning from Chula's mother's funeral. She had been unwell for several years and appeared no worse this Xmas, but died very quietly 3rd January. Hin was very good to her and looked after her most patiently until the last.*

Tredethy, 23rd January 1960. *I've just returned from Pontresina, where I had lovely skiing and fortunately good snow. We are all well, Chula being as usual. He has been very quiet about his mother. As you of course know, theirs was anything but a happy relationship and they never really had any great happiness together. I hope you are well and all goes smoothly. It seems amazing that we are in another 'decade'. With love, Lisba.*

Aunt C died in January 1959. I was staying with Aunt Ray when Uncle Harry rang up with the sad but not totally unexpected news. I had just been staying with her; she was looked after by Louisa who had been with the Aunts since she was a girl. Way drove me back to Devon for the funeral.

In September of that year Henry Tyszka came to stay. We had remained friends since I first met Henry in Buenos Aires in 1949. My nephew Phil was also staying and for his 18th birthday treat we all went to Monza, where Henry and I felt very nostalgic. I had been booked up all that summer with guests and it was sometimes rather a squash - until 1960 when we built a new wing to the villa. Bruno did the design - an enormous glassed-in veranda overlooking the lake - to be used in the summer as our living area and to house my orchids; with two new bedrooms and a bathroom over it. Bruno also designed a glass wall to divide the garden in half, with a sliding door allowing cars to pass up the drive. It was to protect the orange, grapefruit, lemon and tangerine trees from the fierce morning north wind. Work was started in the autumn of 1960 and the workmen and dust were with us for nine long months. It was well worth it, and when Bira next came to *Campagnola* it was finished. He was enchanted by it all.

30th December 1961 I received a telegram - "ARE YOU AT HOME? WOULD LOVE TO SEE YOU AM STAYING FLAT 63 AVENUE MIRAMONT 15 GENEVA LOVE BIRA".

I had heard from Evelyn Haccius that Bira had arrived in Switzerland. She had been to see him at the Bellevue in Berne, where he told her he was on the verge of becoming a millionaire. He came to see us; full of stories of his coming prosperity, but when Bruno and I heard more about his plans we feared he would be in for many disappointments.

It was tragic that Bira, a really talented sculptor, had given it all up for a life of commerce, for which he had no talent or training whatever. If only he had opened a studio in Bangkok (as we had planned when we were young), he would never have been without work, money or satisfaction, and without doubt would have achieved fame as one of Thailand's leading sculptors. About that time, I had a letter from someone who was preparing a new catalogue of the portraits belonging to the university and the colleges in Cambridge. They wanted more information about the excellent head of Field-Marshal Smuts at Christ's College, which Bira had done. How many of those portrait heads he could have done in Thailand!

In February 1962 I received a letter from Rumer Godden, whose books I had always enjoyed so much. It seemed she had got to know Dr. Helena Wright, who was a great friend of mine and came to stay every year. Helena was a pioneer of contraception and had been asked to write an article in a woman's magazine giving the 'family planning' point of view on birth control. The following week, Rumer, a Roman Catholic, was to present that side of the argument. Through this they had got to know each other:

Little Douce Grove, 19th February 1962. *This is a letter from a complete stranger. My only excuse is that Helena Wright suggested that you might be able to advise me. I understand from her you have a villa on Lake Garda, just beside Malcesine where we have often stayed, and that you know the lake from end to end. As Helena may have told you, I am a writer and am at my wits end as to how, in the pace of life in England, I can finish a novel. In order to do this and work in peace and quiet, I am seeking a villa - large or small, where we (my husband and I) could come and be in seclusion.*

I wrote that the big villa next to mine was sometimes let in the summer, and Rumer Godden and her husband James Haynes-Dixon took it for a month to work on *The Battle of the Villa Fiorita*.

From Chula came news of Bira -

Tredethy, 3rd January 1963. *Darling Ceril, 1963 was the first year since I have known him, that I never saw Bira. I saw him in*

London in November 1961, when he said his business plans would soon mature and he would be a millionaire. He was away in Switzerland all the time I was in Thailand. I have very bad news about him now. You may have heard that his third wife Salee left him and that they were divorced. He has not married again. His business plans have not prospered. He has fallen under the influence of old type Brahmanic Buddhist teachers and now believes in supernatural help from some dead Buddhist saint. To achieve this, he has shaved off all the hair on his head, does not eat after midday and does not touch women - although he is still looked after by his girlfriend and her mother. When he meets people, he talks some gibberish purporting to be the Buddhist doctrine. His second wife, Chelita, is now living in Buenos Aires very precariously with their son, to whom Bira does not send one penny. It seems he is not certifiable, but the future looks very bad. With love always, Chula.

It transpired that Chula had been rather too gloomy about Bira, for when I next saw him his hair had grown again and he was absolutely his old self - also rather affluent.

Chula's subsequent letters came from the Royal Marsden Hospital -

26th February 1963. *Darling Ceril, I insisted on being told the truth from the first, and when I was told it was cancer on 30th January, I faced it with the resolve that either I would die soon or I must fight hard to get cured. I did not have the moral uplift from others, including Lisba, as you think. They are all so unused to my being ill and feeble, so accustomed to my own moral support, that they all collapsed around me, and it was I who had to calm them. This was very tiring. The treatment began on the 18th. As there were no ill effects, I went to London for the w/e. It is very sweet of you to suggest seeing me. The best thing is to come to see me at my temporary flat.*

The Hospital, 12th March 1963. *The rays have given me a sore throat and made me very hoarse, but I was able to go to London for the w/e. I therefore hope to be able to do so again 15th-17th. In that case, come to see me at the flat. Bira came to see me last Sat/Sun.'*

Chula died on 30th December 1963 at Tredethy when he was 55 and Narisa was only seven. She was also to lose her mother from cancer when she was 15 as Lisba died in November 1971 at the age of 56. It was indeed a sad period, as Aunt Ray also died in the spring of 1964.

Rumer Godden wrote from Copenhagen -

4th January 1964. *Your letter followed us here. Since I read of Prince Chula's death, I knew how rushed and strained you must have been on your short visits. I meant to write before, as I knew how deeply sad you must have been. About Fiorita; it seems to be rolling along very happily; the film rights just sold.*

From the time Bruno expanded his yachting business life had become more hectic. We would start the year by going in January to the London and Paris boat shows, where Bruno would place his orders, have a busy season with his large chandler's shop in Riva, importing, facing frustration with the Italian customs, selling to the trade and exhibiting at the Italian boat show at Genoa. Bruno ran it all with the greatest enthusiasm and enjoyment and, I must say, with success.

Hartshorn House, Tuesday 11th January 1966. *Probably you and Bruno are again at the boat show. Your wonderfully vivid description of the boat chandling made us laugh, but I can imagine how he is enjoying himself! Can also see how immersed you are - it must be truly hard work. Did you ever dream you would become secretary to a boat chandler? Our love to you both and all good wishes for the New Year and the new enterprise. Rumer.*

By now, Bira too had a new enterprise - *Bira Air Transport Ltd.* Years later, in his obituary the *Times* wrote "He had latterly run an airfreight business and his navigating exploits on the Bangkok-London run were legendary". With both Bira and Bruno so busy, the three of us seldom met. In February 1970 Lisba wrote -

You mentioned you could be coming to Cornwall for your nephew's marriage to a Cornish girl. If you are going to do this, you must come and stay here. I cannot remember if you told me the date of the marriage. Narisa is home from school in March and April, and we are visiting Paris together the second week of April. Much love, Lisba.

My nephew Philip was marrying Tamsin Trefusis at Trefusis near Falmouth on 4th April 1970. It was too far from Tredethy for me to stay there over the wedding, but I hoped to stop for a few days on my way back to London - only it turned out to be just when Lisba and Narisa were in Paris.The following year Lisba became ill. The last letter I received was just over a month before she died -

Tredethy, 7th October 1971. *My dearest Ceril, I realised that for the first time in many many years, I'd not sent you a card for your birthday. So I felt I must write you a line. I am unwell again and in* fact was up in London, then down here battling with my various maladies. I am rather worn out with being ill which is now nearly a year. I so hope you are bearing up, as Bruno has been really unwell. What a bore it all is; one does not mind getting older with a modicum of good health. Tredethy is as nice as ever, and Narisa is back at school for her last year. She has done well with 3 'O' levels this summer. She will have a nice half-term when we can meet, as I find I'm too feeble to travel at the moment. Much love and best wishes for your 55th year. Lisba.

Ronnie Potts wrote -

Tredethy, 30th November 1971. *I have the sad task of having to tell you that dear Lisba died during the early hours of Saturday, 27th November. Her immense courage and characteristic concern for others was an inspiration to those of us who were fortunate to be near her. A private family cremation is being held at Truro and her ashes will then be interred together with Chula's in Bangkok.*

As Lisba had become a Buddhist there was a memorial service in London at a Buddhist temple and I went to it with Daphne and Helena.

Since Aunt Ray died I was without a London home, but my distant cousin Helen Curling (known to the family as 'Deddie') came to my rescue. Her parents and my Faudel-Phillips grandparents had been friends as well as relations and, as a girl, Deddie stayed with them often. She shared a flat with Freda Edwards at Baron's Court, near the Royal Ballet School, where Freda taught. In her youth she had danced in Anna Pavlova's company and later in America with Kosloff of the Imperial Ballet of Moscow. She and Deddie had met during the war, doing Red Cross work in London. Their spare room was therefore to be my London home for the next 20 years.

I saw Shura and Nan whenever I stayed there - his business was doing well - and we still wrote -

19 Coleherne Court, 17th March 1968. *Darling Ceril, you will probably know that* Romulus *is at Beaulieu (The Montagu Motor Museum). Oddly enough, they asked me to manufacture colour transparencies of some 22 vintage and veteran cars, and* Romulus *was one of them. There he stands in a corner with the round red sign behind, saying: 'Stop immediately' and the signal board telling Bira that Parnell is leading him by some three minutes and 50 seconds!!! Someone must have turned in his grave several times. Pots of love to you, darling Ceril and I <u>do</u> hope à bientôt. Love to Bruno and good things for the season. Love from Nan. Yours, Shura.*

Stanley Holgate, who was still running the *White Mouse Garage* as his own business, sometimes helped Shura mount transparencies. I also saw Evelyn in London now, as her husband, Colonel Helmut de Frisching, was Military Attaché at the Swiss Embassy and I had introduced them to Shura and Nan and Daphne. It was in London that I met Brian Boden for the first time - he was to marry my niece Dolly - and Bruno and I took them both out to dinner.

In the winter of 1970 when he was 60 Bruno had a stroke and was forced to give up work. His business was bought by two young sailing enthusiasts, who moved it to Genoa but retained Bruno's name.

CHAPTER TWENTY TWO

One very hot summer morning in 1971 I was weeding under the orange and lemon trees by the small gate of my villa when I heard a familiar voice call out "It's me, darling" and there was Bira; completely unchanged, except perhaps a bit heavier (but weren't we all?). I noticed his car was parked in the full heat of the sun and that Lom and someone else was in it, so walked down the drive to open the big gate for him to park it under the olive trees in the shade. Then Bira rushed off to the house, saying he must 'phone Bruno at once as he needed his advice.

I opened the car door and asked Lom to come and sit on the terrace and have a cool drink, and then saw there was a sweet little Thai child in the back with a young woman. I congratulated Lom who said "Oh, she's not mine - I can't have children". I asked who the little girl was and she said "She's hers and Bira's." A bit taken aback, I didn't continue the conversation but just seated them in chairs overlooking the lake and went to the kitchen for drinks. Bira joined me, saying Bruno was on his way, so I asked him to please explain his new domestic situation.

He told me the young woman was called Lek and that she had lived for some time with the son of a well known lawyer in Bangkok, whom he knew, but when she had a baby the family threw her out and kept the child. Lek had come to him and Lom for help and they had taken her in: she went to work in the office of his air transport firm. She had been heartbroken at having her baby taken away, so Bira said he had felt it only kind to give her another. However, the little girl called Lom "Mother", not Lek, who she called "Aunt". I asked Bira to whom he was married and he said "No-one". He had tried three times and failed; that was enough ...

He asked if I could give them lunch but I said I didn't feel like cooking on a hot day. Bira said he had never expected me to cook for them - it would have been unthinkable - that 'they' (meaning Lek and Lom) could get us a meal. I said "No, Bira dear, not in my kitchen", and so when Bruno arrived he took us all out.

Bira was very abrupt and off-hand with the two women - I regretted both that and the fact that he no longer spoke his former Etonian English but mixed it with a sort of American slang. However, with Bruno and me he was exactly the same as before; very pleased to see us, as we were to see him. Bira was now 57 and seemed very fond of his pretty little daughter.

He had come to Europe to start preparations for sailing in the 1972 Olympics in Germany, had stayed in London at the Hyde Park Hotel, bought a car (a Sunbeam Rapier) and then came to get Bruno's advice as to where to buy a new boat. To the dismay of all devoted 'Star' owners like Bruno and Bira, the 'Star' was not this time to be an Olympic class although, happily, for the 1976 games they returned and remain Olympic to this day. Now a new boat had been chosen in its place - the 'Tempest', designed by Ian Proctor - and as Bruno had been Ian Proctor's agent for Italy and had imported the first 'Tempest' to exhibit on his stand at the Genoa Boat Show, he was able to tell Bira all about it and where to buy one in Italy.

As Bira no longer had a home on the French Riviera he wanted to make his European base with us and took to leaving his car and boat at *Campagnola*. He wrote -

Bhanurangsi House, Sukumvit Road, Bangkok, 30th September 1971. *Dearest Ceril, I have returned home about 12 days now and found work stacked up on my desk. First, let me wish you a happy birthday in your peaceful and quiet villa. I enjoyed spending brief moments there! Now that we are connected again, I hope to be coming to Italy more frequently; depending on the cash situation of course.*

In Beirut, I did a lot better than in Sweden, so the morale is up again, and I should like to go on with International sailing of some kind. With the Tempest *class, it is certainly very limited because of the crew question. However, with the* Fireball *Asians like me, with their light weight could sufficiently cope, so after a regatta, I bought the* Fireball *I was sailing and had it sent back to England. Sometime next year, I hope to come to Riva and pick up the* Rapier *to go to England and fetch it, and return to have a few regattas with it.*

In the meantime, please ask Bruno if he sees any possibility of selling my Tempest (with a proviso that I can sail her in Kiel Olympic Games). I loved being back in Riva and meeting up with old friends, though it was a little nostalgic. I am much relieved to have a good reliable friend like Bruno to look after my boat and car. Now I can rest quietly without anxiety. When I write next time,

I will send photos of activities over here. In the meantime, lots of love to you; and to Bruno thanks again. Your Bira.

After Bruno's stroke life had to slow down, though he made a good recovery. It was a very happy period for us both. We were able to be together the whole time. He kept the hedges beautifully cut at *Campagnola*, also the grass - but not weed-free, as we loved it purple with giant violets and full of mountain flowers from the seeds blown down from the Monte Baldo range behind us. He helped to pick the olives after Christmas, covered part of the vegetable garden for us to have salads all the winter and his workshop was a 'do it yourself' man's dream. He could turn his hand to anything.

Bruno now lived all the time at *Campagnola*. He and his sister Tosca had sold their villa in Riva and also their library and gift shop. It was taken over by a young couple, Ettore and Graziella Bondi, who owned a large and beautiful house next door to the Tomasoni villa. Tosca went to live with them in a ground floor flat looking onto the garden, next to where Graziella's sister Elda Benvenuti lived. Bruno went to see Tosca nearly every day and to watch a new block of flats going up nearby where he had bought one to be our home, when *Campagnola* became too big for us in our old age.

Bira came over to sail in the 1972 Olympics at Kiel. He needed a heavy man to crew for him in the *Tempest*, so had gone to a Thai general to ask if he had any weighty officers (Thais being mostly rather light). The general found him a colonel, whom he wanted to reward for great bravery in the jungle fighting on the frontier - but to Bira's dismay the man had no sailing experience at all. Still, they didn't completely disgrace themselves, and after the races went to Munich for the closing ceremony. Bira 'phoned me to say that they would be with us early the following afternoon, but they didn't arrive until late in the evening. This was the time of the terrible murder of the Israeli Olympic team by Palestinian terrorists, and when Bira and the Colonel reached the frontier they fell under suspicion and were held there for five hours. It was dark when they finally arrived; angry and hungry, and while I got food Bruno helped them unhitch the trailer.

At breakfast, Bira said he would leave the car and boat with us and fly straight back to Thailand; so while Bruno and the Colonel got everything out of the car and boat, Bira and I sorted it all on the veranda to see what they could take with them and what to leave behind. I took letters, bills and money out of Bira's pockets for him, and he showed one of the letters to me, which shocked and upset me very much. It was from Chelita to tell him that their sixteen year old son, Biradej, had died of cancer: again, that terrible disease striking the family. Some years before Chelita had married an elderly American and they lived in Buenos Aires where the boy went to boarding school. Her husband had been very good to Biradej and had seen that he received the best possible treatment when he became ill. It was most tragic for poor Chelita and she and her husband came for a trip to Europe afterwards and called on me.

I told Bira how sorry I was, and he said he would try to have another son. Indeed, the following year when he was nearly sixty he and Lek had a little boy.

Later that year, Bira rang from Switzerland to say he was there on his own. His air business had closed down and he was back in international finance with an office again in Geneva. He wanted to know if Bruno had sold the *Tempest*, and when I said he had, asked if we would send him the money? I pointed out that exporting money from Italy was a criminal offence, so he said not to worry; he would come and fetch it. He turned up the next morning for breakfast and spent the day telling us all about his new project. He wanted to be the first person to fly the Atlantic in a glider, starting from Brazil. He drew maps for us, talked about prevailing winds, finding a sponsor, a ship to follow him, and so on. He asked Bruno to buy a villa for him near us, as he was again on the verge of becoming very rich indeed and wanted to spend his summers with us sailing on the lake, returning to Thailand in the winter to be with his children. These particular plans for getting rich never materialized, but he went on trying, certain of success. As always, he kept in touch with letters -

Geneva, 25th May 1974. *Dearest Ceril, I only just came back from Paris - extremely busy, but I hope to achieve some result!!! Tentative programme: Geneva 1st June - 5th July. Dijon 6th July - 7th July. Amsterdam 7th July. Bergen 8th July (on cruise to N. capitals, birthday on board!). Riva 25th July-10th August. I hope to get some sailing during Riva stay. Please excuse this great rush (as usual!). Love as always.*

After seeing Bira during the summer of 1974, we didn't meet again for several years, as he returned to Thailand.

Early in the morning of 1st March 1982 Bruno died quietly at *Campagnola*.

In 1983 I went to stay with Freda Edwards at Baron's Court. I hadn't been for a year or two (not wanting to leave Bruno), but had heard from Nan and Shura that Bira was now in London, going through a very unsuccessful period but sure he was once more on the verge of making an immense fortune. Shura said it was not entirely imagination - he had shown them bankers' letters. Something really big was in the air! I met Bira at their flat and he was very upset to hear about Bruno - they had been good friends and fond of each other ever since their first meeting. Bira had often told me that if he couldn't be with me himself, Bruno was the only man he knew who he would want me to be with.

I saw him again in London the following year. This time he had his son with him and Nan asked me to come to tea as they too would be there. Thinking "Like father like son", I visited Harrods' toy department on the way. Bira called the boy 'Birdi' - he was about twelve, very nice looking, had good manners and spoke perfect English - but I heard from Nan that he was a bit of a handful for his seventy year old father. Bira told him that here was someone who had always been very important to him, and the boy went down on his knees, bowed his head and, with his folded hands against his forehead, touched the floor with them, then sprang up to open the Harrods bag. Bira said he adored his son and wanted to send him to school in England. Then he changed his mind, which was a good thing as at that moment, he would have found it impossible to manage the school fees. Not that it worried Bira; his big fortune was always just round the corner ...

He asked me what I was doing now. I told him I had moved to the flat Bruno had bought in Riva as I didn't want to live alone in the villa. I said first Way and Ygerne, then Philip and Tamsin with their son Tom (the same age as Bira's boy) had come to help me move. Bira took out his diary and wrote down the address, saying he promised to come and see me soon. He never did.

My brother rang me at home in Italy late one night to tell me Bira was dead. He had suffered a heart attack, collapsed and died on the platform of Baron's Court underground station two days before Christmas 1985 - just opposite the block of flats where, for the last 20 years, I had always stayed during my London visits. He was seventy one.

I first met Bira when I was seventeen and he was twenty. Three weeks later he asked me to marry him ...

INDEX

221